THE BROWNSVILLE REDEMPTION

Theodore Roosevelt's Wrongful Disgrace of the
All-Black Infantry in Brownsville, Texas, 1906

THE BROWNSVILLE REDEMPTION

Theodore Roosevelt's Wrongful Disgrace of the All-Black Infantry in Brownsville, Texas, 1906

Lieutenant Colonel (Ret) William Baker

Copyright © Bettye F. Baker 2023

The moral rights of the author have been asserted.

All rights reserved. No part of this publication may be reproduced, stored in or introduced into a retrieval system or transmitted in any form or by any means, electronic, mechanical, photocopying, recording or otherwise without prior written permission from the publisher.

Events, locales, conversations and dates have been recorded to the best of the author's memory. Some names and details have been changed to protect the privacy of the individual/s involved.

This edition published by Vulpine Press in the United Kingdom in 2023

First published by Red Engine Press in 2020 in the United States under the title *The Brownsville Texas Incident of 1906: The True and Tragic Story of a Black Battalion's Wrongful Disgrace and Ultimate Redemption*

Cover photo property of Bettye F. Baker

ISBN: 978-1-83919-204-3

Praise For *The Brownsville Redemption*

"William Baker's riveting narrative rips the scab off one of the most disgraceful episodes of racism in the annals of the American military—and one of the shameful low points of Theodore Roosevelt's otherwise progressive presidency. The book—and perhaps our very history—are redeemed by the author's patient personal quest to exonerate and compensate the African American "wrongdoers" who in fact did no wrong in Brownsville, Texas, in 1906. Justice deferred is of course no justice—especially when it is so hard to achieve—but this book goes a long way toward exposing, and righting, a terrible wrong. Baker proves not only an able chronicler, but a tireless crusader. He emerges as a key character in what turns out to be part biography, part history, and part memoir—all of it well worth reading."

– Harold Holzer, Winner of the 2015 Lincoln Prize

This is an important story that needs to be told with accuracy and from the perspective of the Black soldiers who were victimized by the fears and prejudices of the white residents of Brownsville, Texas. The work does both; it strives to set the record straight, and it gives the soldiers the voice they were denied when the incident occurred. It also reveals the extraordinary effort of the author to uncover the truth and to restore the reputation of the men who were betrayed by the government they had sworn to protect and defend. His research is comprehensive and meticulous.

Lt. Col (Ret.) Baker uses his understanding of the history of racial prejudices in the military to explain the injustice visited upon the men of the 25th Infantry both in the early 20th century and as he attempted to redeem them a half century later.

The Brownsville Redemption is engaging and informative, even inspiring. It is both a tribute to the men who were grossly wronged as well as a reminder of the importance of the pursuit of truth.

– Edna Greene Medford, Professor of History Emerita and former Associate Provost for Faculty Affairs, Howard University

"For nearly forty years of his life, the late Lieutenant Colonel William Baker devoted himself to the meticulous investigation of the Brownsville, Texas, Incident of 1906. This volume is the result of his brilliant analysis, which led to the full exoneration of the 167 Black soldiers involved. More than an expertly written history, this volume is a fascinating chronicle of a military man's 'quest for justice.' Readers will thank Dr. Bettye Foster Baker for her critically important role in the publication of her husband's book."

– Henry Louis Gates, Jr., Alphonse Fletcher University Professor, Harvard University

"Both Colonel Baker's imaginative recreation of the Brownsville Affair and his account of his fight to redress the wrong done to the disciplined Black soldiers add considerable depth to this important story. Although several books have been written about this unfortunate piece of America's racial history, Baker demonstrates that there is more to be learned. His is a remarkable tale of courage, persistence, and conviction. Get the book: it is a great read."

– Tweed Roosevelt, University Professor, Long Island University; Chairman, Theodore Roosevelt Institute

"An inspiring story of one honorable man's commitment to correct a 'gross injustice' and to remind Americans that these lessons transcend race and time: 'Innocence before guilt. Due process of law. These basics of constitutional protection cannot, should not, be superseded by anyone, including the president of the United States.'"

– Sam Roberts, New York Times

"Colonel Baker skillfully interweaves two distinct stories. First he offers an imaginative reconstruction of a shameful and widely reported 1906 incident: the events that led President Theodore Roosevelt to discharge without honor 167 African American soldiers for allegedly participating in—or refusing to identify the participants in—a shooting rampage in Brownsville, Texas. (Doris Kearns Goodwin's *The Bully Pulpit* calls Roosevelt's action 'a permanent scar on his legacy.') Second, he gives a first-person account of his own ultimately successful efforts—sixty-six years later—to exonerate those same soldiers. Racism, sectional tensions, political machinations, careerism, and sheer human malevolence all rear their ugly heads in Colonel Baker's fascinating narrative."

– Professor Baird Tipson, Adjunct Professor, Gettysburg College

"With a keen eye for truth and justice, Lieutenant Colonel William Baker provides a road map for those with the courage to successfully fight the most powerful political institution in America."

– Judge Greg Mathis (Ret), First cousin, Lieutenant Colonel William Baker

"LTC Baker has written a book that should be required reading in all military schools. As an analyst, historian, critical thinker, and philosopher, LTC Baker has fashioned the most comprehensive story of the Brownsville Affair to date. His efforts led to the redemption of 167 African American soldiers whose lives were forever altered and ruined by racism.

The Brownsville Affair had implications that ultimately fleeted up to the White House. Included in this group of innocent soldiers was Master Sergeant Mingo Sanders, who was considered to be one of the best leaders in the Army. LTC Baker's magisterial efforts led to a modicum of vindication and justice for these soldiers' unjust treatment. His remarkable scholastic ability and moral courage set a high standard for all future investigations into this matter and may provide a moral compass for similar investigations going forward."

– Dr. Benjamin Swinson, LTC (Ret) Infantry, U.S. Army

"Two sad things emerge from Lieutenant Colonel William Baker's phenomenal research in The Brownsville Texas Incident of 1906: The True and Tragic Story of a Black U.S. Army Battalion's Wrongful Disgrace and Ultimate Redemption: first, that only two of the 167

Black soldiers dishonorably discharged lived to know of Baker's determination to exonerate them; and, second, Baker did not live to see his book to publication. Still, there is one great thing readers can derive from Baker's relentless drive and a discipline annealed in the military is the satisfaction that he corrected a terrible wrong. Lieutenant Col. Baker, Presente! And let the 21-gun salute begin."

– Herb Boyd, Adjunct Professor, City College of New York; Author, *Black Detroit: A People's History of Self-Determination*

To the men of the First Battalion, Twenty-fifth Infantry, U.S. Army, from whom justice was denied for more than 66 years.

May my grandchildren, Julianne Frances Walker, Andrew Bryant Walker, and Wesley Baker Walker, come to understand that it is only by standing up for justice that one can find true freedom.

"Truth, crush'd to earth, shall rise again."

— William Cullen Bryant

Contents

Foreword	i
Preface	1
Book I: The Brownsville, Texas, Incident of 1906: A Reconstruction	9
One	11
Stranger at the Door: *The Beginning*	
Two	14
Thirty-Five Years Later: *The Pentagon, June 1, 1972*	
Three	22
Brownsville, Texas, 1906: *Anger and Fear Take Over*	
Four	28
Brownsville Awaits *the Final Decision*	
Five	46
Buffalo Soldiers *Are Coming to Brownsville*	
Six	56
The Troops *Go to Town*	
Seven	80
"The Yellow Rose of Texas"	
Eight	96
Midnight Attack *on Brownsville*	
Nine	120
Did the Soldiers *Shoot Up the Town?*	

Ten 134
    Panic in Brownsville

Eleven 141
    A Citizens' Committee *Investigates*

Twelve 150
    The Blocksom *Investigation*

Thirteen 154
    A Texas Ranger *Comes to Town*

Fourteen 170
    Departure from *Fort Brown*

Fifteen 176
    Fort Reno: *Days of Forced March*

Sixteen 182
    Judge Parks Fails to Keep *His Appointment*

Seventeen 184
    A "Conspiracy of *Silence*"

Eighteen 190
    The Grand Jury *Investigates*

Nineteen 194
    The Ultimatum

Twenty 211
    President Roosevelt *Makes His Decision*

Twenty-one 215
    A Public *Outcry*

Twenty-two 224
    Without Honor: The Drumming Out

Twenty-three	**237**
The Gridiron Club *Dinner Debate*	
Twenty-four	**246**
The Last *Investigations*	
Book II: Years Later	**257**
Twenty-five	**259**
The Pentagon, *June 1972*	
Twenty-six	**267**
The Search for Evidence of a "Conspiracy of Silence"	
Twenty-seven	**279**
Writing the *Nonconcurrence*	
Twenty-eight	**296**
JAG Sets the *Legal Parameters*	
Twenty-nine	**303**
Disproving a *Negative*	
Thirty	**307**
The Leckie and Wiegenstein *Experiments*	
Thirty-one	**315**
The Eyewitnesses *to the Shooting*	
Thirty-two	**326**
Finding the *Proof*	
Thirty-three	**332**
Pardon or *Exoneration?*	
Thirty-Four	**348**
The Old Man's *Claim*	
Book III: Aftermath	**369**

Thirty-five	371
Compensation or *Reparations?*	
Thirty-six	394
Who Actually *Did the Shooting?*	
Thirty-seven	406
The Officers' Fates and *Seeds of Doubt*	
Appendix A	408
Author's Biography	416
Source Notes	420
Selected Media Resources and Abbreviations	422
Backstories	428
Acknowledgements	449
Index	451

FOREWORD

My Connection to This Story and the Author

It was 1993 when this book began to find its voice, after incubating for more than 18 years in the mind of my husband, retired Lieutenant Colonel William Baker. You would think that such important stories as the Brownsville Redemption are immediately recognized the moment they reach a publisher's desk or, more significantly, the eyes of an agent. That was not initially the case in *The Brownsville Texas Incident of 1906: The True and Tragic Story of a Black Battalion's Wrongful Disgrace and Ultimate Redemption*. Several publishing houses viewed the manuscript, but they had no interest. Who would buy it? How would they make money?

Publishing history, particularly Black history, is rife with stories that never see print, and those that do barely squeak by. We understand that these are not stories that white America welcomes or digests easily, whether they take place on battlefields or cotton fields. However, they all lay bare a stark reality that demands telling.

Brownsville, in particular, is a classic example of how truth was ignored and even subverted—by a president of the United States no less—to advance a political agenda or deny Black justice. Colonel Baker pushed ahead against institutional opposition and threats to his career to uncover the hard facts of the incident and reveal a hidden truth that was disbelieved for nearly 70 years. It is also a story of the deep and abiding pain that was levied on the men and families of the First Battalion, 25th Infantry (Colored), most of whom went to their graves disgraced, never knowing that their innocence would one day be proclaimed.

A Story Determined to Be Told

Brownsville was a story determined to be told. And because of that imperative, I was successful in securing posthumous publication of my husband's manuscript. From start to finish, he carefully researched and documented this work, which consumed nearly 40 years of his life. But it was Bill's painstakingly accurate research that led both the Pentagon and President Nixon to correct the gross injustice of President Theodore Roosevelt's discharges without honor against the soldiers.

The Brownsville tragedy transcends racial boundaries and time. The universality of its themes—due process, fair play, and the presumption of innocence—are enduring principles. For that reason, it should have wide appeal to all who value justice, especially among African Americans, soldiers, and former soldiers of all stripes.

Because of its similarities to the Dreyfus Affair and the Japanese internments, this book provides a poignant chronicle of our past that demands that those who ignore history and the stunning impact of racial discrimination and injustice shall have the task of establishing why race and social justice matters.

The foundation and tentacles of what moved my husband to correct the Brownsville injustice reach back to the inception of this country, long before the nation had set its ideals and laws on paper.

Yet, it is clear that his motivation stems from his life experience growing up in the Jim Crow South, in Attapulgus, Georgia, the grandson of a freed slave named Ned Keaton. It was Keaton who would first tell him the story of the Brownsville debacle.

The notion that Black men are dispensable and undeserving of the same justice, opportunity, or consideration as their white brethren

The Brownsville Redemption

defined Bill's circumstances but not his upbringing or belief system. It was for this reason alone that Bill decided—once Brownsville officially came to his attention—that he would dedicate his life to vindicating these innocent men.

This work begs the question: What is it that makes a man stand up—in spite of threats to his livelihood, to his career, and yes, even to his life?

Bill Baker will tell you:

> Knowing that Might Makes Right had won in Brownsville and Washington for 66 years has caused me to distrust certain judicial expressions that often give the illusion of justice, the sort of stereotyped bromides that politicians and judges are given to, such as: 'All men are equal before the law,' and the inscription over the U.S. Supreme Court building, 'Equal justice under law.' President Roosevelt made similar statements, even as he rationalized his actions against the Brownsville soldiers.
>
> Roosevelt's statements were barren then, and such lofty pronouncements are barren now, and will always be barren, for they assume the law is just. But they are just platitudes—reminders of how things should be, rather than how they really are.
>
> I am convinced that justice is not always inspired or achieved by the law, and certainly not by well-meaning clichés, and not even by just having constitutional rights. Those rights must be activated. It was goodness, the God within, and struggle that achieved a measure of justice for the soldiers. What they got was delayed and imperfect but redemptive. Truth prevailed. 'Truth, crush'd to earth' did 'rise again.'

Lieutenant Colonel (Ret) William Baker

Note: Lt. Colonel Bill Baker died on September 24, 2018, just weeks after the ink on the final page of his manuscript dried.

Relevance Today

The story of Brownsville is powerfully relevant today. Back in 1906, claims that the Black soldiers were innocent would have been labeled "fake news." There was compelling evidence to prove their innocence, but there was no imperative to find and interpret it. In today's parlance, the 167 men of the 25th were guilty of acting as soldiers "while being Black."

It wasn't until Bill Baker made the effort to dig up the evidence and analyze it decades later that a true and accurate account of the incident could be told.

On July 17, 2014, Eric Garner, a Black man, died in the New York City borough of Staten Island after a New York City Police Department officer put him in a chokehold while arresting him. Before he died, Garner is heard on video saying, "I can't breathe" eleven times while lying face down on the sidewalk. Despite his role in the incident, Daniel Pantaleo, a New York City Police Department officer, remained on desk duty, collecting a salary and pension benefits, and avoided any legal punishment for his role in Garner's death. Pantaleo was ultimately fired—five years later, in August 2019.

Garner's crime? He was suspected of selling loose, unlicensed cigarettes.

The list of the victims of such lethal and unlawful incidents continues to grow. The year 2020 alone saw the deaths of George Floyd and Ahmaud Arbery, to name just two. Floyd's last words were the same as Eric Garner's: "I can't breathe"—an apt metaphor for a society caught up in a chokehold of perpetual stereotypes and racism. We cannot "say [all] their names" simply because there are too many.

But while the incidents pile up, so do the efforts to counter them to get to the truth of what really happened. That's why Bill Baker's effort must be recognized, applauded, and cited as an example of the ongoing need to continue to fight for Black justice.

Bill Baker is America's Émile Zola, the man who fought for justice in the infamous Dreyfus Affair at the turn of the 20th century. Both men faced seemingly insurmountable odds, risking their livelihoods to rail against hidebound conservative societies, and both succeeded in their goals. The main difference is that Zola helped vindicate one man: Bill Baker vindicated 167.

Justice is not automatic. It must be fought for. It must be believed in. And it requires men and women of good conscience to step forward and do the hard work, just like Bill Baker did. Refer to: https://www.nytimes.com/2018/10/08/obituaries/william-baker-dead.html.)

Dr. Bettye Foster Baker

PREFACE

A Night of Terror

Midnight, August 13, 1906. Unidentified bandits viciously raid the town of Brownsville, Texas, where the First Battalion, 25th Infantry of the United States Army, a unit of 167 Black men, is stationed. The raiders unleash a 10-minute barrage of bullets that kills a young bartender, wounds a police lieutenant, shatters windows, studs the sides of houses, fells a horse out from under its rider, and causes widespread panic among the white townspeople.

The next day, the August 14 edition of the *Brownsville Daily Herald* newspaper proclaimed, "DASTARDLY OUTRAGE BY NEGRO SOLDIERS." This patently false headline set the tone for subsequent media coverage as well as the arc of events that would lead to what could be called "President Theodore Roosevelt's biggest blunder."

For nearly seven decades, the true facts of those deadly few minutes were buried in obscurity. This important historical episode does not even have a fixed name. Terms used have included the Brownsville, Texas, Affray—or Affair—or Raid—or Riot—or Incident. I have chosen to call it the Brownsville, Texas, Incident. But, whatever one calls it, the harrowing event resulted in a rush to judgment that tragically changed forever the lives of those 167 men and their families.

Roosevelt charged that all 167 Black soldiers of the First Battalion, 25th Infantry, who were stationed in Brownsville that day were responsible for the carnage. The men were subsequently discharged without honor and without trial. Their pain and suffering, however, did not end with that humiliation. They also lost their pensions and were barred from any future government service. Worst of all, they were forever stigmatized with the dishonor of a crime they never committed—a tragic mistake that set me on a decades-long quest for justice.

My grandfather first told me the Brownsville story when I was a child. He never believed the Black soldiers did the shooting. Further, he accused Roosevelt of not only deceiving the soldiers but disgracing the entire "Colored race." I recall the deep sadness in his voice when he recounted what he called the president's betrayal of his brothers-in-arms. Some of these same Black soldiers had fought with then-Colonel Roosevelt during the Spanish-American War in 1898. They helped him capture Kettle Hill by first capturing the village of El Caney near San Juan Hill. And they faithfully served him during the Philippines insurrection. They deserved better.

The 25th Infantry marching in the Philippines during the Spanish-American War (1898). The soldiers also fought in Cuba, where they helped Theodore Roosevelt capture San Juan and Kettle hills.

The Brownsville Redemption

A Reconstruction

This book is divided into three parts. Book I is a reconstruction of the events surrounding the Brownsville Incident, using newspaper reports, court documents, and depositions from the National Archives, Library of Congress and the Pentagon Law Library. I created conversations between the players in Book I with the help of these sources, plus my own knowledge and experience in military protocols. Book II is a memoir of my quest for justice and my search for the real story of what happened on that fateful day in Texas. Book III details the aftermath of my successful discovery of the innocence of the Black troops and the long-delayed compensation for the affair's one known survivor—a payment 66 years in the making.

I believe this investigation worthy of national record and provides much needed closure to an important event. To a limited extent, it is also autobiographical, in that it portrays a glimpse of a particular slice of my life.

Government reports constituting the official records of the Brownsville Affray included: Three presidential messages War Department reports Hearings of the Senate Military Affairs Committee Courts-martial records of the white officers—Battalion Commander Major Charles W. Penrose and Company Commanders Captain Samuel P. Lyon and Captain Edgar A. Macklin

Military court of inquiry proceedings published by the U.S. Government Printing Office in Washington, D.C.

These published reports included many volumes, some of which constituted thousands of pages. They purported to tell the story of what really happened at Brownsville and, in fact, offered valuable information.

However, as I reviewed and analyzed them, I grew to distrust much of what they presented and eventually rejected many of their conclusions. Other sources included telegrams, cablegrams, memoirs, contemporary newspaper accounts, letters, and autobiographical materials of some of the major characters.

Official reports I studied were from the Law Library in the Pentagon. I also used U.S. National Archives original source documents located in boxes numbered 4499 through 4504, adjutant general document file number 1135832 and newspaper accounts. Sworn affidavits; depositions; testimonials of the Black soldiers, white townspeople, and officials; court-martial records from the white military officers who commanded the Black troops; technical reports by ballistic experts; and other documents of special legal significance. *Book II, Years Later: My Quest to Exonerate the Innocent*, is based largely on the strength of the evidence upon which I relied to tell my story. They include the same government records and the same original source documents in the National Archives, official government letters and memoranda from 1971–1974, my private papers, my own memory, and some of the official documents purporting to tell the story of what happened at Brownsville.

Notwithstanding my distrust and rejection of some of my source information, I am satisfied that I have been fair and true to all of my sources. However, I have not been able to keep myself out of the story. It was impossible. My quest to exonerate the innocent has become itself an integral part of the whole story.

Background to the Early 1900s

Before reading, it is helpful to review the politics, events, and sentiments of the times.

When Theodore Roosevelt assumed the presidency in 1901 after the assassination of William McKinley, he did something no other president had done—he invited a Black man, the educator and former slave Booker T. Washington, to the White House for dinner. The public expressed outrage. Nevertheless, Roosevelt further signaled his intention to promote civil rights for Black Americans by appointing Blacks to Federal positions.

Theodore Roosevelt proved to be a man of contradictions, suggesting a conflict in his nature. His father, Theodore, Sr., whom he idolized, was a New Yorker and a Unionist during the Civil War. His mother, Mittie, however, was a high-born Confederate from Georgia, who ran a southern-style household that was presumably racist in nature.

Roosevelt's invitation to Booker T. Washington, coupled with his actions and his public statements condemning the lynching of Blacks, created hope within the Black community. Consequently, in the elections of 1904, the Black electorate flocked to Roosevelt and the Republican Party.

It appeared that all would be well.

But the Brownsville Incident crushed those hopes and brought the progress of the Black community to a sudden end. Just one month later, the Atlanta Race Riot (September 22-24) occurred, during which up to 100 Blacks were massacred in retribution for an alleged assault on two white women. As we shall see, the unwarranted blame in the Brownsville Incident almost certainly lent credibility to the white's fury in Atlanta. Even its very name, the Atlanta Race Riot, somehow implies the riot was an uprising of Blacks against whites. One has to wonder whether that riot would never have taken place had Roosevelt rejected the theory of a "conspiracy of silence" and made the correct and honorable decision in the Brownsville ruling. But once he had announced his decision, nothing in the world would make him change his mind, at least in public. In fact, he would double-down on his prosecution of the Brownsville soldiers, signaling that the persecution of Blacks was A-okay.

Interestingly, the Wikipedia article at present on the year 1906 does not include the Brownsville incident. It does, however, reference the birth of Hazel Bishop, the "inventor of no-smear lipstick" (August 17) as well as "the first legal forward pass in an American football," (September 5) and the "invention of the muffuletta sandwich" (exact date unknown). In the age of global searching capabilities, the omission of Brownsville is inexcusable.

The two most famous events of 1906, however, were the San Francisco Earthquake and fire (April 18) and the military exoneration and reinstatement (July 13) of the French Captain Alfred Dreyfus, who had been falsely accused and imprisoned for treason. The Dreyfus Affair remains the most infamous scandal of the 19th century.

In 1894, Dreyfus, an officer and the only Jewish member of the French General Staff, was accused of spying for Germany, France's bitterest enemy. On flimsy (and perhaps manufactured) evidence, Dreyfus was quickly convicted and sent to a hellish prison on Devil's Island.

Dreyfus was the perfect scapegoat. He was the single Jew among high-ranking conservative Catholics. Who would defend him?

It was later proved the real culprit was another French officer, an aristocrat named Esterhazy. But in 1898, a closed military tribunal pronounced Esterhazy innocent. The tribunal, unwilling to admit its original error, entered into a "conspiracy of silence" and doubled down on Dreyfus, pronouncing him guilty a second time.

The ruling shocked many, most notably Émile Zola, the most popular writer in France at the time. The obvious injustice prompted him to write what is perhaps the most famous newspaper article in history, "J'Accuse!" ("I Accuse!"), an open letter to the president, citing the facts of the case and demanding Dreyfus's exoneration.

"J'Accuse!" tore France into two intractable factions and nearly caused a civil war between the powerful pro-Catholic, anti-Semitic authoritarian conservatives and the lowlier anti-religious, pro-republican liberals. The higher powers convicted Zola of libel. But his letter lived on and ultimately led to the justice he had championed: Dreyfus was officially exonerated and reinstated in the army on July 13, 1906.

On the occasion of Zola's burial in the nation's Panthéon of national heroes, the literary giant Anatole France declared, "Zola deserves well of his country for not having lost faith in its ability to rule by law." He also rightly asserted, "[Zola] was a moment in the history of human conscience."

It appeared that all would be well.

But the 12-year ordeal had unleashed a virulent wave of anti-Semitism in France that soon transcended borders, all because of a lie and a "conspiracy of silence" within the highest reaches of government.

Universal Importance

To me, the historical importance of the Brownsville Incident lies in the universality of its themes. They transcend racial boundaries and time. When Americans are charged with committing a crime, they are entitled to a trial and all of the rights associated therewith. Innocence before guilt. Due process of law. These basics of constitutional protection can~~not~~ *should* not—be superseded by anyone, including the president of the United States. In addition, the underlying theme of redemptive justice—craving it, pursuing it, and finally getting it—flows throughout this book. It is never too late to correct injustice. This story, chronicled here in three sections, illustrates that powerful truth. Together, they form the chronicle of my fight to exonerate the innocent, and the ultimate triumph of justice.

BOOK I

The Brownsville, Texas, Incident of 1906:
A Reconstruction

ONE

Stranger at the Door: *The Beginning*

Southwest Georgia, 1936

Decades after the Brownsville Incident of 1906, the stigma of dishonor still haunted the soldiers of the 25th Infantry. In the empty years that followed their release from the U.S. Army, they wandered around the country like ancient mariners, proclaiming their innocence to anyone who would listen.

My grandfather, Ned Keaton, a former slave and storyteller himself, had heard the Brownsville story and passed it along to me when I was a boy of just five or six. It was during the depths of the Great Depression.

Late one evening, I sat on the front steps and watched a stranger walk up the dirt road toward my Grandpa's house. The old man carried himself with an air of dignity. He advanced with a deliberate and precise cadence, suggesting he had once been a soldier. As he walked, his shoes kicked up little clouds of red dust. His clothes were clean but old and tattered and dotted with holes that had been patched many times. He wore a funny-looking wide-brimmed hat, a kind I had never seen before.

I scampered up the steps, ran into the house, and told Grandma Angeline that a beggar was coming. She took a hoecake from the cupboard, wrapped it in newspaper, and went to the door. When the stranger saw Grandma's face, he retreated and apologized, saying something to the effect that he was sorry, and called her "Miss." He said that he didn't mean anything and begged her not to holler for the sheriff. She assured the man she was a "Colored woman" and that she had some bread for him.

The stranger looked at me and a faint smile came over his face. He reached into his pocket and pulled out some pennies, offering to pay. Angeline told him she wouldn't take anything for it, but the stranger insisted, telling Angeline that he was not a beggar. She told him to take the bread and said, "May the good Lord be with you." He accepted it gratefully, then turned and left.

The next day in town, Grandma Angeline and I stood on the corner near the Country General Store, waiting for Grandpa to return from the Gulf of Mexico with oysters. Evening shadows were beginning to fall. We expected to see him coming over the hill at any moment.

Suddenly, I heard the screeching sound of a car skidding on the road, its brakes squealing as it tried to stop. The smell of burning rubber permeated the air. I saw an old man about to cross the road. Someone shouted at him, "Watch out! Car! Car!" But the warning came too late. There was a dull thud and a cry of pain. The car dragged the man several feet, then sped away. I turned away and buried my face in Grandma's apron. I recognized the man as the stranger who had come to our door.

Grandma held on to me tightly. But I soon broke free and ran across the street to pick up the old man's hat. Then I rushed into the crowd, working my way through to the inner circle. I looked at the dead man lying on the ground, motionless, face-up, and eyes wide open. People stood around talking and shaking their heads. Their voices were hushed and respectful. But no one tried to do anything.

All the commotion drew the attention of Mr. Kauffman, the white storekeeper at the meat market. He pushed his way into the crowd, elbowing people out of his way. When he got through, I ran to him, grabbed the corner of his apron, and pulled him toward the man on the

The Brownsville Redemption

ground. I looked up into his face, wanting so much for him to help the stranger. Kauffman stared down at the man quizzically, looked up at the crowd, and asked, "Who's the dead nigger?"

My grandfather knew. Suddenly, he appeared through the crowd and knelt beside the man. He lifted the stranger's hand, felt his wrist, then looked off into the distance. I approached Grandpa slowly and handed him the hat, which he placed over the dead man's face. Then he told me that he knew the old man from a long, long time ago.

He had been one of the Brownsville soldiers.

Lieutenant Colonel (Ret) William Baker

Two

Thirty-Five Years Later: *The Pentagon, June 1, 1972*

The Brownsville Papers

Fast forward three and a half decades to June 1, 1972. I am a staff officer in the U.S. Army at the Pentagon. On this day, I am sitting at my desk, engrossed in a letter addressed to me from the White House staff. The letter is full of petty complaints and projects that President Nixon's special adviser wants me to work on. I had been away in Europe on a White House project. By the time I returned, the papers on my desk had mounted to an impressive height.

The phone rang and I answered, not knowing that call would change my life forever. It was my boss, Colonel Harry W. Brooks, Jr. I detected a sense of crisis in his voice. He told me to come to his office right away and to bring the Brownsville papers.

What was he talking about, I wondered? I told Colonel Brooks thatm I didn't know anything about any Brownsville papers. "Helen said she put the file on your desk weeks ago. Find it and bring it over to my office immediately."

When I did not find the Brownsville file among the pile of papers, I tore my office apart. It wasn't really an office at all, but a cubicle painted in ugly government green. It had one desk, an old typewriter, an old-style black telephone, a chair, and several metal six-drawer file cabinets in assorted shades of drab beige and gray.

My office was a part of the newly established Army Department of Equal Opportunity Programs. The department was a lowly stepchild in the Pentagon—understaffed, generally ignored, and poorly housed. The layout reminded me of those endless cubicles at the U.S. Post Office, where I had worked during the Christmas recess in 1954. There I'd seen low-level clerks (many with college educations) who had grown old working long hours in the mailroom, hunched over long tables, leaning with one shoulder lower than the other, sorting huge piles of mail. These men would hobble down the marble steps at the end of the workday. But once they hit the streets, they straightened up and strutted with exaggerated pride, casting off the drudgery of the day. They walked the be-bop walk, heads held high, with one shoulder higher than the other, one arm swinging stiffly.

These men belonged to the Army of Inopportunity, living with broken hopes and lost dreams. I worried I'd become one of them. But I escaped up the ladder of equal opportunity. It wasn't a self-made ladder—my opportunities were made available by others.

When I opened the last of the old metal cabinets, I caught sight of a document with a red tab attached to the top with a paper clip. I took it out, leaned against the file cabinet, and read a document with big, bold letters emblazoned on the top, "H.R. 6866, 92ND CONGRESS, 1ST SESSION." It was a bill proposed by Congressman Augustus F. Hawkins of California. (Hawkins was the first Black politician west of the Mississippi River elected to the House of Representatives.) His bill had been referred to the Committee on Armed Services. If approved by Congress and signed into law by the president, it would direct the secretary of defense to rectify certain official actions taken as a result of the Brownsville Raid of 1906.

Brownsville! The name transported me back to my boyhood in southwest Georgia and awakened memories I had tucked away. One day, while fishing on the banks of a creek, my grandfather had told me about a violent shooting spree in Brownsville, Texas, and that President

Lieutenant Colonel (Ret) William Baker

Theodore Roosevelt had accused an entire regiment of Black soldiers of getting drunk, breaking out of their army camp, and shooting wildly into people's houses. My grandfather did not believe the Black soldiers had been involved in the shootings. He said that Roosevelt had cruelly misjudged the soldiers and disgraced the Colored race. I recalled the sadness in his voice as he explained the president's betrayal.

I pulled the folder out of the drawer, went back to my desk, and continued reading. I knew that Colonel Brooks wanted the file immediately, but I couldn't pull myself away.

Attached to the bill were three intriguing letters:

The first letter was from Congressman F. Edward Hebert of Louisiana. It was addressed to Secretary of State Melvin Laird, requesting his views on the proposed legislation H.R. 6866. The bill proposed to overturn the Discharge Without Honor meted out to the 167 members of the 25th Infantry who'd been charged in the Brownsville Incident. The resolution was the culmination of nearly 66 years of effort by the country's Black leadership to reverse what many believed had been a gross miscarriage of justice.

The second letter, the response to Congressman Hebert's, had been written by army lawyers in the Judge Advocate General's office (JAG) on behalf of Secretary of State Laird. It said that Laird opposed the bill.

As I probed deeper into the opposition, I found the army's official version of what happened:

> The Brownsville Affray occurred on the night of August 13-14, in 1906, in Brownsville, Texas. Some 16 to 20 unidentified soldiers of Companies B, C, and D furtively left the garrison and ran amuck through town, firing into homes and stores. One man was killed, two men were wounded, and the horse belonging to the lieutenant of police was killed.

The Brownsville Redemption

The letter went on to explain that because none of the soldiers had come forward to identify themselves as participants or to offer any evidence to incriminate others, President Roosevelt accused the entire regiment of participating in a "conspiracy of silence." He punished them by discharging them **all** "without honor."

It appeared to me that the alleged "conspiracy of silence" had constituted the legal basis for Roosevelt's blanket punishment of 167 soldiers. It was also the basis for JAG's current opposition to Hawkins's bill.

JAG's negative stance disappointed me. But I was gratified to see that George P. Shultz, the director of the Office of Management and Budget (OMB), had returned the letter to JAG, requesting additional reasons for the army's opposition.

The third letter was JAG's reply to Shultz. It had yet to be sent but was on its way out the door. The letter showed that the army refused to offer any additional reasons for its opposition except to assert that the discharges were supported by ample historical precedents.

I was afraid that if that letter got out, it would kill the bill.

The letters of opposition, having been approved by a maze of high-level department heads, had reached the end of the line for agreement. They were now on my desk. I looked at the date of the bill: March 29, 1971; the congressman's letter was dated April 9, 1971; and JAG's response was dated April 23, 1972. These papers had been kicked around for a year now—first to the OMB, then to the White House, the Justice Department, and then back to the Pentagon. It was now June 1, 1972. The deadline for response was upon us.

We had only three days remaining to concur or nonconcur. While studying the legal arguments in the letters, I sensed a presence around me. I looked up and saw my boss, Colonel Brooks. I blurted, "What's the matter with those lawyers over there in JAG? I know you can't agree with them, Colonel. I don't agree with them.

We *must* non-concur!"

Brooks wanted to know where I had found the Brownsville papers. He and Bob Dews had been looking all over for them for some time now. I told him that I found them stuffed in the file cabinet.

I handed the papers to Brooks. "Here, you take 'em."

Brooks didn't take the papers. He smiled slightly, and his face settled into a relaxed expression. "Let's get Bob Dews and go to my office and talk about this," he replied.

On the way to Brooks's office, I stuck my head into Dews's office. I told him I'd found the Brownsville papers and motioned for him to come with us.

Lieutenant Colonel Robert Dews, the senior staff officer in our department, was a brilliant, savvy, and experienced man. Brooks relied heavily on his judgment in critical matters.

We were barely seated at the conference table before Dews glared at me and said, "You want this project?"

"What's the matter, Bob?" I said, still holding on to the Brownsville file. "Don't be sensitive. I just want to help."

"Do you know something about it?" he parried. "You can have the whole damn thing."

I spared Dews an excursion into the past by simply telling him that I had just read the file and I'd like to work with him on the project.

Brooks intervened. He wanted to know whether we were going to agree with JAG's opposition to Hawkins's bill. "Bob, can we concur with JAG?"

"We can't do it!" I cried before Dews could answer. "We just can't do it!"

"Wait a minute, Bill," Brooks said softly. "I was talking to Bob." He asked Dews again, "Can we go along with JAG?"

The Brownsville Redemption

"I'm not sure. I haven't had time to do much on it," said Bob. Turning his attention to me, Brooks asked me what I knew about Brownsville. I still clutched the folder in my hand.

"I've read most of the papers in this file, sir. We have an issue with JAG."

Now, more excited than ever, I felt confident. I wanted to take on this fight with JAG. I wanted to persuade the army to drop its opposition to Hawkins's bill, and I volunteered to take the case. I showed Colonel Brooks that, without our assent, JAG had already sent a letter stating that their opposition was not controversial in the Department of the Army.

"Look here." I pointed to the document. "Nowhere on this piece of paper can you find our signature agreeing to that statement. They bypassed our office. I think they must be hiding something."

Brooks picked up the telephone and called Colonel Wade Williamson over at JAG and told him he was sending Bob Dews over to resolve some issues on the Brownsville case. When the call ended, Brooks turned to me and said, "Sorry, Bill, I want Bob to handle this."

Early the next morning, around six o'clock, I stopped by Dews's office. He was sitting at his desk, having a cup of coffee. I could tell from his expression that he was in a sour mood. He was angry and wasn't trying to hide it.

"Those bastards' skirts aren't clean," he said. "You were right. They *are* hiding something." He, too, believed that JAG had deliberately bypassed our office. They had sent that first letter out to OMB without our concurrence.

Dews was certain that JAG's Colonel Williamson wouldn't support Hawkins's bill because of his distaste for the Congressional Black Caucus. Dews described Williamson as adamant, dogmatic, and unyielding in his position. He asked whether I still wanted the case. I told him, "Yes, by all means."

Later that morning, Colonel Brooks called me into his office, where he and Dews had been meeting for some time. Brooks didn't even ask me to sit down.

He looked up from his desk and said, "We'll non-concur. Bill, you have the Brownsville project."

That assignment led to my own investigation of the strange story of a town seized by fear and anger, a web of lies, deep-rooted racial passions, prejudices…and murder.

A Violent Beginning

The town of Brownsville, Texas, founded in 1846 during the Mexican-American War, was fathered, birthed, and nurtured by the guns of the United States Army. General Zachary Taylor, while leading his troops against the Mexicans, had constructed an earthen bastion on private property that was later named Fort Brown, after a fallen U.S. soldier of the war. The tiny civilian settlement nearby became Brownsville. In 1848, U.S. congressman Abraham Lincoln of Illinois questioned the genesis of Brownsville and sought to determine whether the United States had committed an act of aggression against Mexico in prosecuting the war.[1]

Brownsville sat in the lower Rio Grande Valley in a flat river delta, in the farthest reaches of southeastern Texas, just north across the Rio Grande from Matamoros, Mexico. Fort Brown, located on Garrison Road at the end of town, nestled within the big bend formed by the Rio Grande as it flowed toward the Gulf of Mexico.

---

[1] This account was taken from Carl Sandburg, *Abraham Lincoln: The Prairie Years, Volume One*. p. 372.

The Brownsville Redemption

In 1906, Brownsville was a rough-and-tumble town of poor dirt farmers who barely eked out a living. Ranchers, shopkeepers, and saloon owners depended heavily on the patronage of the soldiers from nearby Fort Brown.

The town's 6,000 inhabitants were saturated in deeply rooted racial prejudices arising from the old cotton field, tobacco road, and the unreconstructed South. As there were just a few African American families in Brownsville, Anglos tended to blame lawlessness, violence, and most all other ills on the much larger Mexican population and on itinerant gunslingers, rough-neck newcomers, and smugglers. But all that changed on July 25, 1906, when the all-Black 25th Infantry came to town.

THREE

Brownsville, Texas, 1906: *Anger and Fear Take Over*

The Announcement

Weeks had passed since Dr. Fredrick J. Combe, the mayor of Brownsville and also a medical doctor, announced at a special town meeting that the War Department was planning to send Black soldiers to Fort Brown. They would replace the current battalion of white soldiers.

Not long after the announcement, Mayor Combe started hearing rumors that his citizens would not accept "nigger soldiers." Some white citizens were making violent threats, boasting that all they would have to do was kill a few niggers and that would drive the other niggers out of town in a week or two. William Howard Taft, secretary of war under President Roosevelt, received many complaints. They all said the same thing: "Do not send Colored soldiers to Texas. Change the orders!"

While assuring his citizens they had no reason to fear the potential new arrivals, Mayor Combe neglected to tell the townspeople that he had served with some of these very soldiers. He had been their doctor. *Perhaps*, he thought, *it would be unnecessary since it was taking so long for the War Department to make a final decision.*

Afraid that Taft would not heed the warnings, Combe set up several meetings with his police chief, George Connors, to plan a strategy. He wanted to do anything he could to prevent trouble, which might soon be on its way.

The Brownsville Redemption

Mayor Frederick J. Combe in his military uniform, c. 1903. Courtesy of the Brownsville, Texas, Historical Association

Meantime, Brownsville was on the verge of a general panic. For weeks, families had congregated around their kitchen tables, conjuring alarming fantasies fueled by rumor, anger, and fear. *The Black heathens will rape, rob, and murder us in our beds,* they thought. People felt the coming of a reign of terror. One would have thought that foreign conquerors were advancing to occupy their town.

Captain Benjamin J. Edger, Jr., the doctor for the white unit that was leaving Fort Brown, told Mayor Combe that all the white people he had spoken to, even his friends, didn't want "Colored soldiers" in Brownsville. And they were loud and insistent in their denunciations.

Mayor Combe believed their fears were groundless. He had to find a way to quiet them.

"They'll get used to the Colored soldiers, for sure, with time." He tried to sound reassuring.

Chief Connors shook his head and said he didn't know about that. Talk was getting violent. Threats were being made.

"My policemen tell me that they heard a group of roughnecks talking about joining a posse to meet the train and stop the soldiers from getting off," he said.

The mayor wanted to know who was behind it and what their names were. Connors believed the saloon keepers were behind it, down to the last pissing details.

"They are an unhappy lot. They're afraid their businesses will fold when the white soldiers leave because they'll refuse to serve the Negro soldiers. I heard Joe Crixell say that all he wanted in his saloon was white officers' business."

The chief then remarked that one of the policemen had heard another saloon owner, H.H. Wellers, say to a crowd of rabble-rousers, "The people will get rid of the niggers some way."

"Then," continued Chief Connors, "there's John Tillman. He just opened the Ruby Saloon, and it's only now beginning to take off. His business will go under if he doesn't serve the Negroes. I heard him say he might have his bartender set up something in the back for the Colored soldiers. If he can't make money that way, he threatened, he'd have the Negro soldiers 'run out of town in three weeks.'"

"That's nonsense," the mayor said. "Who's he going to find to do that? Who's going to shoot first? And they damn sure better aim straight. They won't get a second shot. I knew these soldiers in Cuba." The chief continued his report, "And, oh, yes. There's something else I heard. The preachers are calling for a mass meeting next week."

"Keep your eye on them," said Combe. "When they stir up trouble, they wrap it in the sanctity of God."

The Brownsville Redemption

This conversation took place while Brownsville was still waiting on the final decision from the War Department.

The chief leaned forward. "You'd better get some kind of answer soon. You saw the crowd gathered near City Hall the other day. It was getting pretty ugly when Captain Kelly stepped in and cooled them off a bit."

"I saw Captain Kelly addressing the crowd," said the mayor, "Now there's a man I can count on."

"Kelly is a good man," Connors agreed. He then warned the mayor, "You'd better watch out for your political enemies, especially Sam Wreford. Don't take your eyes off him. He'll use this thing to embarrass you."

The chief finished his report and stood up to leave. "The streets are quiet today. I'm going fishing."

As Combe walked the chief to the door, his thoughts turned to the 25th Infantry. Companies B, C, and D were units of the 25th United States Infantry Regiment (Colored), an all-Black battalion except for its white officers. At present, the soldiers were stationed at Fort Niobrara, on the plains of Nebraska, near the small town of Valentine. The Plains Indians and other western tribes held the Black warrior-soldiers in such high regard that they honored them with the name of their sacred buffalo, calling them "the Buffalo Soldiers."

Combe began to brood. He would rather not have Black soldiers stationed in his town if his citizens didn't want them. But he knew these soldiers. He especially knew First Sergeant Mingo Sanders and was friends with some of the white officers. He had served with them in 1898 as a combat medical officer in Cuba and the Philippines during the Spanish-American War. He knew them as honorable, well-disciplined fighting men.

An Anxious Wait

It was a hot and humid day in mid-July. The air barely stirred in the sweltering heat. Many of the townspeople had scurried off to the beach near Point Isabel, on the Gulf of Mexico, to cool off. Mayor Combe was at work, performing his doctor duties. But there had been few patients that morning.

Still troubled by the chief's report from the week before, Combe decided to close his medical office early and go to his other office at City Hall. He worried that he still hadn't received any final word from Washington. He'd been promised that the secretary of war would give his reply "any day now." That was weeks ago.

While walking, Combe saw Captain Edger, the post surgeon for the departing white soldiers. Edger waved him down from across the street and approached him. "Fred, got a minute? I've got something for you."

Combe sensed some urgency in the captain's voice. He greeted his old friend. "Sure, Ben, what have you got?"

They walked up Ninth Street toward City Hall.

"I have the army contract for you to sign to act as post surgeon until they can get a new doctor here to replace me," said the captain.

Edger followed the mayor and waited for him to unlock his office. The two men walked in, closed the door, and sat down. Edger reached into his black bag, pulled out the contract, and offered it to Combe, who made no move to take it. He hesitated for so long that Captain Edger let his hand and the contract fall to his side. "What's wrong, Fred?"

Combe felt uneasy, but he managed to say, "Oh, it's nothing. Give it to me. I'll sign it." He took the contract, signed two copies, and handed the army's copy to the captain. Edger stood up. "We're leaving the day before the 25th Infantry gets here, Fred. Word is that they'll arrive on the 27th. Between now and then, there'll be lots of packing to do, so I'd better be going."

Combe dropped his copy of the contract on top of the pile of papers waiting for his signature. He then sat down and signed paper after paper, resigned that there would always be something more to sign. When he finished, he placed the finished work in a basket on a small corner table near the stately grandfather clock. He used to love the sound of the clock's ticking and had often marveled at the enormous golden pendulum that moved with such marked precision. But now, it disturbed his thoughts.

Combe relaxed into his brown leather armchair and propped up his feet. He took a deep breath and reflected on his two years in office. It seemed that all of the progress he'd made was about to go up in smoke. Just as he was feeling good about the strides he'd made, trouble was heading straight for him. He feared rioters would rip the community apart. Why hadn't he told the people at that special town meeting that he knew some of the soldiers? Maybe that would have eased their fears.

Who was he kidding? He knew why he hadn't told them. Now he regretted it.

Lieutenant Colonel (Ret) William Baker

Four

Brownsville Awaits *the Final Decision*

The Telegram

On the 23rd of July, Mayor Combe was alone in his City Hall office. He was reclining comfortably in his great leather armchair, reading the *Brownsville Daily Herald,* when he heard a light tap on the door. It startled him. He had grown edgier every day, awaiting word from Washington. He didn't respond immediately but took a deep breath. *Was the final decision waiting at the door?* Finally, he said, "Come in." His clerk opened the door and smiled. "Doctor Combe, I think this is what you've been waiting for." He handed him a telegram. Combe took it, and the clerk left the room.

Combe stood up and walked to his desk. He stared at the envelope in his hand and paused for a few seconds before ripping it open. As mayor of Brownsville, Combe had seen many telegrams, but this one appeared more official than any other. As he read the first line, he slumped back into his big chair, sagging beneath the weight of the news: They'd made the decision. The Colored soldiers were coming.

Taft had simply refused to change the orders, but his response intended to allay the fears of the townspeople:

> The fact is that a certain amount of race prejudice between white and Black seems to be universal throughout the country, and no matter where Colored troops are sent, there are always some who object to their

coming. It is a fact, however, as shown by our records, that Colored troops are quite well disciplined and behaved as the average troops, and it does not seem logical to anticipate any greater trouble from them than from the rest. Army records also showed that white soldiers averaged a greater degree of intemperance than Colored ones. Sometimes communities that objected to the coming of Colored soldiers have entirely changed their view and commended their good behavior to the War Department.

Combe, of course, objected to Taft's decision, but he readily agreed that Black troops were well disciplined. He thought that the townspeople's fears were overblown, although he had to admit that even he, a combat veteran and a medical doctor, had allowed himself to fall into the fear trap. Then he had a revelation: It wasn't the soldiers he was afraid of; It was his own citizens—and the potential consequences of the looming frenzy.

The News Gets Out

Even before Mayor Combe could inform his policemen and his staff, word had hit the streets that Taft had refused to change the order—and that Black soldiers were indeed coming to town. *How could the word have leaked out?* Then Combe remembered. It must have been through his nemesis Sam Wreford, who'd probably heard it from his ally in Washington—former Texas governor, and now U.S. senator, Charles Allen Culberson.

Combe wanted to organize a citizens committee to calm the people's fears. He rang up the chief of police to discuss his plan.

"The preachers are one step ahead of you," said Chief Conner. "They're holding a protest meeting tomorrow in front of the federal courthouse."

"Do you think they'll draw a crowd?" asked the mayor.

"Yeah, they've been whipping them up for weeks now."

Combe felt he must act quickly. "Get hold of Captain Kelly. Tell him to round up some stalwarts and meet me here tonight at eight o'clock. Tell him it's urgent." At ten minutes past eight, Mayor Combe was sitting alone at the head of a large mahogany conference table when Captain Kelly arrived, thundering, "Damn fools! They'll incite a riot!"

The mayor called out to Kelly and the group of men entering the lobby. "Captain, in here! In the conference room."

Captain Kelly had invited some of the town's most prominent officials to the meeting—the county judge, John Bartlett; the city attorney, Frank W. Kibbe; the editor of the *Daily Herald*, Jesse Wheeler; and the sheriff, Celedonio Garza. Police chief Connor was also in attendance.

Mayor Combe got down to business. "You all know why you're here. We've got to get control of this situation before the rabble-rousers spin it out of control. How can we stop them?"

Chief Connor said, "I don't have anything on the preachers. I think they're pretty straight. I think Sam Wreford's the one behind this rally."

"Get me some charges, and I'll throw his ass in jail!" Judge Bartlett said. "Well, what have we got on Wreford?" The judge looked around the table. "Anybody? I can smell shit a mile away. Got to be some shit somewhere."

"He's dirty all over," agreed Kibbe

"I need specifics," replied the judge.

Then Connor announced, "He's been fornicating with a Mexican woman!"

Under Texas law, "fornication"—defined as sex with a woman other than one's own wife—was considered a crime.

"So what!" cried the judge. "There are a lot of men in this town fornicating with Mexican women."

Then Jesse Wheeler spoke up. "I have proof he's not a resident and hasn't paid taxes in several years."

Judge Bartlett peered over his glasses. "Now we're getting somewhere."

"Just listen to this," said Wheeler. "A few years back, Sam Wreford tried to smear Jim Powers, the superintendent of the local, national cemetery, by accusing him of embezzling cemetery funds. Jim came to me to help clear his name. While looking into the matter, I found some interesting stuff on Sam, including a court record in Cameron County that confirmed he'd been found guilty of living in sin with a Mexican woman. No penalty had been imposed on him on the condition that the woman return to Mexico. But get this. The record also revealed that Sam Wreford has paid no taxes in Brownsville for several years and that he is, in fact, a resident of *Mexico!*"

The judge immediately turned to the city attorney. "Kibbe. Go to Sam. Get him to call off the meeting tomorrow."

Mayor Combe interjected, "The momentum for the meeting is probably too great to stop it now. Besides, somebody responsible needs to address the citizens—and that man is me."

Combe turned to Kibbe. "Tell Wreford that we appreciate the preachers' leadership in calling the meeting, but the mayor needs to talk first—after an opening prayer, of course. After I finish, one of them can give the benediction, and then I'll leave."

Combe's strategy was to marginalize the preachers by confining them to the opening invocation and the closing benediction. He then instructed Kibbe to strike a deal with Wreford: Combe would support his interests if he would simply agree to a joint meeting under the auspices of the mayor's office.

"Tell Wreford that he must get the preachers to tone down their rhetoric. Persuade him to go along. And don't bring up any 'dirt' unless you have to."

A Unique Distinction

The next day, by five o'clock, the square in front of the courthouse was packed, with people still coming. Mayor Combe sat on the hastily erected platform, conspicuously apart from the rest of the dignitaries. It was his practice to have his massive, overstuffed brown leather chair transported from his office to wherever he was speaking. As he intended, it dwarfed the other chairs, with their rickety backs and caned seats.

The rest of the dignitaries—Captain Kelly, John Fernandez, Jesse Wheeler, Judge Bartlett, and Sam Wreford sat behind a table draped with red, white, and blue bunting. A pitcher of water had been placed in the center of the table, with a glass set out for each of them. The mayor had his own fruit jar filled with water, which sat on the floor beside his great chair, as it did during all of his speeches. Whenever he was lost for words or needed to get his thoughts together, he took a sip or two, using it as a distraction. There was a joke around town that one could tell whether the mayor had made a good speech or a bad one by measuring the amount of water left in the jar. A good speech left the it nearly full. A bad speech left it empty.

The Brownsville Redemption

The courthouse square was decorated with all the trappings of a political rally rather than a protest meeting. Patriotic bunting was tacked up everywhere. Old Glory and the Texas state flag rippled in the Gulf breezes. The air was electric with expectation as if some political heavyweight were about to announce his candidacy for office.

After a few more late arrivals elbowed their way closer, one of the preachers stood poised at the podium to offer up a prayer to Almighty God. "Let us bow our heads." Then he offered up a short invocation—so short, in fact, it probably set a record in that part of Texas.

Then Fred Combe rose to address the crowd. "My good citizens, my friends, you know me. I am your mayor, and for some of you, your doctor. Our relationship is long, close, and deep. Like most of you, I was born here in Brownsville. I grew up here. This is home. My roots are deeply embedded in the soil of our ancestors who were born and died here—strong men who built this town up from nothing but a cotton patch. Our ancestors loved this town. You love this town. And like you, I love this town—its traditions, the way we talk, our food, the soil from which it comes, and the salty air we breathe. I love this part of Texas!"

The crowd broke out, chanting "Texas! Texas!" A man up front yelled, "Tell it, Fred!"

The mayor was encouraged.

After several more rounds of chants, Combe then reminded the crowd of how much he had accomplished since he'd become mayor just two years before and how well off they'd been under his administration.

"Since becoming your mayor, I have reformed the city administration, cleaned up the streets, and brought order to our town. I dressed our policemen in military-style uniforms to bestow on them the dignity they deserve. So now, as you know, they look like soldiers. And that's good, for like the soldier, they are here to protect our mothers, our wives, and our children.

"I witnessed the transforming magic of the uniform while I was a soldier. The uniform brings discipline, honor, and respect to the soldier, his community, and his country. I knew the uniform could do the same for our policemen. With a more professional police force, you, the citizens, feel more secure, and I feel more secure. There has been less open display of weapons, less shooting and gunplay in our streets, and fewer casualties than ever before.

"I know you all own guns. You love your guns. I love my guns. I see you toting Winchesters and Remington rifles, shotguns, six-shooters, and even a few old Krag-Jørgensens you bought from the soldiers leaving Fort Brown, willing to sell one for a buck or two. But, as we all know, a gun is not the way to settle a dispute."

Then the mayor dropped his voice and eased into the crux of the matter:

> Now we are being consumed by a crisis of fear, a contagion, spreading hate among us. Irrational fear that has invaded our minds, our bodies, our [community] spirit, and is about to invade our very souls. It is a fear that threatens our Christian way of life and propels us toward the gun, toward the destruction of our town, urging us to believe in salvation through the gun instead of salvation through our God.

Sam Wreford, sitting on the platform with the other dignitaries, grew increasingly uneasy at the tone of the mayor's speech.

A heckler near the front shouted, "Git to the point, mayor! The Colored soldiers are coming. What are we gonna do about it? I thought this was a protest meeting. We're not here to talk about our souls!"

The Brownsville Redemption

Looking directly at the man, the mayor replied cooly, "I know what we're here for. I'll get to it in a minute."

"Deal with it now, Combe," the heckler called out. "We're tired of waiting! Why are you making a campaign speech?"

Mayor Combe recognized the heckler as someone who had supported his opponent in the last mayoral election. Combe turned his head away and looked straight ahead at the sea of people before him. Then, as if speaking confidentially and privately to separate groups, the mayor first addressed the middle, then the left, and finally the right.

"You have nothing to fear from these soldiers," he said firmly. "They wear the uniform of our United States Army. They are coming to protect our border from thieves, smugglers, and bandits. And remember, it was the ancestors of these soldiers, who, as soldiers themselves, drove many Mexican bandits from our land, from our Texas!"

"Liar!" the man shouted. "White men drove the bandits out of Texas. White men!"

Again, Mayor Combe ignored the man. "And, my dear citizens," he continued, "I want you to know that the very soldiers coming to our town fought the Spaniards in Cuba. They captured El Caney! They tore down the Spanish flag and raised Old Glory—your flag! my flag!—in its place! They shared their rations with Colonel Roosevelt and were fighting alongside him when he captured Kettle Hill."

The crowd gasped at this astonishing revelation, and the mayor thought he was beginning to win the people over. Now was the time to call on Jesse Wheeler, editor of the *Daily Herald*. Combe waved him up to the podium. "Come on up here, Jesse. You tell 'em."

Wheeler walked over to the flag-draped podium and stood at the mayor's side.

"The mayor is right," he said. "These are the very soldiers who captured El Caney." He held up a copy of the *Daily Herald* and waved␣␣t at the people. "It's in today's paper. You can read it for yourselves." A woman in the crowd, stretching and standing on tiptoe, called out politely, "Mr. Wheeler, would you read it to us?"

Wheeler nodded. "It's a long article, but I'll read a few lines." He began:

> The 25th United States Infantry, which laid over in San Antonio yesterday on its way from Nebraska to a different post on the Texas border, enjoys a unique distinction in the military Annals of America.
>
> It was that body of troops, composed entirely of Negro Soldiers, that charged El Caney Hill in the face of continuous fire, pulled down the Spanish ensign, and, with the assistance of the Fourth and Twelfth regiments, made prisoners of the Spaniards that survived the attack.

After reading these short passages, Wheeler added, "It goes on to say the Negro soldiers then rushed to join Colonel Roosevelt and his Rough Riders and helped them capture Kettle Hill."

Still skeptical, the heckler turned his back on Mayor Combe, and facing the crowd, he hooted, "It's a fake, folks. They say anything in the newspapers." Then he turned and, pointing at the mayor, challenged him again. "You don't know, Combe. How would you know? You weren't there!"

An old man standing on the ground near the corner of the stage, who knew the heckler, looked over at him and said scornfully, "You ain't been there, neither. So shet your mouth."

Sam Wreford, sensing that the mayor was turning the crowd in his favor, decided to speak out. He was sure he had an ace in the hole to turn the crowd around. *Best use it at once,* Wreford thought, *or Combe will surely win.*

"As I was trying to point out, my good citizens," Combe continued, "these soldiers' records demonstrate that we have absolutely nothing to fear."

Wreford shot out of his chair and pointed accusingly at Combe. "Their records be damned! It sounds like you've gone over to the enemy, Fred. Sounds like you're in favor of the soldiers coming! Oh, and I've got a question for you. Are you going to be the medical surgeon at the post when those Coloreds get here?"

Mayor Combe reached down and took a sip of water. *How the hell had Wreford found out he'd agreed to act as post surgeon?* He was to go on an emergency basis only, and nobody was to know about the contract. He didn't believe his old friend Captain Edger would have told anybody about it. And Edger had assured him that nobody in the departing white battalion knew about it, not even the commander. So, who else knew? He would find the snitch later. For now, he had to deal with Sam Wreford's question. But before he could answer, Wreford went on, "Didn't you sign a contract the other day, knowing in all likelihood that you'd be serving the Colored soldiers, that they'd be coming? You signed that contract, didn't you!"

The mayor turned away from Wreford, faced the crowd squarely, and spoke. "Now folks, Sam knows, and you all know, that I go to the post on an emergency basis when I am called. I've been going for years. They never asked me to sign a contract before, but this time they did. Yes, I signed it, but it doesn't say a thing about Colored soldiers coming to the post. It just says 'soldiers,' and anybody can come by my office and read the contract for themselves. I have nothing to hide."

The mayor was relieved to see the people nodding in approval at his explanation. He felt the sentiment of the crowd returning to his favor.

Having defused the contract issue, the mayor decided it was time to disclose his past connection to the 25th Infantry—the Black soldiers' regiment. Getting back to the heckler, he asked, "Sir, would you please repeat your question?"

The man shouted, "I asked you how you know that Cuba stuff in the paper is true! How could you know? You weren't there!"

Standing erect, Mayor Combe squared his shoulders, looked directly at the crowd, and said, "I served with them. I was their combat medical officer. And some of the white officers are my friends. I do not fear these men, and you should not fear them. They are honorable men, good United States Army soldiers. I came back from Cuba with them on the same boat. The boat stopped in Tampa, Florida. There was no…"

When he saw Sam Wreford stand up again, the mayor stopped in mid-sentence. He looked directly at the troublemaker and said sarcastically, "Okay, Sam, I guess it's your time to speak. Come on over here before you pee in your little britches."

Then the mayor raised his voice, "Don't tell too many lies, and keep the poison out!" The crowd broke into laughter.

Wreford glared at Combe as he walked to the podium. He reached in his pocket for his prepared speech and, not finding it, began fumbling about. He started to sweat. He faced the crowd and said, "Folks, I lost my speech, but…"

Before Wreford could finish, the mayor interjected, "But what? Did a little bird steal it?"

The crowd broke out laughing again. The mayor was making a fool out of Wreford. If he didn't get it together quickly, he was going to be the laughingstock of the town.

Someone shouted, "Quiet! Let him talk!"

The crowd settled down, and Wreford began again.

"Well, I don't need a piece of paper to tell you that the mayor is selling out to the enemy. He's selling out to Roosevelt and that

The Brownsville Redemption

Republican crowd up yonder in Washington, D.C., who's trying to foist these Colored soldiers off on us."

"For your information," Wreford continued, "*my pastor and I* called this meeting today. The mayor jumped aboard our bandwagon and sent his man—begging us, sweet-talking us—to let the mayor speak first. Out of respect for his position, we agreed, thinking we had a common purpose, to keep the nigger soldiers out of our town. Now, the mayor used to be my friend. But no more. He's done switched sides. He's gone over to the enemy."

Wreford leaned over the podium and looked intently at the crowd. "You know, all he really did was give us a campaign speech, telling us how much he loves our town and how much he loves Texas."

He then turned his head toward the mayor and continued. "Well, Fred, we all love our town. We all love Texas. But we didn't come here today to talk about love or to lick our own boots. We're here to send a message to Washington that we're not going to allow any niggers in here! Folks! Don't believe him! If he loves us so much, he'd stop them from getting off that train. But, by God, we'll stop 'em, with or without him!"

The crowd stood silent. In the quiet, Wreford dropped his voice almost to a whisper but continued firmly, "I'm a good Christian. I know there's a lot of good Christian men out there among you. God said, 'love your neighbor.' But he never said nothin' 'bout lovin' niggers. Them nigger soldiers are just like rats. You let 'em in your home, and they'll infest the whole place. You don't hafta hate rats to kill 'em. You just kill 'em."

Raising his voice to an emotional pitch, Wreford shouted, "They don't want our land! They don't want our money! Gentlemen! They want our women! I say, let's go meet that train and clean 'em out!"

The people stirred and murmured among themselves. Wreford waited for the reaction to what he thought were the most powerful words of his speech. When a response was not forthcoming, he repeated, "Gentlemen! They want our women!"

But there was only silence.

Finally, a man near the back shouted out, "Oh, shet up, Sam! You ain't nothin' but a barnburner."

Wreford held his hand to his ear. "Speak louder. I didn't hear you."

The man called out again. "I said you're a barnburner! You talkin' 'bout gittin' rid of rats. You're jest like the Dutchman who burnt down his barn jest to git rid of the rats. You risk all these people's lives if you attack them soldiers. Don't listen to him, folks. Don't go down to that train. You'll all git killed."

"Coward!" Wreford yelled. "You're a coward, old man."

"Yeah!" shouted another man in support of Wreford. "I could take fifty men and go clean out the whole nigger outfit. Let's march on the train!"

Captain Kelley was boiling. He could not sit any longer and listen to such foolishness. Furthermore, it infuriated him to hear United States Army soldiers being compared to rats. He rose abruptly from his seat and said derisively, "Stop the train? With what? With that old rifle you keep around the house to shoot squirrels? The soldiers got the new Springfield rifles. They're trained to fight. None of you've ever been a soldier."

Wreford, sensing that he was about to lose control of the situation, figured he had better get in a few last words. He needed to slam the mayor for good, and this was the moment: "Folks, we got a rat among us, and we all know who he is. He just finished talking to us, and there he sits!" He pointed at the mayor.

"It's plain as the hair on his head," Wreford said emphatically. "He's a double-crossing, double-dealing rat! He's a traitor to the purity of our white women. He's a traitor to the chastity of our girls!"

The crowd grew silent again. They squirmed at this venomous attack on their mayor, whom most of them honored and even loved. They stood stone-faced, in total disbelief.

Wreford fired off another volley of attacks. "And why won't he go to that train station with us? I'll tell you why. 'Cause he's made his bed with them. And I want to tell you—he's still in that bed with 'em. By his own admission, he's lived with 'em!"

Seething with anger, Mayor Combe leapt to his feet, crying, "That's enough, you son of a bitch! You assaulted my honor! You impugned my character and integrity! You called me ugly names! Now you're trying to take the law into your own hands and incite my citizens to riot! You have completely crossed the line. I will not let you destroy this town!"

Combe strode over to Wreford and, standing chest to chest, stared intently into his eyes. "I promise, you'll regret this day, you rascal," he growled as he brushed past Wreford's shoulder and started to walk away.

He stopped cold when he heard Sam yell, "You double-dealer! You asked for it!"

Mayor Combe swung around to confront Wreford and jabbed him in the chest with his index finger, backing Wreford up against the table and chairs, yelling, "You…you…you!"

Wreford fell back into his chair. He tried to get up, but the mayor hovered over him. "Sit down," he seethed. "And shut up, you…you fornicator!"

The crowd let out a gasp.

"Oh my God!" cried one woman, standing in the front row. Aghast that he'd let the word "fornicator" slip out, the mayor knew that he had to offer some proof of Wreford's crimes. *I can't stop now*, he thought. *I must destroy him completely.*

Wreford flinched, astounded that the mayor would make such an accusation in public. Visibly shaken, he tried to hurry off the stage. But Combe blocked him and shoved him back down into his chair. He had more for him. "Oh, no," he cried, "you're not going anywhere, you tax cheat! You dirty the chair you're sitting in. You defile this stage!"

Map of Brownsville and Fort Brown, drawn by craftsmen in the Office of Quartermaster General, December 1909. Modified by Lt. Col. (Ret) William Baker. NOTE: Garrison Road separates Brownsville from Fort Brown.

The Brownsville Redemption

Mayor Combe walked back to the podium and addressed the crowd, "My good citizens. My friends. I apologize for my language, but there's more you should know about this man, and I regret it has to come out this way. All this time, he's been pretending to be one of us. But I've got to tell you; he is not a resident of Brownsville, not a resident of Texas, not even a resident of these United States. He's a resident of Mexico! Also, the court in Cameron County found him guilty of fornicating with a Mexican woman. The judge ordered him to get out of this country and take the woman with him or be thrown in jail. He didn't obey the law. Yet curiously, here he remains, stirring up trouble and poisoning your minds. The record also shows he hasn't paid any taxes in several years. If you don't believe me, go down to the courthouse and see for yourselves."

The mayor paused and took a deep breath. Then, buoyed by his fury, he launched into a rhetorical flight of fancy, all the while pointing at Wreford: "And there he sits—still in this country. He's a bad man. He's a liar. He's a notorious introvert. And he was a dangerous celibate before he met that Mexican woman," he said with righteous conviction.

He then lowered his voice and said dramatically, "And my friends, I'll tell you something else! He even practices nepotism with his sister!"

Another collective gasp came from the audience.

One of the preachers was devastated upon hearing that his favorite deacon was being accused of what he misunderstood to be taboo offenses. He could excuse a tax cheat, a liar, and all those other shameful things the mayor had said. There was redemption for those sins. They could be forgiven. But not fornication. God would never forgive a fornicating deacon. And neither would he. To think that this man—a deacon in his church—was a fornicator. That was altogether too much for him.

The preacher walked over to the mayor at the podium and tapped him on the shoulder. The mayor turned, and the preacher whispered in his ear. The mayor shook his head in disagreement, then said, "Please give the benediction, Reverend. This meeting is over."

But another distraught preacher in the crowd wouldn't hear of it. His faith required that he disavow Sam Wreford—the fornicator—right then and there.

The mayor let the preacher speak. He'd already won the crowd, and Wreford had been disgraced. He turned to the audience: "My good citizens, my friends," he said. "I thank you for coming and for your understanding. The Reverend has a few closing remarks to make."

The crowd shouted and applauded.

On his way back to his chair, Combe whispered to Kelly, "After I leave the stage, stay up here, take all questions, and keep that crowd pacified, got it?" Kelly nodded silently.

The preacher held both sides of the podium to steady himself. His face was stern as he faced the crowd.

"Good Christians, you should know, I will not tolerate my deacons fornicating with Mexican women who are not their wives!" He walked over to Wreford and pointed directly at him. "You're no longer a deacon in my church! And git off this stage! You ain't fit to sit here, neither!"

But Wreford didn't get up. So the preacher moved in on him and, wagging an angry finger in his face, yelled, "Git! Git! You ought to be horsewhipped!"

Wreford swayed so far back in his chair to avoid the threatening finger that he tumbled back and hit the floor.

The preacher dropped his arm, stepped back, and watched the fornicator struggle to get to his feet.

"Git up! Git up!" the preacher shouted.

The Brownsville Redemption

The sheriff stepped in to prevent a fistfight from breaking out between the new adversaries. The preacher backed off, and the sheriff escorted Wreford from the stage.

"My good Christians," continued the preacher, "there goes my worst sinner."

In the commotion, the mayor slipped from the stage and began making his way through the audience, shaking hands as he went.

As the crowd slowly dispersed, the preacher shouted after them, "Let the slackers go! All the God-fearing people—stay! God's on our side! We'll stop that train!"

# FIVE

Buffalo Soldiers *Are Coming to Brownsville*

July 23, 1906, Valentine, Nebraska

Despite the continued warnings of military officials and Texas senator Culberson not to send Colored troops to Brownsville, the War Department issued its final directive on May 26th, 1906: The Black soldiers must depart Nebraska for Texas on July 23rd.

A throng of well-wishers, mostly whites, along with a few Indians and Blacks, gathered at the train station near Valentine, Nebraska, to say their goodbyes to the Black soldiers of Companies B, C, and D of the 25th Infantry. They'd been stationed at Fort Niobrara for the past four years. (Company A was out in Montana, protecting settlers as they seized land from the Indians.) The citizens of Valentine hated to see these men leave, for they had found them to be good neighbors, and some had become good friends. Owners of saloons, cafés, and restaurants in Valentine had never refused them service, nor had the townspeople ever made racial distinctions against them.

When the soldiers boarded the train for Brownsville, the townspeople stood on the platforms, waving goodbye and calling out, "We're going to miss you!"

Just as the train was pulling out, an elderly white woman shouted a warning, "The people in Texas are gonna give you hell! Don't go down there!"

The Brownsville Redemption

Leaning his head out of the window of the train, Private John Amos Holoman shouted back, "If the Texans bring hell, they gonna get hell!"

The men of the 25th Infantry left for Fort Brown without any trepidation. Many of them were seasoned veterans of the Spanish-American War in Cuba, the Philippine Insurrection, and the Indian Wars on the Great Plains. They had also seen action in the hills of Montana and Wyoming. Their records acknowledged their fine character, military skills, and acts of heroism. They were the sons of both Northerners and Southerners. They were sharecroppers, farmers, musicians, carpenters, bricklayers, mechanics, cooks, and laborers—and all shared the common bond of honor, duty, and country as Black soldiers of the United States Army.

Unlike the Black soldiers, their five white officers dreaded taking the troops to Texas: The soldiers of the 26th Infantry stationed at Fort Brown had passed along to them all of the ugly racial talk emanating from Brownsville. They would soon be hearing it for themselves.

The officers of the 25th Infantry were highly qualified professionals. Two were graduates of the United States Military Academy at West Point, and two others had come up through the ranks. The fifth had received his commission by direct appointment.

The battalion commander was Major Charles W. Penrose, an ambitious soldier who had aspired to become a general ever since receiving his commission. He had always been thoroughly committed to his military career. Penrose saw the military as a stepping stone into Michigan politics, a move he hoped would lead to the governorship.

From the standpoint of health and physique, Penrose had been scorned by the gods at his birth. He was a slender man with a puny build and little strength. He weighed about 130 pounds (59 kilos), stripped, and never seemed to be able to gain weight, no matter how much he ate. He had a pallid complexion and suffered from frequent bouts of illness, including recurring attacks of typhoid fever, diarrhea, and amoebic dysentery—all of which made him irritable. He wore glasses. He was also a heavy smoker and moderate drinker. Yet, despite all of his obvious infirmities, he still aspired to become a great general.

The train was nearing Austin when Penrose suddenly remembered something that had bothered him. It was something his father had said. He vividly recalled that evening last summer when his father had returned home from a Republican political meeting at the Union League in Philadelphia. Their conversation had been unsettling, even chilling.

The old general had told him, "Charlie, you've got to change regiments."

The sense of urgency in his father's tone seemed ominous. "What do you mean, change regiments?"

"Your career's in jeopardy, son. It's as simple as that."

"What do you mean? I'm in the finest regiment in the army. We proved that in Cuba!"

"Undoubtedly. But it's a Negro regiment," the old general said.

"I know that, sir." Penrose tried to sound respectful but belied his impatience. "Dad. Cut to the chase."

"It's the uniform, son. There's resentment, and it's growing—resentment against the Colored man wearing the U.S. Army uniform."

"That's petty prejudice. What's the uniform got to do with it?"

"The uniform is a symbol, a powerful symbol of honor. It represents acceptance of the Black man, even deference to him. It dignifies and ascribes nobility to him. It's the acknowledgment by official policy that the Black man is equal and entitled to wear the same uniform as the white man."

The Brownsville Redemption

The younger Penrose stiffened. "You mean the Black soldiers have the same rights and privileges under the constitution to fight and die in war? But not the right to our respect or gratitude?"

But his father had no interest in debating the rights of Negro soldiers. His only concern was his son's career and future. "Command of Black troops by white officers is considered inferior duty," he said. "It's a drag on your career. Many senators are unlikely to confirm you for promotion above major if your principal duty has been commanding Negro troops."

Last summer's conversation would stick with him for a very long time.

Knowing that the protests from Brownsville had reached Washington, Penrose now worried that his battalion had come to the attention of the top officials in a negative way. Stern-faced and serious, he stood up, smoothed the front of his uniform, and went to check on his men. He was aware that he and his troops would be arriving in Brownsville under protest from the citizens of the border town his command was supposed to protect. He worried what form those protests would take. How unfair, he thought, that his command was being rejected for doing nothing more than being born Black.

The Texans' prejudice flew in the face of the contributions his men had made and still could make. It shattered his belief that they would be measured by their military performance, not by their color. But his father had undoubtedly spoken the truth, and he felt a new sense of foreboding. Fortunately, he had one friend in Brownsville he could rely on for support—Fred Combe.

When the troop train stopped in Austin, Penrose decided it would be unwise to allow his men to get off to stretch their legs and get a breath of fresh air. Previous threats of violence by the Texas militia in

Austin and warnings by the military authorities made the idea seem foolhardy.

July 25, 1906, Brownsville, Texas

In Brownsville, crowds of people lined Garrison Road, leading to the main gate to Fort Brown. Split-rail fence barriers were set up along the route to control the crowd.

Mayor Combe and his police force waited at the depot for the train to arrive. The mayor was tense and anxious. He stood near the station, in the background, watching for any sign of a posse. Wreford and the preacher might yet show up to carry out their threats. Although he didn't see them or any other sign of trouble, he was still apprehensive. Searching for shade from the hot July sun, he moved to a cooler spot by an orange tree in a vacant lot. Things were quiet thus far, and he relaxed.

His mind drifted back to the days he'd spent during the war with his friend, Charlie—Major Charles W. Penrose. They had first met in Cuba in 1898 and had developed a respectful, warm, and genuine friendship. Now he wondered what his old friend would look like and whether he'd still be the same old Charlie. It will be a good reunion, he thought. He was sure that together they could work out any difficulties that might arise among the townsfolk and the soldiers.

Combe had heard that First Sergeant Mingo Sanders, a Black non-commissioned officer who also fought in Cuba in '98, was still in the 25th Infantry Regiment. Combe recalled Sanders's reputation as a combat soldier—in battle, he was heroic under fire, and, as a professional soldier, a strict disciplinarian who brooked no foolishness from his men. He was fair, reasonable, and one of the best soldiers in the army, Black or white. Although Sanders had to be getting old and nearing retirement, Combe was sure that he and Major Penrose could count on him to keep any troublemaking soldiers in line.

Elizabeth Street, looking toward Fort Brown. U.S. Archives, AG File 1135832

Mayor Combe had thought about planning a public welcome, a warm greeting for the troops, but changed his mind for political reasons. An outward show of friendship, even for his old friend, might be misunderstood. But how could he stand in the background and watch his friend get off the train and say nothing?

Two years ago, when the white soldiers from the 26th Infantry Regiment arrived, greeting the troops hadn't been a problem. Combe and the townspeople were right up front, shaking hands, smiling, and welcoming them to Brownsville. Now he was uncertain. Should he come forward and greet the soldiers? He decided he would go to the post later and welcome them in private. The decision pained him, and he was a little ashamed for having to do that. It reminded him of his childhood when he had to hide with his Colored playmates in the backyard or the kitchen. These rules were forced on him by his parents. He now forced the same rules on himself.

The 25th Infantry Arrives

When Combe felt the ground shaking under his feet, he recognized the heavy vibrations of a train radiating down the tracks. He heard the screeching whistle, signaling everyone to stand back, get out of the way, and let the train rumble in. The rust-colored iron engine, pulling the troop train behind, rolled into Brownsville, puffing clouds of black smoke high into the air and blowing billows of steam as it jerked to a stop. The Black troops had arrived.

Sergeant Sanders was the first soldier to appear. He was in charge of the security detail. Sergeant Sanders was a tall, wiry Black man with chiseled features, high cheekbones, long arms, and large hands. He had the look of a fiercely protective African warrior-king. His posture was stern and formal—even regal. His eyes were black and deeply set, yet they somehow remained friendly. He had entered the army in 1891 and fought in Cuba and the Philippines. He was a brave soldier and an honorable man. He loved the United States Army. He'd spent 26 years in devoted service and was just two years away from retirement.

After disembarking from the train, Sanders looked around. He scanned the streets and studied the crowd of people near the station. He took notice of the policemen standing at the intersection of Levee and 12th streets. He imagined how he could best use the split-rail fence barriers for security. He looked for any sign of people carrying guns. Then, with a commanding tone, he ordered, "Security guards, disembark! Take up your preplanned positions."

The Brownsville Redemption

The 25th Infantry Arrives in Brownsville, Texas, July 25, 1906

At Sanders's command, twelve armed soldiers jumped off the train, took up positions on both sides of Levee Street, and stood at parade rest. Combe was reassured as he observed these precise military moves. The leadership of the old 25th Infantry was still in charge. Nothing untoward was going to happen in his town between these soldiers and his citizens, he thought.

Penrose saw no smiles. He heard no clapping, no bands playing. He saw nothing but hostile, suspicious faces glaring at his soldiers as they marched along the streets of Brownsville through the large black iron gate guarding the main entrance to Fort Brown.

What a cold reception, he thought. *It's not going to be easy for us here.*

The wives and children of the officers and noncommissioned officers were the last to get off the train. They followed the troops, carrying suitcases, hat boxes, and an assortment of belongings. Some of the children had their pets with them—dogs, cats, and even birds in cages. Assisting them were their personal military orderlies and cooks.

Main Gate, Fort Brown, Texas, c. 1906. Courtesy of Professor René Torres, University of Texas at Brownsville

Under the regimental organization, the unit was a closely knit collection of soldiers, wives, children, and sometimes other close relatives, all of whom lived together as a big family. It was a military tradition to allow the married men's families to accompany them except on extremely dangerous campaigns.

While the lower-rank soldiers lived in barracks, the married noncommissioned officers and their families lived in separate quarters. The commissioned officers and their families also lived in separate quarters.

Each company unloaded their stash of military supplies: boxes of ammunition, boxes of spent cartridges, fired shell casings, and ammo clips they had used on the rifle range at Fort Niobrara. Then the teamsters came, loaded everything onto horse-drawn wagons, and hauled it off to Fort Brown for storage. When space ran out, they placed the overflow of boxes filled with empty cartridges, shells, and clips on the back porches of the barracks.

As the men began to unpack their personal belongings, four families from the local Black community came to welcome them. But they also came to warn them that the white people weren't happy and had made it clear that they did not want "these damn niggers trading down here" or even coming downtown.

That warning turned out to be prophetic.

Six

The Troops *Go to Town*

A Breeding Ground for Mosquitoes

The next day began with a heavy rain, which did nothing to cool off the sweltering town. Sheets of water fell onto hot pavement and rose back up into the air as steam. The old soldiers hadn't experienced such insufferable weather since their sweaty days in the Philippines.

With its low-lying topography, lagoons, ditches, and semi-tropical climate, Brownsville was a fertile breeding ground for mosquitoes. They attacked at any time of the day—morning, noon, and night. Typhoid fever was rampant.

That afternoon, Private William E. Jones was in the kitchen, preparing dinner for Captain Lyon and his wife. Willie, as Mrs. Lyon called him, was busy trussing a chicken. As he pinned its wings back and tied the legs together to hold in the stuffing, he stopped to scratch his arm, now peppered with red welts from mosquito bites. But scratching brought only temporary relief. He picked up a box of bicarbonate of soda, added a little water to make a paste, and smeared it all over his arm, trying to get some relief. Mrs. Lyon gave him an occasional stare as she observed him plastering his arm with the white paste.

Finally, she said, "Willie, that looks awful. Why don't you go to the drugstore in town and get some salve after dinner?"

"It'll be all right, Miss Lyon. My mother used to put soda powder on her arms all the time to stop the itching."

The Brownsville Redemption

"You should go get the salve, anyway," she said. "Besides, I need some."

After dinner, Mrs. Lyon handed Private Jones some money and cautioned him, "Don't linger. Be careful. Don't forget. You're in Texas."

Private Jones walked out the iron gate, crossed Garrison Road, and hurried up Elizabeth Street looking for a drugstore. This was the first time he'd been to town. As he walked, he studied the store signs on both sides of the street.

In the middle of the first block, he saw a short white man with a heavy mustache standing outside on the sidewalk. He was smartly dressed in a dark suit, white starched shirt, black vest, and a white bow tie.

As Private Jones neared the man, he called out, "Evening, sir." The man said nothing, but his face turned hostile, and he turned to block the entrance to the store behind him. Jones looked up at the sign, which read, "Dotgrain Drug Store." Then he looked at the man—and realized he was not wanted there.

He had been told Black soldiers weren't welcome in the beer joints. But this was a drugstore.

The man folded his arms across his chest, his eyes squinting with loathing.

"Damn you; we don't sell beer here."

"I don't want no beer," the private answered. "I want some of that salve I hear you got to stop this mosquito itching." Jones stretched out one arm, still whitewashed with soda paste.

With clenched teeth, the druggist growled, "I don't want your business. Leave!"

"Mister, I got money. I can pay." Jones held out a quarter.

"Boy, are you some kinda idiot? Don't you get it? I'm not selling you a damn thing."

Jones put the money back into his pocket and turned away, crestfallen and puzzled. "It seems kinda funny I can't buy salve in a drugstore," he mumbled to himself.

"...don't you know this is a white man's town?"

Resigned to a night of discomfort, Private Jones headed back down Elizabeth Street to the fort. A white man was walking just ahead of him, so he felt comforted when he saw two fellow privates, Williams and McGuire, coming toward him. As they approached, Jones picked up his step. He wanted to warn McGuire and Williams how he had been treated at the drugstore because he thought they too might be looking for something to stop the itching.

McGuire, who was ahead of Williams, passed the white man on the narrow sidewalk, and their shoulders brushed lightly.

The man got angry, stopped, and whirled around, pointing at McGuire. "Why, you Black son of a bitch, *don't you know this is a white man's town?*"

McGuire liked to avoid trouble and quickly moved on. Williams moved on, too.

Jones, who had seen and heard the whole thing, ran up to meet them. "What's wrong with these people? The man at the drugstore wouldn't let me in the store. He wouldn't sell me salve. We ain't done nothing to them. What with the mosquitoes and all, I'm about tired of this place already."

McGuire looked back over his shoulder. "Our shoulders barely touched. Hell, they don't even want us to walk on the sidewalk!"

The Brownsville Redemption

When Jones returned to Captain Lyon's quarters and told Mrs. Lyon what had happened, she shook her head but said nothing. A confused feeling of guilt mixed with denial came over her. She was a white woman, the daughter of a general officer, who was accustomed to privilege. She'd been with the 25th Infantry for many years. She knew first-hand that the men were good, disciplined soldiers and wouldn't cause Brownsville trouble. Why wouldn't the druggist sell Willie some salve? She had a strange feeling that it was she who'd been denied the salve, not Willie.

She sat at the dining room table and looked down. "It's not right—not right for a drugstore." When she looked up, she saw Jones's outstretched hand offering her back the money. She put the coins in the pocket of her dress. "I'll go tomorrow, myself, and get the salve."

Not knowing what had happened to McGuire, John Holoman led a group of soldiers into town that evening to quench their thirst. Among them were Dorsie Willis and James Newton. Holoman wished he could have also brought along an old buddy, an ex-soldier named Bugs. Legend had it that Bugs had joined the army because he liked fighting. It was said that he would rush into hell looking for the devil, find him, fight him, split his head open, piss on his brain, and roast him for supper. But Bugs wasn't with them. Unsurprisingly, he wasn't in the army anymore.

They walked up Elizabeth Street and stopped in the first saloon they came to—the Ruby Saloon, owned by John Tillman. They walked in, stepped up to the bar, and ordered beer. Frank Natus, the bartender, looked over at Tillman, who shook his head.

Tillman leaned back against the whiskey racks. "Sorry, boys, I can't serve you here in the front. I'll set up something in the back of the saloon. You boys go 'round the back to the alley. I'll have Frank put some beer back there for you."

Turning to the bartender, Tillman said, "Get some crates for chairs and tables and set them up in the back. That'll do for now. We'll fix it up better tomorrow."

But the men refused to go to the back of the saloon. They left and crossed Elizabeth Street and entered Crixell's Saloon. Joe Crixell was standing in the door as if he had been waiting for them.

"Boys, we have the officers' trade," he said. "Some of 'em are in the back drinking. We like it that way. My guess is you boys would rather drink by yourselves and not mix with the officers."

Private Holoman caught his drift. "Never mind, fellows," he said. "There's another joint across the street. Let's go there."

They had started out the door when Lieutenant Lawrason stepped out from behind the curtains of a back room, holding a bottle of beer. "Aw shucks, Joe," he called to the owner, "Get 'em the beer. We just got in town, and we're all thirsty. They got money. These are my men. I don't mind."

"Yeah, lieutenant, but some folks in this town *do* mind," Crixell replied. "I can't serve 'em. They'll kill my business."

"That's all right, lieutenant," said Private Newton. "We'll leave." The men then went next door to H.H. Weller's Saloon, the rowdiest, toughest tavern in town. Half drunk, H.H. stood at the bar. The place was filled with locals. It was standing room only.

"Well! Well! Well! Look what we got here, folks!" H.H. announced in a slurred voice. "A bunch of nigger soldiers looking for Mexican whores. I tell you, boys, we don't serve no Mexicans, no whores here. And I damn sho' ain't serving no niggers. Just keep walkin' till you think you can't walk no more—that's the tenderloin section. You'll find the Mexican bars and all the whores you want out there."

Then H.H. staggered over toward them.

Private Holoman stepped forward. "Stand back, fellows, he's mine," he commanded. "Y'all just go on down to that Mexican bar and git your beer like this here man says. As soon as I take care of this here business, I'll catch up with you."

"To hell with that," said Private Boyd Conyers. "We'll wait for you outside."

Several toughs wearing faded black 10-gallon hats got up from their table and stood behind H.H. to back him up. The bartender reached under the counter for a pistol and slid it down the bar to a man waiting at the other end. Holoman saw the gun. Instinctively, he grabbed a beer bottle off one of the tables and threw it, striking the pistol a split second before it reached the man's outstretched hand. The firearm fell behind the bar and shattered a bottle, sending glass shards flying everywhere.

"I'll be damned!" H.H. stood in awe. However, he was not impressed by the crashing beer bottle. Bottle-smashing was a common occurrence in Weller's saloon. What got his attention was Holoman's glaring eyes inviting a fight, his quickness, and, most of all, the power of his arm.

H.H. muttered to himself, "Where the hell did he learn to throw like that?"

Holoman gave the room a menacing look.

"We might not git beer here, but we sho' gonna git respect," he declared. "We are men of the United States Army, soldiers, and don't you forget it."

He opened the door and calmly walked out.

Holoman and his friends continued walking up Elizabeth Street toward the tenderloin district. Holoman slapped young Willis on the back and, with a loud belly laugh, roared, "We scared the hell out of 'em, I can tell you that! You should have seen us fight those Texans back at Fort Riley. Ever heard about it, Dorsie? Bugs was with us then."

Holoman then grew quiet. He hoped to God that they hadn't done too much damage. They hadn't come to town to cause trouble. They had come for beer. It was damn hot, and they were determined to find a bar that would serve them.

After walking a fair distance, Willis saw a sign that read White Elephant Saloon. "Look, there's another bar. Let's go there." The proprietor of the White Elephant was V.L. Crixell, Joe Crixell's brother, who ran a combination beer joint and pawnshop. It was also a place where white men could meet women. Crixell advertised that part of his business euphemistically as "Polite Attention."

Behind the bar next to the whiskey bottles was a big notice, WE BUY AND SELL GUNS. Accordingly, along the walls were racks with a variety of guns and rifles—Winchesters, Krag-Jørgensens, Springfield 03s, shotguns, pistols—you name the gun, and it was there.

"I don't know. It looks more like a pawnshop to me," Conyers said.

With an overly friendly gesture, Crixell waved them in. "Come on in, boys. You got them new Springfield rifles, I hear. You come to sell me some guns?"

"No, sir. We're thirsty. You sell beer here, too, don't you?" Holoman asked.

"Yeah, but…"

"But what?"

Crixell's friendly disposition changed abruptly. He looked Holoman up and down with a quizzical, scornful air and motioned to the bartender. "Looks like we got John Henry here. He's a big Black steel-driving man. Wants a beer. He just scares me to death," he said. "Bartender! Get the big man a beer!"

The Brownsville Redemption

The bartender handed Holoman a beer. Holoman looked in the glass, inspected it carefully, then swallowed the cool liquid in one gulp.

Crixell looked up at Holoman in amazement and said, "Give me the glass. You need a refill, BOY."

"No, I don't," said Holoman.

He paid 15 cents for the drink, but Crixell demanded more money. "For what?" Holoman asked.

Crixell snatched the glass from Holoman's hand and threw it to the floor, smashing it to pieces. "For the glass, you idiot! White people don't drink after Colored!"

Holoman was ready to fight again. "You called me 'boy!' You called me 'idiot!' I'll rip your heart out, you cracker!"

He advanced and Crixell retreated, backing up against the gun racks. The other soldiers jumped between the two men, but it took all of their strength to restrain Holoman.

That bout of excitement increased their thirst for anything cold— beer or water, anything. It didn't make much difference at that point. "Let's push on," Holoman said. "Couldn't be much farther. I haven't felt this kind of heat and humidity since I left Luzon Island."

Several blocks on, they heard Spanish music drifting across the railroad tracks. They had finally reached the tenderloin district, which was lined with mostly Mexican bars. It was like stepping into an oasis.

Hot and sweaty, the men piled into the first saloon they saw. A Mexican bartender welcomed them, offering a shot of something stronger than beer. But they ordered beer and drank up. After emptying several glasses, the soldiers paid up and walked back to Fort Brown. All went but John Holoman.

Holoman stopped at the Ruby Saloon, the closest bar to the fort, to speak to the owner.

Lieutenant Colonel (Ret) William Baker

A Talent for Making Money

Private John Amos Holoman was a tall, lanky, athletic man with curly brown hair and a heavy mustache, who had a talent for making money. He was the hard-nosed, premier money lender in the outfit. He was also the company's fastest runner, its lightning-fast outfielder, and the captain of the baseball team. He'd been a sergeant but had been "busted," as soldiers would say, and he'd been demoted the previous year for fighting with another soldier named Arvin over money—a debt of $1.50.

Holoman's story was that Private Arvin owed him money but refused to pay. When Holoman attempted to collect it, Arvin ran off. Holoman ran him down, threw him to the ground, and punched him several times. Then he took a $5 bill out of Arvin's pocket and threw him the change.

Holoman had operated a business at every post at which he had been stationed. Fort Brown would be no different. Coming up with unique schemes to make money from the soldiers and local merchants was his specialty. No one in the battalion came close to his financial prowess. In Nebraska, he had set up a "pay for a ride into town and back" service to carry his fellow soldiers from Fort Niobrara into Valentine. There the men paid for wine, whiskey, beer, and women on credit, charging almost anything to Holoman's account…for a fee.

Holoman's account was a line of credit he had set up with the local Valentine merchants. All a soldier had to do was sign a handwritten note and present it to receive whatever he wanted on credit until payday. Holoman also lent the soldiers hard cash, charging 25 percent interest for any fractional part of the month until payday. He also ran gambling games and took a cut of the winnings.

Holoman saw a ripe opportunity before him in the saloon business. With the four white bars in town refusing service to the Black soldiers, there was quick, easy money to be made, he thought. He knew that the soldiers would be too tired after their grueling duty to make the long trip to the Mexican bars. But more important, he knew the men had too much pride to buy beer from Tillman at the Ruby Saloon. They would never agree to sit in a makeshift room, hidden away in the back. Now if he had his own bar, Holoman's Saloon, the problem could be solved—and he'd make a killing. All he needed was a local white saloon to supply him with beer, soda pop, cigars, and tobacco.

He had this proposal in mind when he dropped in to speak to the owner of the Ruby Saloon.

He told Frank Natus, the bartender, that he wanted to speak to Mr. Tillman. Natus stopped wiping off the bar and looked up suspiciously at Holoman.

"Did I hear you say you wanted to speak to Mr. Tillman?"

"You got that right."

"You don't have to see Tillman. I can take…"

"Yes. I do," Holoman interrupted.

Natus pointed to the back room. "I got the place set up in the back. Just go around back, and…"

Holoman interrupted him again. "I'm not here to drink beer. I want to see Mister Tillman, the owner."

"What do you want to see me about?" Tillman suddenly appeared from the back room.

"I'm John Holoman. Can I talk to you alone? It's kinda private."

Tillman studied Holoman's face for a second. "Come around to the back door."

Crate tables and chairs had been placed haphazardly around a dingy, windowless storage room. Unopened crates of beer and liquor were stacked along one wall, held securely with ropes. There, Holoman laid out his plan to Tillman.

"I figure over half the soldiers won't buy beer here if they have to drink it in the storage room. Weller and both Crixell brothers have refused them, and the Mexican saloons are too far away."

Tillman looked at Holoman quizzically, surprised he had remembered his name. He was unaccustomed to this kind of conversation with a Black man.

Holoman continued. "Both of us can make money. You help me get a license, supply me with beer, soda pop, cigars, and tobacco at five percent over your wholesale price, and we got ourselves a new business." Holoman gestured toward the boxes and crates. "Looks like you got plenty of everything I need."

Tillman listened with interest, and his face relaxed some. "Go on."

"I understand you have a little dry goods business going on, too. I want to set up a line of credit with you. Some of the boys run out of money before payday. I want you to give them credit and charge it to my account. You don't have to worry about being paid by them. I'll pay you, and we'll settle up at the end of the month."

Tillman replied with a smirk, "Where'd a Colored boy like you get an idea like that?"

Holoman said nothing.

Tillman was beginning to take him seriously. "And how are you going to get your money? What's your take?"

Holoman leaned back on a crate, looked Tillman directly in the eyes, and shoved his right hand in his pants' pocket. He rattled the five gold coins he always carried and calmly replied, "You don't worry about me. I'll get my money." He jangled the coins once again.

Tillman looked at Holoman with both interest and skepticism. He felt uncomfortable and was intimidated by the boldness of the proposal. Tillman thought, *This is one smart nigger, talking about percents and things.* It was a full minute before he spoke.

"You got some nerve, trying to horn in on my business," he said. "I can't believe your nerve. Colored boys have had their asses kicked for less. What did you say your name was, nigger? Yeah, I remember, you said, 'Holoman.'"

Holoman bristled at Tillman's insults. *I'm going to bust 'im upside his head,* he thought. But he had to avoid trouble in this new town and focus on starting his business.

A Deal is Made

Holoman's anger took him back to '04 when his outfit was on maneuvers with the Texas National Guard at Fort Riley, Kansas. One night, the Texans had brought their own entertainment for a floor show at the Junction City Saloon—a so-called "Colored" man with a banjo. When the "Colored" man began singing offensive coon songs, Holoman went after him with a vengeance. He took the old man's banjo and smashed it over his head. That's when the fight with the Texans began. Three burly militiamen beat up Holoman until Bugs joined the fight. Bugs picked up two of the Texans and hurled them through the air like toys. They crashed against the whiskey bottles and glasses lining the shelf behind the bar and fell to the floor.

What felt momentarily like triumph later dissolved into a sense of shame, and he pitied the old man. Holoman regretted having hit him and destroying his banjo, his only means of livelihood. He realized the old man only sang those songs to make money.

Although quick to anger and to fight, Holoman was usually a patient man, and he was not easily discouraged when he really wanted something, like closing a business deal.

After his failure at the Ruby Saloon, he walked across the street to Joe Crixell's place. The same man who had been standing in the doorway earlier was still there. Holoman asked if he could speak to the owner.

"That's me."

"You're Joe Crixell?"

"Last I heard, I was Joe Crixell. What do you want now? I told you earlier we had the officers' trade."

"I don't want to talk to you about drinking beer in this here saloon. I want to buy it by the crate and take it to my place."

Joe Crixell was immediately intrigued. Perhaps he could make up some of the business he'd lost when the white soldiers left.

"Come on 'round back," he said. "Let's talk about it."

Holoman was heartened by Crixell's interest and laid out the same deal he'd just offered Tillman. Crixell could see a way of making himself some good money and was impressed with Holoman's plan. He made his mind up right on the spot.

"I'll do it. You pay me a nickel on the bottle above my cost for beer, two cents on the bottle above my cost for soda pop, and two cents above my cost per cigar. I'll work out something later on the cost of tobacco."

Holoman reflected and made some quick calculations in his head. "No." he said, "I'm buying by the crate. Give me crate prices for the beer and soda pop and big-box prices for the cigars and tobacco."

Crixell hesitated. He was not in the mood to negotiate—still, he was tempted by this potential new source of income. "Boy, are you trying to *bargain* with me?"

"You know I can't make any money at the prices you want me to pay," Holoman said. "If I can't make money on this proposition, there's no point to it. But, if I can make money, so much the better for me, and so much the better for you."

Crixell admired Holoman's reasoning and decided to show him some respect. "Alright, you can have it by the crate and boxes. I'll work out the prices so you'll make a profit. By the way, where do you plan to set this up?"

Holoman did not answer but rather stretched out his hand. He and Crixell shook on the deal. A gentleman's agreement. "I'll find a place and let you know." He shoved his hands deep into his pockets, rattled his five gold coins, and walked out the door.

"Get Off the Sidewalk!"

Sunday evening, August 5th, was hot and humid. Fred Tate, a US federal customs inspector, and his wife were standing on the sidewalk on Elizabeth Street, talking to half a dozen white women. They were all hoping to catch an evening breeze from the Gulf of Mexico. Two Black soldiers, Private James W. Newton and Private Frank J. Lipscomb, were walking down the sidewalk, approaching the group. Newton, walking slightly ahead of Lipscomb, passed between Fred Tate and the women.

"Hey, Boy, don't you know how to get off the sidewalk when you see white people?" Tate called out to him.

When Newton said nothing, Tate took it as an insult. He pulled a pistol from his jacket, rushed up behind Newton, and struck him on the head with the butt of the gun, knocking him to the ground. Then he began pistol-whipping him about the head and shoulders. Newton curled up into the fetal position, holding his head, trying to protect himself.

Private Lipscomb ran up to intervene. When he saw blood streaming down the side of his friend's face, he pleaded, "Don't hit 'im anymore, mister! You gonna kill 'im!"

Tate pointed the gun directly at Lipscomb's face. "Get back, BOY," he warned, "before I BLOW YOUR HEAD OFF."

Lipscomb looked down the barrel of Tate's .45 caliber Colt pistol and stepped back.

Tate turned back to Newton, who was still lying on the sidewalk, holding the side of his head. He held the pistol over Newton. "Get up, you BLACK BASTARD. Get away from here. GO! I've got a good mind to BLOW YOUR BRAINS OUT."

Dazed, Newton said nothing. He struggled to his feet, holding his hand over his right eye. He staggered on down the sidewalk. Tate ran up behind him and shoved him into the street. "That'll teach you to get off the sidewalk when you see white ladies standing there."

On Monday morning, Private Newton stood in formation, waiting for the routine morning inspection with a grossly swollen face and a half-closed black eye.

Sergeant McCurdy stopped in front of him, looked closely at him, and said, "What in the hell happened to you, Newton? Been drinking and fighting again?"

Newton was known to be a heavy drinker and frequently found himself on the losing end of a fight. But, before he could answer, McCurdy brushed him off.

"Go over to the hospital and get that face fixed up," he said as he moved on down the line.

Two days after the pistol-whipping, another private, Clifford J. Adair, returned from Matamoros, Mexico, after spending the day shopping and sight-seeing. As he was getting off the ferry in Brownsville, he was stopped by a U.S. Customs official.

The Brownsville Redemption

"What are you bringing back from Mexico, boy?" the customs officer asked.

"I have a pen I paid fifty cents for," Adair said.

"Let me see it," the customs officer said. Adair took a little blue pen from his pocket and started to give it to the officer. But before he could, the man snatched the pen out of his hand.

Wanting to avoid trouble, Adair said, "I'll pay the duty on it. I got money. It's for my mother back in New York."

"You're not in New York," said the agent. "You're in Texas. I don't care how much money you got, and I don't give a good goddamn about your mama."

With that, he flung the pen into the Rio Grande. "Swim for it, you damned nigger." Then he turned and walked away.

When he got back to the fort, Adair told his commanding officer, Captain Edward Macklin, what had happened. But Macklin just told him to be a good soldier and not make waves.

The abuse the soldiers were taking in Brownsville didn't sit well with Holoman. It made him more determined than ever to find a place he could turn into a saloon. He wanted to give the soldiers a space they could call their own, where they could drink freely, tell war stories, and raise hell among themselves.

After days of intense searching, Holoman found a place to rent at Sixteenth and Monroe, not far from the fort. It was an old wooden crackerbox of a building that looked like a small barn. Its adobe foundation rested on 4 x 4 wooden pilings, and a steep-sloping wood-shingled roof slanted to within a few feet of the ground on one side. It had rough-hewn, vertical clapboard siding with wood-shuttered windows and three doors affixed with metal box locks. Plain wooden steps led up to each of three separate entrances. Some folks called it ugly, but it had character and certainly stood in sharp contrast to the garish saloons on Elizabeth Street.

Holoman named his bar "Allison's Saloon" after Private Ernest Allison, a recently discharged soldier Holoman hired to serve as bartender.

Holoman and Allison worked feverishly to get the old building ready for business. They scrubbed it down with homemade liquid potash soap made from Red Devil lye and hog lard. If the saloon became a success, Holoman would have the money to send for his son, Robert, who lived in Macon, Georgia, with his mother, who was barely able to support herself.

"How old is he?" Allison asked.

"He's nine—fine boy," Holoman said, smiling.

Holoman's wife declared a long time ago that she was through following him from post to post while he chased Indians, and Holoman had given up trying to persuade her. But he thought if he had enough money to offer her, he could talk her into letting the boy go with him. And if she agreed, he swore he would never give up his son again. He had already made plans to bring a housekeeper he knew in Nebraska to Brownsville to care for the boy.

"Think your wife will let the boy go?" Allison asked.

"I'm sure she will when I offer her money," Holoman responded. "She'll take the money. I know she will."

The two finished scrubbing down the building. Next, they set up the bar and counter in the front room, which served as the main part of the saloon. They set up tables for gambling in a back room and converted the smallest room into a storeroom.

Friday, August 10th, 1906, was John Holoman's big day—the day he was to open his saloon. He went behind the bar and checked the icebox to make sure the beer was cold. Then he pulled out his record book to see who owed him money. Tonight, like never before, the soldiers would drink at Holoman's bar. They could get whatever they wanted from him—loans for gambling, money or credit to buy beer, and anything else they might need. They had received credit from Holoman at other forts and towns, but the money had always been spent at somebody else's saloon. The difference tonight was that the men would buy directly from him.

Opening Day

Allison's Saloon. Saloon of Private Holoman, Company B, 25th Infantry.

A swell of pride ran through Holoman. Then he glanced at his watch. It was time for him to head back to the fort to stand inspection and prepare for the five o'clock retreat ceremony, with the lowering of the flag, signaling the official end of the day.

Anticipation, expectation, and excitement filled the air. Word had gotten out that Holoman's saloon would open that evening after retreat.

The men polished their boots to a high spit shine and wore their best and cleanest uniforms for the ceremony. They were anxious to get to the parade ground. No soldier wanted to be kept on post that night for failing inspection. They lined up and stood at rest on the field, facing the flag, with B, C, and D companies standing in that order. The red, white, and blue flag snapped and rippled in the light breezes coming off the Gulf.

Finally, it was almost time to sound retreat. The bugler, Private Hoyt Robinson, strutted out onto the field like a proud peacock, took his position, and waited for the command.

The officers took their positions. Major Penrose gave the order, "Sound retreat!"

A moment later, the haunting music signaling the end of the day flowed over Fort Brown. The music enveloped the newly arrived companies, evoking powerful emotions—a deep sense of patriotism, duty, honor, and country, and pride in wearing the uniform of the United States Army.

On the last note of retreat, the evening cannon fired. The gun barrel lurched forward, then recoiled. The blast created the sound of war without war. It shook the ground and filled the air with black smoke and the smell of gunpowder. The smoke slowly drifted with the breeze over and away from Fort Brown until it finally dissolved into the sky.

Major Penrose brought his battalion to attention and saluted the flag. The soldiers snapped to attention in unison—so precisely that 167 pairs of boot heels clicked as one. When Private Robinson blew the first note of the national anthem, the soldiers all saluted, and the color guard started slowly lowering the flag.

The Brownsville Redemption

First Sergeant Mingo Sanders stood ramrod straight and felt a rush of emotion. His throat swelled, his lips quivered—and he choked up. He tried to fight back the tears. Feeling an urgent need to cover his face with his hands, he struggled not to lower his salute. He looked straight ahead, motionless, except for the tears flowing down his face. He was thinking that he would soon have to retire from his beloved army, the army he idolized. He wished he could stay forever.

The music was coming to an end. The flag reached the bottom of the pole and fluttered into the outstretched hands of two soldiers, who completed the folding ritual. Robinson lowered the bugle and tucked it under his arm. With the flag folded into a neat triangle, retreat was over. The troops were dismissed.

After retreat, all were free to go into town—and town that evening meant going to Allison's Saloon. The soldiers poured in, filling the place to capacity within just a few minutes. Private Newton, who had been pistol-whipped by Tate just two days before, was one of the first soldiers through the door. When he saw an empty spot at the bar, he grabbed a bottle of beer, yanked out the cork, and climbed up on the counter—his head almost reaching the rafters. Raising his beer in a toast, Newton looked around and called out, "Here's to the soldier! We're all soldiers! Let's drink like soldiers!"

Holoman was late getting to his saloon on opening day. He had gone to the Western Union office to send a telegram to his wife. He wanted to tell her about his good fortune and to ask her to at least let young Robert visit him before school opened in late August.

By the time he got to the saloon, the place was packed. Soldiers stood elbow to elbow at the bar. There were so many people that they spilled outside into the yard. Holoman made his way through the revelers, slapping them on the back, greeting them like a politician running for office. Once inside, he put on his apron, went behind the bar, and checked the cash register. Then he helped Allison and three other bartenders fill orders.

Everybody was drinking, laughing, and having fun. Some told war stories—recounting their military exploits in Cuba, the Philippines, and on the western plains. Some went outside and sang the old cavalry songs they had sung when riding with the 9th and 10th cavalries.

There was friendly banter about how long it had been since Company C had won a baseball game. Company B's team had won last year's championship and let everybody know it—rubbing it in and making the other teams relive their losses. Private Conyers proudly passed around a photo of the champion baseball team. Mingo Sanders was so proud to be on the team that he'd worn his dress blue uniform for the picture.

Somebody shouted, "Hey, Holoman, when you gonna get some whiskey and women in here?"

"Damn the whiskey, just git the women," another soldier yelled.

"You know where the whores are," Holoman called back. "Catch the ferry, go to Matamoros. The girls are just waiting to take your money."

Private Newton hadn't stopped drinking since Allison had opened the place.

"Newton, stop drinking," Conyers yelled. "You as full as a pig that's been in the slop all day. You gonna be big as a barrel. Ain't you drunk enough?"

Newton, his eyelids almost fully closed, turned on his stool and nearly fell off. "Yeah, I'm drunk, and I like it." The crowd roared with laughter.

The designated bouncer sat on a stool in a corner, watching everything, looking like a giant Buddha with his huge frame overlapping the stool. He wasn't drinking beer that night. And he was moody.

Holoman came out of the gambling room. He saw Newton, looked at the bouncer, and nodded toward Newton. The bouncer got up, walked over to the sodden private, picked him up, and threw him over his shoulder like a sack of rice. He then carried the squirming lump back to the barracks and dumped him on his bunk.

"Stay here, and don't you come back," he growled. "You drunken coward. You let that cracker beat your head. If you come back tonight, I gonna whip your ass!"

Newton mumbled something and fell asleep.

Meanwhile, every kind of gambling was going on in the backroom at the saloon— poker, blackjack, craps, you name it. Holoman went in and out of the gambling room, carrying drinks, picking up the house share of the pot, and lending money. As he moved around, he heard fragments of gambling talk, which he would later describe in his deposition:

> "Put my money down."
> "I put five down there."
> "And I put ten."
> "Put your bones in the pot."
> "Shoot the dice or snake eyes."

It was getting late, and most of the soldiers had already gone back to their barracks. Many had gone to bed but were still talking about the good time they'd had. When the bugler sounded taps at eleven o'clock, the lights were put out, and all was quiet when the sergeant in charge of quarters conducted bed check.

As John Holoman lay awake in his bunk, thinking about the day's events, he was struck by the changes he had observed among the men— a new spirit and vitality, an esprit de corps he had not seen in them since they'd left Nebraska. It had started at retreat. He sensed that the tensions of Brownsville had faded. There were no outward signs of bitterness in the soldiers over their treatment and rejection by the citizens.

However, the soldiers' attitude was more than just an absence of ill will. A cohesive spirit was rising, a brotherhood that went beyond the common bonds of the soldier, some kind of burgeoning racial pride. The men seemed to have more respect for each other, honor for each other, honor among themselves. What was it? It's something about the saloon. He was sure.

The saloon was a living thing, and it had become one of them—a soldier, a buddy, a welcoming friend. *Yes, that's it!* Now they had a place where they could relax and mingle, a place owned by one of them: A place of their own. It had worked magic on the men that night. Each soldier felt as though he owned a piece of the saloon, even though he owned none of it.

A powerful sense of ownership, possession, and control seeped into Holoman's psyche. *What is it in men that evokes that deep emotional drive for control?* he asked himself. *What ignites it, drives it, perpetuates it?* The answer came to him just as he drifted off to sleep: It was simply man's craving for respect, honor, and recognition.

No soldier would have to enter *his* saloon through the back door. The Ruby Saloon was quiet that Friday night. Saturday and Sunday also came and went, and still no soldiers.

Late that Sunday night, August 12th, John Tillman boiled in anger as he looked at his empty saloon. He'd lost a lot of business, and he knew why. Joe Crixell was selling beer and other goods offsite to the soldiers.

After they had heard that the Black soldiers were coming to town, all of the saloon keepers and merchants got together and pledged not to

The Brownsville Redemption

do business with them. They agreed to work together to bring the white soldier back. Now Crixell had double-crossed them all.

Tillman walked out of the front door of the Ruby Saloon and looked down Elizabeth Street toward the fort. He spat in the street, and with a voice fueled by vengeance, he growled, "I'm going to see Joe Crixell about this!"

Seven

"The Yellow Rose of Texas"

"Them niggers done gone too far."

It was ten o'clock, Sunday night, August 12th, when Private Oscar W. Reid and Private Jimmy Brown ferried back to Brownsville from Matamoros, Mexico. They had taken the advice given the previous night at Allison's Saloon to go there and get some women. And they did just that. Having had a bit too much to drink and feeling no pain, Reid and Brown sang some old ribald cavalry songs as they crossed the Rio Grande, back to the dock at 14th and Levee Streets. They didn't realize that they were about to encounter one of the most dangerous men in Brownsville.

A.Y. Baker, a U.S. customs inspector and former Texas Ranger, sat on his horse on the Texas side of the river, watching and listening to the two singing frolickers aboard the approaching ferry. Baker was a lawman with a hazy past who had been involved in a highly charged case of murder by dragging and mutilation. The crime landed him in jail. He could have been given a long prison sentence or even been sent to the gallows had he not been defended by one of the best and most well-connected lawyers in the state of Texas. James B. Wells of Brownsville, his defense lawyer, had probably saved his life.

The Brownsville Redemption

On this particular night, Baker appeared to enjoy hearing the bawdy old cavalry songs. But that all changed when the Black soldier started singing "The Yellow Rose of Texas."[2]

> There's a yellow rose in Texas
> That I am going to see
> No other darky knows her
> No one only me
> She cried so when I left her It like to broke my heart And
> if I ever more find her We nevermore will part.
>
> She's the sweetest rose of color
> This darky ever knew
> Her eyes are bright as diamonds
> They sparkle like the dew
> You may talk about dearest May
> And sing of Rosa Lee
> But the yellow rose of Texas
> Beats the belles of Tennessee
>
> Where the Rio Grande is flowing
> And the starry skies are bright
> She walks along the river
> In the quiet summer night

As Baker listened more intently, his mood changed from amusement to fury. He raised himself up in the saddle, then looked over toward Fred Starck, another customs agent mounted on his horse nearby.

---

[2] According to the University of Texas, "The Yellow Rose of Texas" was written by a Black man.

"Them niggers done gone too far," Baker called out. "No they're singing about a white woman, I knew it, I knew it! They're lusting for our women."

He pulled his gun, then hesitated, remembering his earlier troubles with the law and his narrow escape from the gallows. He re-holstered his pistol, gritted his teeth, and charged off in a full gallop toward the merrymakers.

As the soldiers stepped off the gangplank, Baker almost rode into them. He pulled up hard on the reins, and his horse reared.

"Cut out that racket!" Baker yelled. "You got no business singing about a white woman! That's our song! Stop singing it! He shoved Private Reid into the shallow part of the Rio Grande and rode off while the ferry captain stood by laughing heartily.

Private Reid landed in the water up to his waist. "Don't know what that crazy man's talkin' 'bout." Reid staggered out of the water onto the riverbank. "That's a Colored soldier's song. We been singing that song all our lives."

The Assault

That same Sunday night, a white woman named Mrs. Evans alleged that she had been accosted by a big Black soldier as she entered her home at about nine o'clock. She claimed the soldier fled when she cried out.

The following Monday afternoon, Lon Evans, the alleged victim's husband, burst into the mayor's office and demanded, "Doctor, as mayor of this city, I insist you go with us to the post to report this outrage on my wife."

Visibly upset, Mayor Combe stood up at once. "Us? How many others do you have with you?"

The Brownsville Redemption

"At least fifty," Evans said.

"No. I will not go with fifty," Mayor Combe replied firmly. "There's no necessity for that. You and I can go down and do just as much by ourselves. I know the major, and I know he will do all he can to find the guilty man. Alright, let's go. You come with me."

Grudgingly, Lon Evans climbed aboard the mayor's carriage, and the two men took off alone for Fort Brown. There they found a noticeably agitated Major Penrose, pacing the parade ground. The gossip mills had already spread the word all over town that a Black soldier had raped Mrs. Evans.

Seeing the mayor's carriage pull up, Penrose approached and greeted them nervously. "I can guess why you're here."

"And you'd be right," the mayor said as he and Evans dismounted without shaking Penrose's outstretched hand.

Before he had even stepped down from the carriage, Evans launched into a tirade. "Major, last night about nine o'clock, my wife was assaulted by a Colored man, who she positively identified as a Negro soldier."

"I have already heard conflicting reports," said Penrose. "What really happened?"

"Well, my wife and I had just gotten off the train when we were met by a friend on horseback. My wife decided to ride home, and my friend and I followed on foot.

"When my wife got home, she dismounted and entered the back gate. She said she was near the steps by the ashcan when a man suddenly seized her by her hair from behind and threw her violently to the ground. She screamed, and the man ran away."

Penrose crossed his arms and asked, "What did the man look like, Mr. Evans?"

"Oh, he was a large, dark Negro wearing a slouch hat, a blue shirt, and khaki trousers."

"Can your wife provide me a more detailed description? I have a lot of large dark men under my command."

"No! She was too frightened." Evans was clearly annoyed by the question.

"Why have you waited so long to report this attack to me?" Penrose inquired.

"She was so upset I was afraid to leave her."

"Well," scoffed Penrose, "somebody was certainly well enough to report it to the newspaper. A reporter called me last night and gave me a detailed account of what will appear in today's *Daily Herald*, and it is precisely the same story you've just told me, right down to the ashcan. Why didn't you bring Mrs. Evans with you today so she could identify the man?"

Before Evans could answer, Penrose spoke again. "I want you to know I have already ordered an investigation into the matter."

Mayor Combe didn't like the way Penrose appeared to be questioning Mrs. Evans's story. Irritated, the mayor decided to say something in support of his constituent. His eyes narrowed, and he shook his head from side to side to indicate his disapproval at the drift of the conversation.

Finally, he said, "Penrose, you're my friend. We go way back." Then he leaned forward and looked the major square in the eye. "But I've got to tell you—you'd better get to the bottom of this thing quickly."

He glanced at Evans as if to measure his reaction, then turned back to Penrose. "I don't want a lynching in my town. You find the man." Although the three men spoke in low voices, Wilbert Voshelle, the corral master, overheard them and caught a little of the conversation.

The Brownsville Redemption

He heard Evans warn, "Major, if there is not an arrest between now and 11 o'clock tonight, every Black enlisted man seen on the streets in Brownsville will be shot."

Penrose became angry. He snapped back, "Mr. Evans, did your wife say she was raped?"

"No, I didn't say that."

"Then what are you saying?"

"I'm saying she was attacked."

"Then you are not accusing my men of rape."

"Rape or no rape, she was assaulted!"

Penrose drew in a deep breath and expressed some sympathy for Evans. "I'm sorry this thing happened to your wife, and I will provide every assistance possible to help you locate this man. But I can tell you right now—that man is not to be found among my soldiers."

Evans's tone turned aggressive.

"I expect more than that. I want the soldier!"

"None of my men has ever been accused of such a thing. We just left Valentine, Nebraska. They never assaulted white women there, and they freely associated with white people all around town…yes, even in bars. And they were on friendly terms with them." Then the major raised his voice. "Why in God's name would they come down here to Texas, in this hostile place, and do such a thing? Besides," he added dryly, "with the number of Mexican prostitutes in this town, I hardly think rape would be necessary."

"Major, could I speak to you privately for a minute?" asked the mayor.

Penrose nodded. "Of course."

"Excuse us for a minute, Mr. Evans." Combe took Penrose by the arm and led him aside. Speaking quietly, he suggested, "Charlie, don't you think it would be best for you to keep your men in the post tonight? Trouble is already brewing in town."

Penrose replied evenly, "I don't think it was one of my soldiers, but they will undoubtedly get the blame. I've already decided to keep them out of town, and I sent out messengers to get everyone back to post by eight o'clock."

Mayor Combe and Mr. Evans climbed back up on the carriage and drove off while Major Penrose thundered back to the administration building. He rushed up the steps and stuck his head into the sergeant major's office. "Sergeant Taliaferro!" he ordered. "Find Captain Macklin. Tell him to report to me immediately!" Penrose then went back to his own office and closed the door behind him.

Sergeant Major Spottswood W. Taliaferro was straight as an arrow—a stern, unflappable, no-nonsense kind of guy who had worked for Penrose for several years. Penrose had chosen him to be the battalion sergeant major for just those qualities. As Penrose put it, "He's just like me—cool under fire—only Black."

The sergeant didn't respond immediately but sat in a thoughtful mood, holding the *Daily Herald* while tapping it lightly on the edge of his desk. Then he got up, walked to his commander's office, and rapped three times, his signal to Penrose that it was he at the door.

"Come in."

The sergeant stepped inside and closed the door. He found his commander standing with his back to him, staring out the window onto the parade ground. Turning around, Penrose said sadly, "It's bad, Scottie."

Scottie was the nickname Penrose had given the sergeant major, but he only used it in private. In all the years they'd worked together, Taliaferro had never seen his commander look so troubled.

"It's the rape gossip, isn't it," he said flatly. "But I don't see anything in the paper about rape. Here, you read it." The sergeant handed the newspaper to Penrose.

Without a word, Penrose took the newspaper, and with sweaty hands and a pounding heart, he began reading the *Daily Herald*, datelined Brownsville, Texas, August 13th, 1906:

Infamous Outrage
Negro Soldier Invaded Private Premises Last Night.
Attempted to Seize a White Lady

After reading the complete article, Penrose sighed, feeling almost relieved. "Well, I don't see anything about rape either. And Evans didn't say anything either." But when he thought about it some more, he slammed the paper down on his desk. "That won't be the end of it, though."

The sergeant major tried to reassure his commander. "What's the matter? There was no rape. You didn't see it in the paper. The paper said, 'Attempted to seize a white lady.'"

"Yes, I know, but the gossip mills say she was raped, and that's what the mob will act on. It's what comes *after* the charge of rape that's worrying me. You know as well as I do, Scottie, a rumor of attempted rape of a white woman by a Black man is a rallying cry for mob violence."

Penrose paced back and forth. "Good God, what if these Texans attack my command! Sergeant, go get Captain Macklin and tell him I want to see him immediately."

Just as Taliaferro turned to leave, Penrose looked out the window and saw Macklin approaching. "Wait, Scottie, I see him."

Penrose stuck his head out the window and yelled, "Captain Macklin! I need to see you right away!"

Macklin was on duty as the officer of the day. In this role, he was in charge of the guards and responsible for protecting the garrison. He also took care of any routine matters that might arise during non-duty hours.

Macklin stepped into Penrose's office, closed the door, and saluted. Penrose came out from behind his desk and only partially returned the salute. "Mayor Combe and Mr. Evans just left," he said. "There could be trouble in town tonight."

Realizing that the captain was still standing at attention, he said, "At ease," and motioned for Macklin to sit down.

"What do you want us to do, sir?"

"See to it that all the officers are informed that all passes are canceled as of eight o'clock tonight. Make sure that all the men are notified of this order at retreat. No one, not anyone for any reason whatsoever, is to leave the post after eight p.m. As officer of the day, send out patrols to round up any stragglers. And you should check all of the bars personally. Especially the Mexican bars. Now you better get going. It's getting late."

Macklin looked at his watch, saluted, and left.

"Excuse me, sir," said Sergeant Taliaferro, "but you did not mention defending the fort in case a mob does attack."

"I've got to run this thing through my mind."

"So do we all."

A Cornelian Dilemma

Penrose stood at the window, staring into the distance across the parade ground, deep in thought. *What do I do if a mob attacks the fort?* He started running military tactics through his head. He knew that his mission came first, followed by the welfare of his men. He was trapped on the horns of a Cornelian dilemma: Two options were available to him, but they were equally loathsome—he could either defend the fort or not defend the fort. *Either way, I'll be damned!*

Penrose began to pace. If he didn't defend the fort, some of his men would surely be taken at random. The only thing that would matter to a mob would be the color of the men's skin. However, not to defend was the path to ignominy. It would dishonor the uniform, the soldier, the fort, and the U.S. Army itself. It would be a shameful capitulation and would undoubtedly lead to a trial by general courtmartial. In any event, he would be disgraced.

Penrose paused at his desk for a moment, then went back to the window. *But to defend means to fire on civilians…citizens!* Then he reconsidered. *Are civilians necessarily citizens?* Technically, they'd remain citizens until they breached the gate or jumped over the garrison wall. *If they do that,* he reasoned, *they'll become the enemy, no different than a foreign invader.*

He turned and walked back to look at the Springfield 03 rifle mounted on the wall. He grabbed it and examined it, patting the stock. He estimated there might be 150 to 300 decent rabbit shooters in town, but they'd be no match for his men.

If a mob crashes the gate, he reasoned, *they'll get all bunched up as they try to funnel through. They'll form a perfect target—a deadly cone of sitting ducks. And if they jump the wall, they'll land with their backs to it—and they'll still create a perfect shooting gallery, like a carnival game.* So, either way, there would be no escape for them. *May God have mercy on their souls if they do such a foolish thing!* Many would die, and it would certainly end his career. But he would not lose his honor.

I will defend this fort, so help me, God!"

He walked back to the window and faced the town. It did not look peaceful. Several men were milling around, openly carrying guns. The major felt compelled to do something, so he left his office and began to inspect the fort.

In town, the crowds were growing. Bizarre and exaggerated stories about the alleged attack on Mrs. Evans circulated on Elizabeth Street. The people freely jeered, hooted, and heckled any Black soldiers that were still in town, calling them "niggers," "coons," and "darkies."

When the Black battalion mail clerk entered the U.S. Post Office to pick up the soldiers' mail, a group of angry white men stopped him and tried to engage him in a conversation about the attack on Mrs. Evans. He tried to get rid of them as best he could, but they were looking to make trouble. As he exited the post office carrying two bags marked "U.S. Mail" slung over his shoulder, one of the hecklers called out, "It's a damn good thing your commander ordered all you niggers in because some of you are going to get killed tonight!"

Back at the fort, the mail clerk immediately went to see the officer of the day, Captain Macklin, and told him, "Sir, the people in town are talking about killing us tonight."

Macklin was feeling the pressure. He had carried out Major Penrose's orders and had notified the soldiers at retreat about the eight o'clock curfew. He had also sent patrols into town to warn those who missed the order.

After retreat, some soldiers hurried to Allison's Saloon to have some fun before the curfew started. Business was brisk and the place was packed, just as it had been for the last two nights. But the frivolity that had characterized those first nights was gone. There was no heavy drinking. Even Newton moderated his intake.

Some of the sergeants were huddled in a corner, sipping beer. Mingo Sanders shook his head. "I don't believe it. Nothing like that ever happened before. What Black fool would assault a white woman down here in Texas?"

Slowpokes, determined to run out the clock, forced Holoman to announce, "Time to go. We're closing early tonight, fellas. You got the word. Curfew starts at eight."

The men grudgingly left the saloon and headed back to the post. Some went to their barracks, while others went fishing in the lagoon, started a baseball game, played cards, went to the library, or shot pool.

Captain Macklin had stationed a guard at the ferry dock to intercept any soldiers coming from or going to Mexico. He himself went into Brownsville and combed the town looking for stragglers until he was satisfied that all but two soldiers had been accounted for: Sergeant George Thomas and Private Edward Lee had been given 24-hour passes and could not be reached.

Unlike earlier in the evening, by nine o'clock the streets in town were quiet and peaceful. Across the street from the garrison, a children's birthday party was in progress at Louis and Anna Cowen's house. Among the young guests were several of the white officers' children.

The Cowens lived in a plain bungalow on 14th Street on the south side of the alley that ran between Elizabeth and Washington. People called it Cowen's Alley. Louis worked as a New York Life Insurance agent and also ran a successful dry goods business on the side.

Purebreds who lived in the white-columned mansions in the better part of town scornfully questioned his ethnicity. His complexion was considered too olive for a white man. Some said he was three-fourths Mexican—by which they meant "not quite white." Others whispered that he really was a Russian Jew who had shortened his name from Cowajiian to Cowen.

No matter what people thought about him, Louis Cowen was undoubtedly a handsome man and a fastidious dresser. He straightened his curly brown hair with a hot iron, then slicked it back from his face with pomade. His drinking buddies didn't seem to care about his ethnicity. Everyone liked Louis Cowen, his jokes, and his self-deprecating humor. But behind the mask of Anna's fast-talking, wise-cracking husband was an impatient striver who was in a hurry to make money and win social acceptance.

Louis and Anna Cowen's House. U.S. Archives AG file 1135832

Anna Cowen, a devoutly Catholic Mexican-American, was always nervous and easily upset. Worn out before the party even began, she abandoned the decorating brigade to seclude herself in a back bedroom.

Louis was unusually jumpy that night. As soon as the party started, he began plotting how to escape to the Ruby Saloon. Finally, he couldn't take it anymore. At about 10:30 he left the house, still full of guests celebrating his daughter's 13th birthday. But first he went to

The Brownsville Redemption

Anna, who was lying down. "I've had enough. I gotta get outta here." As he left, he told the maid, Amada Martinez, to take over.

Louis R. Cowen, Circa 1906. Courtesy of Ralph Cowen, Nephew of Louis R. Cowen. Lt. Col. (Ret) William Baker Private Papers

When she heard the front door open, Anna called out to her husband, "Louis! Bring me back a couple of sandwiches and a bottle of Schlitz!"

Cowen headed for the Ruby Saloon, the place where he felt more at home than anywhere else in town. On his way, an unexpected summer rain began to fall. To avoid getting wet, he stopped at the boarding house of his next-door neighbor, Katie Leahy, finding the rain a convenient excuse to exchange gossip about the attack on Mrs. Evans. Cowen boasted to Katie that if "any one of those niggers" ever touched or insulted his wife or his children or one of his lady friends, he would take out his Winchester "and kill him."

Lieutenant Colonel (Ret) William Baker

After he left Katie's place, he stopped again to engage with a group of men who'd gathered together in some kind of brotherhood over the Evans affair. They offered whiskey to anyone who would stop and discuss what to do about the soldiers at the fort. But tonight, uncharacteristically, nobody greeted Cowan or offered him a drink. It appeared that no one wanted to talk to him or hear his jokes.

When Louis entered the Ruby Saloon, he saw that it was almost empty and thought it strange that none of his drinking buddies were there. They usually beat him to the bar. *Where is everybody?* He climbed up onto the barstool and slouched over the counter, feeling dejected. He looked like he was already drunk.

What he thought would be a relief from the birthday party turned out to be less than a warm welcome from his young friend Frank Natus, the bartender. Frank, who was standing at the far end of the counter, appeared to be ignoring him.

"Where the hell is my beer?" Cowen grumbled.

"I'm looking for the tin cup,"[3] the bartender shot back.

"The tin cup! What're you talking about? I ain't drinkin' out of no tin cup," Cowen cried. "That's only for slaves and niggers. Git me a real glass, a glass of Schlitz. And don't insult me again, you puckerfaced bastard!"

Natus decided to drop the tin cup prank. "I know what you want," he said. But instead of sliding the glass of beer down the bar with his customary flair, Natus took his time. Then he leaned forward with a smirk as he handed Cowen the glass. "I hear talk about 'cha. They say you're doing business with the Colored soldiers and that your girls are getting awfully nice with them. Better watch your back."

---

[3]The tin cup was used as a way of dishonoring any patron who acted up in the saloon.

The Brownsville Redemption

Frank's warning unnerved Cowan. It was true his family had been friendly with the soldiers, and he himself had sold a few insurance policies to some of the Black non-commissioned officers. And, of course, some of the white officers' children were at that very moment attending his daughter's birthday party.

Cowan decided to go across the street to ask H.H. Weller what was going on. He quickly downed his beer, paid the tab, and left. Once outside, he stood erect and broadened his shoulders, trying to summon some courage. Then he marched across the street and entered the saloon. He was heading over to the bar when he saw H.H. frown at him, turn his back, and walk away. Cowen decided he didn't want another beer after all. He slunk into the back room and ordered a ham sandwich.

Although Anna Cowen had gone to bed long before the party ended, she had been unable to sleep. But now that the party was ending and the guests were leaving, and with Louis still out at the Ruby Saloon, she got up and got dressed as if she were going out. She opened her dresser drawer, took out her rosary beads, held them tightly in her hand, and went into the dining room. She sat at the head of the table and asked her maid, Amada, to bring her some hot water.

At ten minutes to midnight, Anna Cowen was still sitting at the dining room table, sweating profusely. She called to her oldest daughter, "Gertrude, don't go to bed. I don't feel well. Stay by me. I'm nervous."

"Don't worry. I won't go to sleep, Mamma." Gertrude came up to her mother and stood next to her at the table.

"Feel my heart, Gertrude," Anna said as she took her daughter's hand and placed it on her breast. "It's thumping. Can you feel it?"

Lieutenant Colonel (Ret) William Baker

Eight

Midnight Attack *on* Brownsville

August 13, 1906

The drizzling rain had just about petered out, but a heavily overcast sky made it more difficult for the sentinels at Fort Brown to see on an already dark night. They walked their posts expecting trouble. When Captain Macklin made his final inspection, he came within five feet of the sentinel on guard post No. 2 before Private Joseph H. Howard challenged him:

"Halt! Who goes there?"

"Captain Macklin, officer of the day."

"Advance, Captain, and be recognized."

Captain Macklin took two steps forward before Private Howard could identify him.

"Captain Macklin recognized."

"Why did you let me get this close to you, soldier, before you challenged me?"

"Sir, it's dark out here. I couldn't see you."

"Anything unusual happening around here?"

"No, sir. All's quiet."

Just then, at 11 o'clock, the bugler sounded taps and the lights went out in all the barracks. In the darkness, each company's charge of quarters (CQ) conducted the check roll call. Shortly thereafter, Samuel Wheeler, corporal of the guard, received the roll call reports and reported to Captain Macklin that all the soldiers in every company were present or accounted for, including Sergeant Thomas and Private Lee, who were away on a three-day pass.

Wheeler reassured Captain Macklin, "Everything is peaceful. None of the men have been drinking, and no one's acting ugly."

Garrison Wall and Barracks, Fort Brown, Texas, c. 1906.

Satisfied that all was in order, Captain Macklin retired to his quarters to get some sleep. It was about 11:30. On the way, he heard a dog growl near the gate to the officers' housing. Then he heard children crying. He unhooked his saber and ran up to where a big black dog had cornered several of the officers' children. They were huddled in a group and backed up to the gate. Some of the little girls were sobbing.

Recognizing the dog as Company B's mascot, he waved his saber, shouting, "Trooper! Get away! Leave 'em alone! What in the hell's wrong with you?" Obediently, Trooper pranced off toward Company B barracks.

"What are you doing out here this time of night?" Macklin asked Wesley Bailey, who, at 13, was the oldest of the children.

"We were over at the birthday party at Mr. Cowen's house."

Macklin escorted the children across the parade ground and pointed to the officers' family housing. "Y'all go straight home," he admonished them mildly.

Macklin went to his quarters, got a bottle of beer from the icebox, sat down on the side of his white iron cot, and drank his second beer of the night. *Maybe Penrose overreacted imposing that curfew,* he thought. Nothing had happened. Then he lay back on the cot and fell dead asleep with his clothes on.

At about ten minutes before midnight, Private Howard, the sentinel at post No. 2, heard Trooper whining and running up and down inside the garrison wall. He called out, "Trooper, come here, boy! What's wrong?"

Trooper ran to the sentinel to acknowledge his command but quickly turned and raced back to the wall. With a low, deep growl, he sniffed along the base of it, following a sound only he could hear.

Private Howard didn't think too much further about Trooper's behavior. He hadn't heard or seen anything of concern. And it was not unusual for some kind of activity to occur outside the fort wall on the town side. But then Trooper started racing back and forth, barking loudly. Howard heard running, and a few seconds later he heard two pistol shots behind him, near the vacant set of barracks reserved for Company A. Howard looked over in that direction, but he still saw nothing.

The Brownsville Redemption

The Shooting Begins

At midnight, a band of some 16 to 20 men emerged from the darkness outside the garrison wall. They moved cautiously like a military patrol probing enemy lines, their heads lowered, chins buried in their chests, and their bodies hunched over in low, military crouches.

Cowen Alley. U.S. Archives file 1135832, Box 4053 Modified: Lt. Col. (Ret) William Baker

The raiders crossed Garrison Road and ducked into Cowen's Alley. There, Louis and Anna Cowen's single-frame house stood alone. Its lights still burned as the birthday party had broken up only a short time before.

Anna Cowen's heart beat frantically. She still wasn't feeling well. Amada came into the dining room with a pitcher of hot water. As she sat down at the table to console Mrs. Cowen, loud shots rang out from the alley.

One of the marauders, apparently the leader, fired several pistol shots into the back of Cowen's House, shattering windows and piercing walls. Then he directed the men crouched behind him to send more fire at the structure. Two or three of the men raised their rifles and took dead aim at the lights. A student lamp sitting on the dining room table was shot out. So was a light shining directly at the raiders through an open window. Another shot shattered the lantern in the kitchen that threw light into the backyard. Another bullet hit the large Rochester lamp hanging in the center hallway that lit the three back bedrooms. Each shot was fired with military precision. The house went completely dark.

Amada Martinez fell to her knees, crying hysterically, "Madame, Madame! It's the day of judgment! The soldiers are going to kill us!"

It was the custom in Brownsville to discharge shots with a gun to signal a fire. The children, thinking there was a fire in town, ran into the dining room, yelling, "Mamma! There's a fire!"

Anna Cowen yelled back to her children, "It's not a fire! It's the soldiers! Go to the bedroom and get under the bed!" But the children stayed with her, hanging onto her dress.

Anna crawled along the floor with the children and Amada in tow. When they reached the dining room wall, they turned around and pressed their backs into the corner. Terrified, Anna held her rosary beads close to her heart and began praying, "Mary, Mother of God, save us from the soldiers." She urged the children, "Pray to God to save us. If we are alive tomorrow, we will go to church and thank God!"

While Louis Cowen's house was being shot up and his family terrorized, he wasn't there. He was wandering around town, in and out of saloons, trying to find out why he'd suddenly become persona non grata.

He was about to eat his ham sandwich when he heard several shots. He sprang out of his chair, fought his way through the instantaneous furor, and ran out of the bar and down Elizabeth Street toward his house. But first he stopped again at the Ruby Saloon.

Flinging the screen door open, Cowen saw Frank Natus still standing behind the bar. "Hey, Frank! Did you hear those shots? You gotta lend me a pistol."

"I heard 'em, all right. What the hell's going on out there? I don't got but one gun, Louis—and I'm keeping it for myself."

Cowen then remembered Teofilo Crixell, Joe Crixell's brother. Teofilo was known for accepting guns for unpaid debts at the White Elephant. Surely Cowen could get one from him.

As Cowen left the Ruby Saloon, he stumbled off the porch into the street, cursing, "Damn! It's dark as hell out here." As the sound of gunfire drew nearer, Cowen was afraid that he might get shot before he made it to the White Elephant, so he changed his mind, hurried across the street, and flew into Joe Crixell's saloon, crying, "There's shooting going on out there!"

Joe Crixell was enjoying a winning poker hand when he saw Cowen come in. In that instant, Crixell heard four or five shots. He threw his cards down and waited. When another shot rang out, he hollered, "There's some shooting, boys!"

"That's what I just said!" Cowen cried. "Joe, gimme a half-pint of whiskey." Holding onto the bar with one hand, Cowen tried to tell the others what he had seen, but he was interrupted by Martin Hanson, one of the poker players. More preoccupied with the game than the shots, Hanson glanced up and said dismissively, "That's nothing but firecrackers, Louis. Come on, Joe, give Cowen the damn liquor and play your damn hand."

Crixell grabbed a half-pint of whiskey from the shelf and tossed it to Cowen, who caught the bottle with one hand. He clutched it to his chest and fumbled with the cork. After taking a drink, he pleaded with Joe: "I need a gun, too. Got to get home to protect my wife and children."

Crixell shook his head. "Don't have no more pistols here. Plenty at the White Elephant." His voice trailed off as he listened a few seconds more. Then he sat down and picked up his discarded hand. Suddenly, ten or more shots rang out, and the players all jumped out of their seats simultaneously, cards flying everywhere. "I'll be damned if those were firecrackers, Hanson," said Crixell. "Those shots came from army rifles!"

Cowen trembled at the sound of more gunfire. "That's what I was trying to tell you when I came in here! I saw gun flashes down toward the fort near my house."

"It's trouble, all right." Crixell pushed the chairs out of his way and hurried from the back of the saloon to the front door. Looking across the street toward the Ruby Saloon, he saw Frank Natus and several other men standing on the sidewalk. "Close up your doors, boys!" he shouted to them. "Here come the niggers!"

Crixell stepped back inside and was about to bolt the door when Hal Shannon spoke up. "Wait! I gotta git my bicycle." Shannon's bike was leaning against a post right in front of the saloon. When he reached for the handlebars, a bullet whizzed past his head and hit the post, barely missing him.

"Get back in here, you damn fool!" Crixell yelled. "You'll get yourself killed out there!"

The Brownsville Redemption

As Shannon stepped back inside, they heard several more shots. Cowen paced nervously and kept moaning that he was trapped in town, saying over and over again, "I've got to get home to protect my family."

Crixell looked at Cowen as though he were crazy. "You got no business out in the street now. No telling what those Black bastards will do. Let's go upstairs. We'll be safer. If those brutes break in here, the first place they'll ransack will be the bar."

Route of the Attack. Modified by Lt. Col. (Ret) William Baker

Lieutenant Colonel (Ret) William Baker

The Route of Attack

At first, Cowen was reluctant to go upstairs and asked Crixell to unlock the door and let him out. He was going home no matter what. But then he realized without a gun he might not get very far, so he stayed where he was.

Cowen went upstairs with Crixell and the other patrons, took another swig of whiskey, and helped blow out the flames of the oil lamps.

I'll go home when the trouble dies down, he told himself. *My family didn't do anything to the soldiers. All in all, they have been friendly to us. I don't guess they will hurt my family,* he rationalized as he sat forlorn in the darkened room.

No lights shone from the Cowen house. It was dark and silent.

From their position in Cowen's Alley, the raiders fired sporadically with high-powered rifles, then took aim at the Western Union Telegraph building, the Yturria's house, and the Martinez's Cottage.

"Fire High"

"Fire high and over the fort," the leader ordered. The raiders raised their rifles and fired several shots in the direction of the fort.

Across the street from Cowen's house, on the corner of Elizabeth and 14th streets, in the raiders' path, stood the rambling two-story building owned by Katie Leahy. She called it the Leahy Hotel, although it was nothing more than an old-fashioned rooming house.

Katie Leahy was a tall, wiry, and ruddy-faced 36-year-old woman. Opinionated, sharp-tongued, strong-willed, and stubborn, she was quick to command. She told absolutely everyone what to do and how to do it. Katie had been married to a soldier from the Eighth Calvary and had spent much of her life in and around army posts. Later, she and her husband had run a saloon in Brownsville. Since her husband's death, she had managed the boarding house. But she planned to get back into the saloon business someday.

Leahy sat on the edge of her bed in her first-floor bedroom, her nightgown pulled up over her knees. Holding a bottle of liniment, she shook small drops onto her aching legs. She'd had a hard day running up and down the stairs, cleaning up after her boarders, and gossiping with Anna Cowen. "That's that," she said with a sigh as she set down the bottle.

Suddenly, she heard the shots. At first, she thought it was a fire alarm. But when she heard several more, she ran outside into the middle of Elizabeth Street to see where the shooting was coming from. She saw gun flashes near the Cowen's house and heard bullets whistle over her head. Horrified, she ran back inside and raced upstairs. She looked out the window and saw two policemen sauntering down Elizabeth Street. They called up to her, asking, "Katie! Where's the fire?" She didn't answer. Instead, she ran back downstairs, opened the door, and urged the men inside. "Come in! Come in! The Negroes are shooting up the town!"

When the policemen heard more shots, they scrambled inside, almost knocking Katie down. "Get in the bathroom!" she ordered. "Get in the bathroom! You'll be safe in there." She pointed and shoved them inside the small room. Before closing the door, she gave them specific instructions: "Under no circumstances do you leave until I tell you. It doesn't matter who comes. You stay here until I give you the all-clear." Then she went back upstairs to watch the goings-on from a bedroom window.

She saw about 16 men wearing khaki uniforms, who she believed to be Negro soldiers. From her vantage point, she guessed that they were about 30 feet (9 meters) away, near the corner of 14th Street and Cowen Alley. It seemed to her that the shooters were firing into the air, not aiming at anything in particular. She could tell by the upward flashes from their gunfire. She later said, "One of the men was having trouble with his gun, and another guy came over to help him."

She didn't see the men's faces, but she heard one of the men whisper to the other, "There's Mrs. Leahy."

"They got Frank!"

Judge Parks was a frequent guest at Katie Leahy's boarding house. He was a tall, thin man, discreet and well respected. He didn't gamble or socialize with any of the other judges, lawyers, or ranchers in his district. When he wanted a little diversion, he'd steal away to Brownsville. From there, he could slip across the border every now and then to have a little fun without risking his reputation.

Tonight, as he did every night he was away from home, even on his escapades, the judge wrote his wife a letter. He was in his bedroom on the second floor when he heard the shooting. He went to the window and would later say he "saw the whole thing." But he couldn't make out who the shooters were.

When the raiders approached 14th Street, they fired off another volley of shots, then divided into two groups. One group dashed across 14th Street at full speed, entering the mouth of Cowen's Alley from the far side. The other group ran up 14th Street and turned left onto Washington, firing into the air as they ran, with flashes of light piercing the darkness. The frightening sounds traveled far through the night, awakening all of the townspeople as well as the officers and soldiers at Fort Brown.

A group of raiders was heading up the alley, when Katie Leahy heard someone pounding on her front door. She got her pistol and listened before opening it. It was a terrified Anna Cowen, her six children, and the maid seeking refuge.

"Get your asses in here quickly!" Katie commanded.

At the time the shooting began, police lieutenant Joe Dominguez had been sitting on the steps of the police station at 12th and Washington, several blocks north of Fort Brown. Believing he'd heard gunfire, he turned his head toward the sound. When he heard more shots, he mounted his horse and set off at a full gallop down Washington Street.

Genaro Padron, another policeman, heard the shooting at the same time as Lieutenant Dominguez. He ran to the corner of 14th and Washington and arrived just in time to see men he decided were Negro soldiers shooting up Cowen's house. Terrified, he bolted around the corner and fled toward 13th Street. Then he saw Dominguez.

The lieutenant shouted to Padron, "Where's all this shooting coming from?" Padron pointed in the general direction of Cowen's house. "The soldiers are shooting up Cowen's," Padron said. Dominguez continued up Washington, then turned east on 13th and headed toward the Miller Hotel on Elizabeth Street.

Meanwhile, the raiders headed down the alley and paused at the back of the Miller Hotel, where a light shone through a window. "Git the light," the leader whispered. A single shot missed it. As they headed farther down the alley, the leader held up his hand and whispered, "Wait, I hear something."

They heard pounding hooves coming down 13th Street. "Git down! Git down!"

The men crouched low.

As Dominguez passed the mouth of the alley at 13th, he looked up and down but didn't see anything.

Then the leader hissed through his teeth, "There goes the son of a bitch! Let's git 'im!"

Dominguez pulled up on the reins as he got closer to the Miller Hotel. Standing up in the saddle, he hollered: *Wakeup! Put out the lights! The Colored soldiers are firing into houses and killing people! Wake up! Defend yourselves!*

While Dominguez's back was turned, the raiders got up and rushed out of the alley. But first, they fired a volley in the direction of the policeman, hitting him in the arm and wounding his horse. Just as they were rounding the corner, headed toward Washington Street, they heard the horse stumble and fall.

"We scorched his ass! Ha! That'll teach 'im!" the leader gloated as the raiders continued down the alley. John Tillman, the owner of the Ruby Saloon, was drinking beer with Paulino Preciado and Nicholas Alanis when he heard the shots. He rushed to the door, reaching it just in time to hear Joe Crixell's warning from across the street. Immediately, Tillman jumped back into the doorway. Preciado rushed to the bar while Alanis ran to the bathroom in the back of the saloon.

Tillman yelled to his bartender, "Frank! Get back in here! Bar the doors!"

Frank Natus rushed right in and slammed the doors shut, locking them by dropping the crossbars in the metal U-slots. Then he remembered that the door to the alley was open. He grabbed a lantern and a pistol from under the bar and ran toward the open back door. Preciado pulled a small pistol from his boot and followed the bartender.

Alanis, who was sitting on the toilet in the bathroom that backed up to the alley, ran out, pants still down. "Don't go out!" he warned. "I heard noises out back!"

Natus stood at the back door of the saloon and held up a lantern, trying to see what was going on. He stepped into the alleyway. A single shot was fired, and Frank Natus fell dead.

A terrified Preciado cautiously closed the back door, then darted back inside where Tillman and the rest were waiting:

"They got Frank!"

Tillman stood amazed as he struggled to process the horror unfolding around them.

Preciado continued, "A group of five or six armed men appeared in the alley and fired. I heard Frank cry out, 'Oh God!' And then he was gone."

Tillman turned on his heels, visibly shaken. He lifted the crossbars and walked outside. It was at the height of the shooting. Undaunted, he headed down Elizabeth Street and turned right on 13th. When he reached Adams, he headed toward his house, which was right across the street from the garrison. His wife, badly shaken, met him at the door. When he told her about Frank, she sank into the nearest chair and held her head in her hands.

"Oh, that poor kid!" she cried. "Who in the world would want to kill *him*?"

Tillman shook his head, "I don't know," he replied sadly. He looked away as though he were hiding something. After checking on his wife, Tillman went next door to see his neighbor, J.P. McDonnel, and they walked back into town together.

Meanwhile, the second group of raiders had been running amuck. On Washington Street they spotted a lantern burning in Fred Starck's house. Suddenly a hail of bullets hit the two-story residence, knocking out the lantern in his little girls' bedroom and ripping through the mosquito net covering their bed. The bullets came within 20 inches (0.5 meters) of killing them. Had Fred Starck or his wife been standing in the children's bedroom, they might very well have been killed.

Mayor Combe was sleeping on a cot on his back porch when he heard the first shots. Startled, he jumped up, stumbled into his trousers, and grabbed his pistol. His brother Joe, also a medical doctor, was sleeping upstairs. Fred yelled up to him. "Joe! I hear pistol shots down the street!"

A sinking feeling flooded over him. Despite his best efforts, his town was about to explode in racial violence. He grabbed a handful of cartridges, pointed the revolver up, rolled the chamber, and saw that it was already fully loaded. Sticking the pistol in his front belt, he went to the window and looked down the street. "Joe," he called, "I can't see anything from here. I've got to go find out what all the firing's about."

"Wait for me, Fred," his brother said, "I'm coming with you."

Now fully dressed, Joe Combe checked in on his father, who was sleeping undisturbed in his room. Then he grabbed his pistol and hurried downstairs to join his brother.

The two men walked to Ninth and Elizabeth, turned the corner, and headed toward the garrison. Fred walked on one side of the street, while Joe covered the other. Gunfire punctuated their every step.

Just as they were coming up on the post office, Joe Combe yelled, "Fred! Hug the wall. They're shooting this way!"

The mayor froze until the shooting stopped. Then both brothers ran. Just as they reached Twelfth Street, they saw a shadowy figure round the corner.

Mayor Combe shouted, "Stop!"

The man skidded to a halt and saw a gun pointed directly at his face. He cried out, "Mayor, it's me! Genaro Padron! Please don't shoot!"

The mayor recognized the police officer and lowered his revolver. "Good God! I almost shot you!" He thrust the gun back in his belt.

Then Genaro placed a hand on Fred's shoulder. "Don't go any farther, Mayor," he warned. "You'll get shot."

The Brownsville Redemption

Convinced that Genero Padron was in full panic mode, the mayor ignored him and continued on. When he reached Crixell's saloon, he noticed José Garza, a local who sometimes worked as a special policeman, standing out front. Tonight, expecting trouble, Chief of Police Connor had hired him as a backup.

The mayor walked up to Garza and immediately detected whiskey on his breath. And he was puzzled to see the man holding a Winchester rifle. *Brownsville policemen only carry pistols.*

"What are you doing with that rifle, Garza?" The mayor grabbed the gun and took it away from him. "Give me that thing!" Mayor Combe then noticed that Garza's pants were splashed with fresh mud.

Combe pulled the rifle bolt back, looked down into the breech, and saw an empty cartridge inside the magazine that had failed to eject. *It sure looks like this gun has been fired recently.*

When he saw the mayor inspecting the gun, Joe Crixell stepped outside. "The damn rifle doesn't work," he said. "My brother took it on a bad loan some six months ago." He went on to explain that Garza had gone to the White Elephant to borrow a gun when he first heard the shooting.

Mayor Combe seemed satisfied with the explanation.

Just then, Chief of Police George Connor appeared with two other policemen. The mayor addressed him at once:

"George, where have you been? And for Christ's sake, where are the rest of your men? Have you accounted for all of your officers?"

"All but three."

"And they are...?"

"Ramirez, Briseno, and..."

In the excitement, the chief couldn't remember the third officer's name. Such a memory lapse by the chief of police deeply concerned the mayor.

Just then, Mayor Combe saw a dark spot on the ground, barely visible in the dim lamplight. He reached down. It felt wet. He held his fingers up to the lamppost.

"Joe!" Fred Combe called to his brother. "Come here. Look at this. It's blood."

Joe Combe stepped closer, and his brother pointed to the ground. "Follow the bloodstains. Somebody's hurt."

The Call to Battle

Just a minute or so after he'd heard Trooper barking, Private Howard, the sentinel at Guard Post No. 2, heard the first shots. Then came a fusillade near Cowen Alley, directly across Garrison Road.

Tamayo, the scavenger—the fort's garbage collector—was emptying ashcans and trash into his mule cart when the shooting began. The frightened mule reared, rattling the chains and traces connected to the cart. Tamayo gripped the reins tightly as the animal struggled to escape the explosions.

Poised for action with his rifle at the ready, Howard ran to the edge of the parade ground and fired three times straight up in the air.

"They're shooting us up!" he shouted to the guard at post No. 3. The rest of the guards picked up the warning and repeated it. "They're shooting us up! They're shooting us up!"

Major Penrose, who had lain awake anxious, sat straight up. "Those are pistol shots," he said to his wife. His sentinels were not authorized to carry pistols on guard duty. Then he heard a high-powered rifle volley. More shots rang out, and then someone was shouting and banging on his door.

"Major Penrose! Major Penrose! They're shooting us up!"

Penrose threw back the covers and jumped out of bed. "I'm coming!" he yelled, as he pulled his uniform over his pajamas, latched his pistol belt around his waist, and pushed his bare feet into his boots.

The pounding on the door persisted. It was Private Charley Hairston, the sentinel stationed nearest to Major Penrose's quarters. "We're under fire, sir!" he shouted.

"How do you know?"

"I heard bullets whistling over my head!"

"Go to the guardhouse immediately and tell the sergeant of the guard to sound the call to arms."

"Yes, sir!" Hairston saluted and raced off to the guardhouse. Penrose was running across the parade grounds when he heard the clatter of the scavenger's mule cart and Tamayo's voice shouting,

"Whoa!"

Sergeant Mingo Sanders and his wife were sleeping when they were awakened by their next-door neighbor Hattie banging on the door, shouting, "Fire!"

At that very moment, Sanders heard the trumpet play the call to arms. He had heard that sound many times over his long military career, calling him and all soldiers to battle. Never uncertain, never doubtful—it was always clear and forceful. Every soldier knew its meaning.

"That's no fire, Hattie! It's a call to battle!" Sanders dressed quickly, ran out the door, and sprinted across the parade ground to the barracks while still buttoning his shirt. He heard bullets whistling overhead, coming from the town, and determined from the sounds that the gunfire was coming from different kinds of pistols and high-powered rifles. When he got to the Company B barracks, Sanders strapped his rifle over his shoulder and across his back. He grabbed a lantern and the company roster and rushed back to the parade ground, where he gave the command, "Company B, fall in!"

Although most of the soldiers lined up in their usual positions, a few men assumed the prone position, lying on their stomachs. Some dropped to their knees to avoid being in the line of fire.

"Stand up!" Sanders ordered. "Stand up! If you get killed, you will die like a soldier!"

Holoman yelled, "I hear bullets whistling over our heads! Dim your lantern, Sanders! You'll get us all killed!"

"Don't you think I hear 'em?" cried Sanders. "Those shots are high and wild. They wouldn't even hit Maggie's drawers."[4]

"Put out that light, Sergeant," Holoman pleaded. "It'll draw fire. You're gonna get us all killed."

Sanders snarled, "Damn the light and damn you too, Holoman! Stand up before I kick your God damned guts out!"

That was enough to convince the ground huggers to get up. All the men fell in line—and while Mingo Sanders called the muster roll, bullets from Winchesters, Mausers, and Remingtons whizzed high over their heads.

Lieutenant Lawrason, the company commander, heard the shots, got dressed, and rushed out of the officers' quarters. He reached his company just as Sanders began calling the roll. Each man in line repeated his name and yelled, "Present!"

"All present or accounted for, sir," Sanders reported.

---

[4] 'Maggie's drawers' refers to the red flag waved at the shooter during rifle practice. The expression is slang for completely missing the target.

The Brownsville Redemption

Lawrason took two steps forward and faced Company B. "Prepare to defend the fort: Issue ammunition! Take up your defensive positions! Hold your fire! Wait for orders to shoot from me!"

When First Sergeant Jacob Frazier, Company D, heard the first two shots, he wasted no time getting dressed. He raced to Company D's barracks, where he met up with his company commander, Captain Samuel P. Lyon.

The noncommissioned officer in charge of quarters heard the call to arms and quickly unlocked the gun racks. Since the men already had their rifles in hand, Captain Lyon issued a quick order. His voice was urgent. "Sergeant! Get the men downstairs. Get them lined up as quickly as possible, call the roll, deploy in a skirmish line facing the town, fire on my order, and shoot to kill!"

Lyon had been in the army for more than 14 years. Hardened in combat in Cuba, he was a no-nonsense officer, a strict disciplinarian, and a man of few words who would rather shoot than talk. He had come up through the ranks and gained instant social status by marrying a general's daughter.

Lyon stood a half step behind Sergeant Frazier, looking over his shoulder as he called the roll. When the roll call was completed, Lyon wasn't satisfied. He had trouble seeing in the darkness, so he ordered, "Do it again, Sergeant! Go down the line! Look into each man's face! Get nose to nose!"

Sergeant Frazier did as he was ordered. He called the roll a second time and reported, "All present or accounted for, sir!"

"Who are you accounting for? Who's absent, Sergeant?"

"Sergeant Thomas and Private Lee, sir!" Sergeant Frazier reminded Lyon that he had signed a three-day pass for the two absent men. With their whereabouts settled, Company D was ready to move to its defensive position.

All the companies were assembling simultaneously as the raiders continued firing high over Fort Brown. All had completed their roll call and accounted for their men except Company C, which was in a state of chaos.

Sergeant Brawner, the Company C officer in charge of quarters, was making routine inspection checks when he heard shots and the call to arms. He immediately went looking for Sergeant Harley, who was acting as first sergeant. Brawner knew the first sergeant's duty was to assemble his men when the call to arms was sounded. Brawner turned the corner from the upstairs hall and was about to go down the staircase when he saw Sergeant Harley coming up the stairs.

"Sergeant Harley, I am going to open the gun racks."

Harley looked shocked. "What for? Are you crazy?"

"We're being attacked!"

Harley was skeptical. "You must be joking. Who's attacking us?" Brawner became impatient with Harley. Determined to open the gun racks, he yelled, "How do I know? The shots are coming from town. I have the keys. I'm going to open the racks."

Sergeant Harley pulled rank on Brawner. "No, you're not. I am the acting first sergeant. Wait for orders! I didn't hear any call to arms. You wait for orders!"

In disgust, Brawner brushed past Harley on his way down the staircase, turned around, and stared at Harley's back. *You bonehead!* he fumed. *You're gonna get shot someday waiting for orders.* Then he took off running toward the guardhouse, looking for the officer of the day, Captain Macklin.

By this time, Major Penrose had made his way to Company C's barracks to find out for himself what was holding them up. The other two companies had already been deployed in defense of the fort. He was on the porch when he heard men upstairs scrambling and shouting.

The Brownsville Redemption

"Sergeant Harley," one of them said, "why don't you open these gun racks?"

Penrose yelled up the stairs, "You men hurry up and get down here!"

Private Rudy, the company gun repairman, shouted back, "We are not going to fall out without our guns! We'll get killed."

"Why don't you get your guns?" Penrose shouted.

Looking down from the second-floor porch, a soldier tried to explain, "Sergeant Harley won't open the gun racks."

"What?!" Penrose couldn't believe it.

"Says he's waiting on orders," the soldier yelled back.

Penrose went to the head of the staircase and issued Harley a direct order, "Sergeant Harley, this is your battalion commander. You get those gun racks open!"

Harley was distraught. He had been given a direct order, but he couldn't comply. "Sir, I can't. I don't have the keys."

"What are you talking about? Who has the keys?"

"Sergeant Brawner, sir. He just left, looking for Captain Macklin."

"Well, get an ax! Break the locks! Go!"

A soldier who heard Major Penrose screaming ran to the woodshed, found an ax, ran back up the stairs, and broke open the gun racks. One by one, the men grabbed their rifles, hurried down the stairs, and finally fell in line.

"Sergeant Harley," ordered Penrose, "get these men organized. Call the roll. Where in the hell is your company commander?"

Harley tried to explain. "I didn't hear the call to…"

"Forget that. Where's Captain Macklin?"

"I don't know. Maybe he's in his quarters?"

Major Penrose approached the first soldier in line and said, "Soldier, you go to Captain Macklin's quarters. Tell him to meet me at his company's defensive position, immediately!"

Then he put Lieutenant Grier in charge of Company C until Captain Macklin could be found.

Penrose issued his final orders to the company commanders: "Defend your sectors of the fort. Do not allow anyone to enter the garrison. You are not to fire under any circumstance unless it is for the preservation of life. Your men are not to fire unless you order them. And you are not to fire unless I order you to do so. I will be stationed at the Central Gate. Return to your companies on the defense line."

After the shooting died down and Macklin still hadn't shown up, Penrose began to worry. Hadn't he heard the shooting? Had some harm come to him? Penrose ordered Captain Lyon to take a patrol into town to search for him.

Lyon took his whole company and formed a patrol. Before heading out of the fort into the darkness, he issued the patrol order: "We are going into Brownsville to find Captain Macklin. This is a search patrol, not a combat patrol, but we will be in combat formation. The situation dictates that I am the point man. Keep your interval, and if fired upon, return the fire immediately. Do not wait for an order. Follow me!"

They searched the lower part of Garrison Road first, then continued up Madison until they reached 12th Street near the county jail.

There the patrol encountered 40 to 50 men armed with rifles, shotguns, and pistols standing out front.

At first sight of the crowd, Private Dorsie Willis whispered, "Captain! Those men have guns!"

With that warning, the soldiers took a defensive posture. They knelt with their guns drawn and pointed at the armed men. Lyon stood at

The Brownsville Redemption

the head of the patrol with his right hand on his pistol. He called out, "Who are you?"

"Officers of the law! Officers of the law!" a man shouted.

Lyon wanted clarification. "Stand back! I want to speak to the sheriff!"

A man standing amongst the men spoke up quickly. "I am the sheriff," Celedonio Garza stepped out in front of the crowd. "It's me, Captain Lyon—Sheriff Garza."

"I'm looking for Captain Macklin. Have you seen him?"

"I don't know anyone by that name. Wouldn't know him if I saw him."

Captain Lyon didn't like the sheriff's tone. "Tell me, sheriff, do you have a white man in your jail?"

"No, I only have one man in jail, and he's Black."

Captain Lyon was curious. "Is he a soldier? What's his name?"

"It's just old Mack Hamilton. I put him in for safekeeping. Who's doing the shooting?"

"I don't know," Lyon answered. And with that, his patrol moved on, turned left on 12th Street, and continued their search for Macklin.

Nine

Did the Soldiers *Shoot Up the Town?*

"He's gone."

As suddenly as it began, the shooting stopped, and the mystery raiders vanished into the night. Fred Combe was bewildered. Who were they? Some of the townspeople were certain they had seen "Colored soldiers." A clamor of voices filled his ears:

"I saw Black soldiers."

"I heard coarse voices."

"I saw big bulky men jumping the wall."

"It was the nigger soldiers, all right. It couldn't have been anybody else. Everybody knows it was the niggers."

"I know it was the soldiers because I saw their khaki uniforms."

"Mayor, we told you to keep them out of our town. Now look what they gone and done."

Fred Combe wanted to believe the townspeople, but he was not yet ready to join the citizen-chorus, blaming the soldiers. There was no question that some of the people had seen the raiders. But had they really seen Black soldiers?

But for now, the mayor was concerned with the safety of his policemen. He stood in front of Crixell's Saloon, receiving piecemeal reports on his officers' status from Police Chief Connors.

"I heard Dominguez got shot out of the saddle," the chief said. "Don't know his condition or where he is. It's rumored that he was killed, but somebody said they saw him crawling away from his horse.

The Brownsville Redemption

Two other policemen are still missing, Macedonio Ramirez and José Coronado."

The disturbing news made Combe wonder if the raiders were trying to wipe out his police force. But he'd better wait for the facts. Saying nothing, he lowered his head and continued walking down Elizabeth Street with a guard of policemen.

In the dark distance, Combe saw something that looked like a pile of bodies stacked up on the sidewalk. As he drew closer to the corner of 13th Street, he realized it was a horse. The animal contorted its body, writhed about, and twitched its hind legs.

"That's Lieutenant Dominguez's horse!" said one of the policemen. He pointed his pistol at the animal's head. "Should I put him out of his misery?"

Combe shook his head. "No need. The poor creature will be dead in a second. We don't need to hear any more shooting."

As the mayor crossed the street headed toward the Miller Hotel, a man called out to him. "Mayor, they can see you from the garrison. Don't go out in the street!"

The mayor walked on, convinced he would not be harmed by any soldier from Fort Brown. In his heart, he still doubted that they were responsible.

A bright light burned inside the Miller Hotel, but no one was in the lobby. Convinced that the frightened hotel guests were hiding, he stood in the courtyard and called out, "Does anyone know anything about these shootings?"

No one replied.

Suddenly, a man in his pajamas bolted through the front door and ran past him without saying a word. In the darkness, the mayor couldn't tell who the man was but guessed from his limp it was the hotel clerk. Then the mayor saw an old man running toward him.

"Doctor Combe!" He gasped, "They need you over at the Ruby Saloon! The Justice of the Peace wants you to examine a dead body."

When Combe reached the bar, he saw a huge but silent crowd gathered near the entrance. As he approached, the people respectfully opened a path to let him through. When he got to the door, it was locked. He was glad to know that Tillman had had the good sense not to let the rubberneckers in.

Tillman opened the door for the mayor and directed him to the alleyway, where the coroner was waiting on him to examine the body. Frank Natus was lying in a pool of blood. The mayor knelt, lifted Frank's left wrist, felt his pulse, and looked at the wound. He noticed that Frank had been hit with a single shot at close range, apparently with a large caliber gun. He shook his head, "Poor fellow." He closed Natus's eyes and removed the nickel-plated Smith and Wesson pistol from his right hand. Natus still clutched the gun fiercely as if he were still expecting it to save him.

When the mayor emerged from the saloon, the people wanted to know if the young bartender was going to make it. Passing through the crowd, he said simply "He's gone."

"Justice comes at the end of a rope."

Katie Leahy and Judge Parks had been looking for Louis Cowen without success. Now they stood on the outskirts of the crowd with Anna Cowen and her children in tow. When Anna Cowen heard the mayor confirm the bartender's death, she began sobbing. "The soldiers tried to kill us, too! They tried to kill us! Where is Louis? Where is Louis?" Katie grabbed her by the shoulders and shook her. "Anna! Get a grip on yourself."

The Brownsville Redemption

Judge Parks spoke up. "Go easy on her, Katie. She's scared." Leaning her head on Katie's shoulder, Anna Cowan made a pitiful sight. Eventually, she calmed down, but her plaintive cries that the Black soldiers had tried to kill her and her children alarmed the mayor. Combe started having second thoughts about the soldiers. Maybe they were guilty after all? The mayor stepped closer to Anna and asked, "Mrs. Cowen, did you see the soldiers?"

"No, sir, I didn't have to see them. Amada Martinez saw them," she said, pointing to the maid.

Before the mayor could ask Amada Martinez, Katie interrupted: "I saw 'em. One of them was a freckled-faced, yellow nigger. I heard him curse when he stepped in a big mud puddle, then I heard him curse again when his gun jammed."

While searching for Louis Cowen, Judge Parks learned that officer Dominguez had escaped serious injury. He had crawled away from his dying horse, and someone had helped him into a nearby drugstore. Judge Parks said, "Dominguez was shot in the arm, but he'll be okay. But two other policemen have been missing all evening. They must have been killed."

Katie, overhearing the judge, suddenly clasped both hands to her mouth and turned bright red. "Oh, Lord! How could I have forgot?"

"Forgot what?" the mayor asked. "They're in my bathroom at the hotel."

"*Who's* in your bathroom? *The policemen are in your bathroom?* Then, for God's sake, go back and unlock the door!"

"Sir, it's not locked, it's just closed."

"You mean...they could have come out anytime?"

"Yes, sir! But I told them not to come out until I told them to."

By then, the mood in the town had grown ugly, and the deference the townspeople had always shown their mayor had vanished. The angry crowd swelled, and many of the men were armed with various weapons—Winchesters, old-style military Krag rifles, pistols, and shotguns. They ran about, shouting, "The soldiers shot up the town! They killed Frank!"

The angry crowd quickly grew into a wrathful mob. Waving their guns over their heads, the men yelled, "We're going to the fort to do those bastards up!"

Arguments broke out between those who wanted to charge the fort immediately and those who urged calm. Tempers boiled over.

"Get the hell outta my way! I'm going now!" one man shouted. He was not alone.

The mayor looked at Judge Parks, who stood a short distance away, and begged him, "Get me a box or something to stand on."

Judge Parks saw a large water barrel nearby that was used to tamp down the dirt on the street. He tilted it, emptied it, then flipped it upside down. The mayor climbed on top.

Fred Combe raised his hands and tried to speak. "People, please calm down, I have something to…" The noise drowned him out. He waved his arms up and down, but nobody paid him any mind. Judge Parks handed him a shotgun, and the mayor fired a single blast into the air. The crowd startled, and the mayor shouted:

"I appeal to you, as your mayor and an ex-army officer, not to rush that fort! As I already told you, I served with those troops. They're as efficient as any in the world. And they are heavily armed. If you go down there, many lives will be lost. Besides that, right now, you are still within the law. If you attack the fort, you'll be attacking the United States of America!"

"Justice comes at the end of a rope for murderers!" one man yelled. "That's right," the mayor shot back. "But after a trial, not a lynching!"

The man countered, "We're Texans! Our honor is at stake! You go tell Penrose to give up the guilty sons-of-bitches now, or we'll go and take 'em ourselves!"

The mayor got the message. "All right, I'll go."

Katie Leahy spoke up again. "Now, how are you gonna do that without getting shot? Don't risk your life, mayor. You're not a stupid man. Don't go acting stupid."

"Go to your homes," he replied calmly. "I'll call Major Penrose. We'll get to the bottom of this thing, and I promise we'll find the guilty parties."

The crowd began to disperse. The mayor went back inside the saloon and telephoned Penrose. But after numerous tries, he still couldn't reach him.

It was now about 1:30 in the morning, and the search patrol, led by Captain Lyon, still had not found Captain Macklin anywhere in town. The patrol was headed back down Elizabeth Street to the fort when it came upon the mayor and the last few stragglers from the crowd.

When he saw the soldiers take defensive postures, the mayor stepped forward and cried out, "Captain Lyon, order your men not to shoot. These men with me are officers of the law! I need to talk to Major Penrose. Take me to him."

The soldiers lowered their weapons at the order of their captain. "I'll provide armed escort for you and your uniformed policemen only," replied Captain Lyon. "Tell the other men to get back!"

The mayor pointed to the other men. "It's okay. You can all go home. We won't need you anymore tonight."

As they started down the street, Joe Combe spoke up. "Captain, I'm Joe Combe, Fred's brother."

"Okay, you can come, too."

The brothers joined the captain, and together they marched down

Elizabeth Street toward the fort.

"Have you seen anything of Captain Macklin?" Lyon asked the mayor.

"No."

The mayor was concerned. He and Macklin were close friends. "We can't find him anywhere on post or in town. We're afraid he's been done away with." Lyon said.

"That's nonsense." The mayor refused to consider such a notion, but the very idea shook him up.

Stationed just back of the central gate, Major Penrose saw Captain Lyon returning with his patrol. Leading the group were the two Combe brothers, but there was no sign of Captain Macklin. He wanted to rush out to meet them, but he froze in place. Finally, he managed to shout out, "Lyon! Did you find Macklin?"

"No, sir," Lyon called, as they marched toward the gate.

"I'm going over to the officers' quarters and look around for him myself."

Penrose sent the patrol back to the company's defensive position and headed across the parade field.

Three different soldiers had been dispatched to Macklin's quarters over the course of the evening. The first soldier had knocked on Macklin's door, shouting, "Captain Macklin! Major Penrose wants to see you!"

"All right," Macklin murmured. Then he turned over and went back to sleep.

When Macklin didn't appear, a second soldier was dispatched to pound on the captain's door. "Captain Macklin! Captain Macklin! Major Penrose wants you to come now!"

"All right," the soldier heard him say. And again, Macklin promptly fell back asleep.

Later, a third soldier tried. He rapped loudly, yelling, "Captain Macklin! Major Penrose is looking for you!" When there was no answer, the soldier left.

The first two soldiers had not mentioned to Major Penrose that they had spoken to Macklin because they assumed he'd gotten up.

The third soldier reported that Macklin didn't answer, but it turned out that he had knocked on the wrong door.

Major Penrose then sent Corporal Burdette to Macklin's quarters. When Burdett came upon Private Hairston, the sentinel on duty near Macklin's quarters, Hairston said, "I know he's in there. But he won't get up."

Corporal Burdett slung his rifle off his shoulder and snarled, "I'll get him up!" The men went to Macklin's door, and Burdette banged the butt of his rifle against it three times.

"Captain Macklin! They're shooting on the officers' quarters!" Macklin leapt straight up, still fully clothed, and stumbled over an empty beer bottle on the floor. He flung the door open.

"What? What's the trouble?" Not waiting for an answer, he bounded down the stairs and ran at full speed across the parade ground.

The Confrontation

Back at the central gate, Major Penrose greeted Mayor Combe and his entourage with a polite but distinct chill. He got straight to the point. "Mayor, I hope you can explain what all this shooting is about."

Fred Combe was stunned. "To the contrary, sir! You and your officers have some explaining to do. Your men have killed one man, seriously wounded the lieutenant of police, killed his horse, and shot into several houses."

Penrose was stunned in return. "Mayor, I can hardly believe that! I am told that the citizens fired on the post!"

"No! Your men fired on my citizens. Several people saw them!"

"Who could possibly identify anyone on such a dark night? I can barely see my own hand in front of my face."

"I'm telling you, Major. Several people confirmed it."

"Well, Mayor, I just don't believe it. We had a roll call. Two roll calls. All the men were present or accounted for. Your people fired at my post!"

Exasperated, Mayor Combe demanded, "Who is the officer of the day? Can he shed some light on this?"

Major Penrose told him Macklin was the officer of the day and that Captain Lyon was looking for him.

"Inspect your barracks for bullet holes."

Captain Lyon walked across the parade field toward the officers' quarters. In the distance, he saw Captain Macklin running toward him.

"Ed!" he cried. "Where have you been? We've been looking all over for you."

"I fell asleep," Macklin answered, surprised at all the activity around him.

"You'd better go report to Major Penrose. He's at the central gate." Mayor Combe and Major Penrose were still arguing about who shot up the town when Captain Macklin rushed up to the two men, interrupted the conversation, and saluted. "Sir, I report!"

"My God! Captain Macklin!" Penrose exclaimed. "Where have you been?"

"I was asleep in my quarters."

"You mean to tell me that you've been sleeping this whole time? I sent three men looking for you! For God's sake, didn't you hear the shooting?" Then Penrose softened his voice, relieved to know that his best friend had not been harmed.

"Take command of your company."

"Yes, sir," Macklin almost whispered, clearly embarrassed.

Combe continued his rant to Penrose. "Major, we've not accomplished anything here except to butt heads. Don't allow any of your men to come into town tonight under any circumstances. As you well know, the people are very much wrought up."

Major Penrose agreed. "I'll issue an order at once that no man is to leave the fort."

Hoping to keep the peace, the mayor readily made a promise that he knew would be difficult to keep. "I'll keep the citizens in town."

Penrose replied, "And no one will be allowed on post except you." The mayor, relieved that they had reached an agreement, left with his group. He was satisfied that the confrontation had ceased, at least for the time being.

Penrose walked over to Company C's defensive position and gave Captain Macklin a new order. "Ed, redeploy your company to maintain defense of the fort. I'm sending B and D Companies back to the barracks. Make sure no man cleans his weapon. Make sure all guns are locked up. Conduct a shakedown inspection at daylight. I want a rifle inspection after reveille. Verify ammunition. And, oh yes: Inspect your barracks for bullet holes."

"Where have you been, you lousy cuss?"

After milling around from bar to bar, restaurant to restaurant, and crowd to crowd, Louis Cowen headed home at about two o'clock in the morning.

Katie Leahy sat on Cowen's porch, waiting for him. He staggered up to the gate holding a brown paper bag containing a sandwich and a bottle of Schlitz. In his back pocket, he had what was left of a half pint of whiskey.

Katie met him at the gate and gave him a piece of her mind. "Where have you been, you lousy cuss?"

"Get outta my way, Katie. I gotta protect my family."

"You been drinking!"

"Gotta protect my family." He stumbled backwards as he tugged unsuccessfully at the white picket fence, thinking it was the gate.

"They're not in there, Louis. Anna and the children are at my hotel."

"I'm gonna sue the government for fifty thousand dollars," Cowen slurred threateningly.

Katie started to walk away. "I'm sick of you. I'm going home."

"I'll stand guard," Cowen said.

"Guard what? You guard me? Don't be ridiculous."

Disgusted, Katie turned on her heel and went back to her hotel, with Louis Cowen in close pursuit. Without uttering another word, she went into her boarding house and locked the door behind her. Louis lit a lantern and sat in Katie's front yard for the rest of the night, without a gun, guarding his family.

"This is a shakedown."

At dawn, Major Penrose withdrew Company C from its defensive position, and Captain Macklin marched his company back to their barracks for the shakedown inspection.

The Brownsville Redemption

The shakedown was kept secret from all the enlisted men and even from the battalion sergeant major. All soldiers were ordered to their barracks and instructed not to leave.

The commanders of the three companies walked into their respective barracks and announced:

> This is a shakedown, a full shakedown. Noncommissioned officers block the doors. Everybody strip down to your underwear. Dump your footlockers on your beds. Dump all bags on the floor.

A most thorough inspection was conducted, but no unauthorized ammunition, pistols, knives, or other contraband was found.

At the end of the shakedown, the bugler sounded assembly. The men hustled into their uniforms and stood reveille at precisely 5:30 a.m. At that time, an inspection of all rifles was made. There was no evidence that any of the guns had been fired, and none showed any residue of gunpowder.

After the inspection, Captain Macklin decided he would venture beyond the garrison gate into Brownsville and look around. At the mouth of Cowen's Alley, he spotted some debris that turned his blood cold. He couldn't believe his eyes. It can't be. He picked up several empty cartridge shells, rolled them around in his hand, looked at them in disbelief, and put them into his pockets. Then he picked up six empty clips. "Oh, no!" he cried. It was no mirage. The cartridge shells and clips had been made for the army's new Springfield 1903 model.

With the damaging evidence in his pocket, Macklin stood up, looked around guardedly, and went directly to the administration building, where he found a despondent Penrose sitting at his desk. Taking the empty shells and clips from his pockets, he walked over to

Penrose holding the curious evidence in both hands. "Look what I found in Cowen's Alley."

Penrose put his glasses on and examined the findings. Then he took his glasses off and dropped his arm by his side, the glasses dangling in his hand. "Well, Macklin," he said sadly. "It looks as though our men are responsible after all."

Penrose was in a state of shock. He still couldn't believe it. All the men had been present or accounted for, and there was no evidence that any weapons had been fired. And yet, here was this bizarre collection of shells and clips. Did his men really shoot up the town? He would have to conduct a preliminary investigation before he could report anything to his regimental commander.

Since Macklin had found those spent shells, Penrose concluded there must be more in the streets that other people would surely find and turn over to Mayor Combe, who would probably return to confront him again anytime now. Penrose dreaded having to admit what he now was sure was the truth.

He debated with himself. *I'll talk with Creager; that's what I'll do. No, I won't talk to Creager. He doesn't like Negroes. But he's all I got. I'll call Creager.*

Renfro B. Creager was an attorney. He was also the United States Commissioner and the Deputy Clerk of the United States District Court for the Southern District of Texas. When Penrose called, Creager immediately went to meet with him at the fort.

Before their meeting broke up, Penrose heard the knock on his door that he had been dreading. It was Mayor Combe. The mayor promptly confronted Penrose with a clip with one cartridge in it and about seven empty shells.

"Major Penrose," he demanded. "How can you refute this evidence? Your men did this!"

The Brownsville Redemption

"Where did you get that?"

"I stepped on these shells at the corner of the Miller Hotel alley at about two o'clock this morning, and…"

"Are there more?" Penrose asked, examining them.

Mayor Combe replied condescendingly, "Uh, yeah, I'd say so. About daybreak, I picked up some empty shells in front of Mr. Stark's house. He also found some others and turned them over to me. And Mr. Houghton turned over some ball cartridges this morning."

"Live ball ammunition?" Penrose raised an eyebrow. "Yeah."

"Combe," he said resignedly, "this looks like conclusive evidence. But who did it, and how they did it, is an absolute mystery to me."

TEN

Panic in Brownsville

"The soldiers have to go."

On their way back to City Hall after meeting with Penrose, Mayor Combe and Commissioner Creager discussed what to do next.

Creager was blunt. "Fred, you got to get these soldiers out of town. You have no other choice."

From past meetings and discussions with Creager, Combe knew Creager was no friend of the "Negro." In fact, he hadn't wanted the Black soldiers in Brownsville in the first place. "I think you're right. But first, don't you think we should have a group of citizens investigate?"

"All that matters right this minute is to get them out of town," Creager insisted.

With shoulders slumped and head hung low, Combe mounted the steps of City Hall, deep in thought. *Creager's right. The town's in a panic. The soldiers have to go.*

Fred Combe had assessed the situation correctly. On Tuesday morning, August 14th, the day after the attack, the town awoke in fear. The air was thick with rumors. People were on edge and believed all kinds of preposterous stories—that drunken Black soldiers were roaming the streets, plundering homes, raping women, snatching babies from their mother's arms, and shooting and killing at will.

White men locked their women and children behind closed doors and ordered them not to venture out for any reason. Some people fled to Matamoros. Anna Cowen and her children were among them. But first, remembering her promise to God to give thanks if He allowed her to survive the shooting, she dutifully took the children to mass before fleeing the country.

White shopkeepers armed themselves after the shooting rampage in Brownsville, August 1906. Courtesy Texas State Library and Archives Commission, Austin, Texas

Armed, angry white men roamed the streets expecting to find that their town had suffered major damage. But they didn't find the pillaging they had imagined. They looked for bullet holes and picked up empty shell casings and clips. They entered the bloodstained alleyway behind the Ruby Saloon and compared stories on how many shots they'd heard and how many raiders they'd seen. And they stared aghast at the dead horse still lying in the street.

By now, a long line had formed in front of Cowen's house, and curiosity seekers inside were going through their private things. Overnight, the home had become a tourist attraction.

After leaving Creager, Fred Combe cloistered himself in his office and listened to his inner counsel. He agreed with Creager that they had to get rid of the Black soldiers. *But not until after an investigation.* He called a meeting in his office to consult with two of the most prominent Republicans in town—Major John B. Armstrong, a former army officer, and E.H. Goodrich, a former Grand Union soldier. The three concluded that the mayor should hold a mass meeting of "the thinking people" in town at the federal courthouse at eleven o'clock that very morning.

Meanwhile, a raving crowd had congregated near City Hall, demanding to see the mayor:

"Fred! Get out here and do something!"

"You get these nigger soldiers out of town!"

"Come out and stop hiding behind your desk!"

"*Behind* his desk?" chortled Sam Wreford at full volume. "He's *under* his desk!"

The mayor recognized Wreford's high-pitched voice and was immediately agitated. *I'd better get outside and lay down the law.* He braced himself and went to confront the crowd.

"I'll arrest anybody who keeps this up!" Mayor Combe cried out.

"And as for you, Sam, I'll have you deported! But the rest of you—my good, law-abiding citizens!—please come to the courthouse this morning at eleven o'clock. I need you to help me resolve this situation!"

Suddenly, the sheriff and two policemen appeared, an unmistakable sign that the mayor was serious about his threat. When the crowd quieted down, Combe went back inside to prepare for the meeting. He didn't want to make a fool of himself. He knew his credibility was on the line.

By eleven o'clock, the courthouse was packed, and people were spilling out into the street. Captain Kelly said to the mayor, "I think all the respectable citizens are here."

"How many do you think?"

"I'm guessing about five hundred, including the folks outside." The mayor took his place behind the podium and began the meeting by calling on the chief of police to review the known damages and casualties. Then he sat down.

Chief Connor approached the podium and looked over the crowd. Earlier that morning, he had gone up and down every street, talking to people and assessing the destruction. He began without preamble. "Pray for Frank Natus. Last night we lost him." He paused for a few seconds before continuing. "Police Lieutenant Dominguez was shot in the arm, but he'll be okay."

Then the chief began to read from his notes. "As it turned out, God almighty was with us. Only a few houses and buildings were hit. Cowen's house took the worst of it. The soldiers shot it up pretty bad. Mrs. Cowen and her children barely escaped death. Fred Stark's house also took some terrible hits that almost killed his little girls."

The chief paused for a few seconds and looked to the back of the crowded room where Fred Starck stood. "Fred," he declared, "I don't have to tell you you're a lucky man."

Fred Starck nodded in agreement, but there was something else on his mind. *Did Avila have something to do with this?*

Starck was a U. S. customs officer with an outstanding reputation for catching smugglers along the Mexican border. His arrest record had been high, and more than 600 smugglers had been jailed. However, his capture rate had recently plummeted. Somehow, he reasoned, the smugglers had learned how to dodge his traps.

Three nights earlier, Starck had chased a smuggler on foot along the border. When he finally caught up with the man, he hit him in the back of the head with his revolver and knocked him to the ground. As he put the barrel of his pistol to the man's head, a familiar voice cried out, "Mr. Starck! Don't kill me! It's me! Avila!"

Appalled, Starck jumped back, his revolver shaking in his now trembling hand, "Oh no, not you! Oh, how could you do this after I gave you a second chance?"

"I needed the money. Please, *please* let me go!"

It was the same convincing voice that had once persuaded Starck to rescue Avila from jail, to trust him, and to give him a job in his house. In time, Avila had become almost one of the family. But it was now obvious that it was he who had been tipping off fellow smugglers about the techniques Starck used to apprehend them.

Starck's anger dissolved into genuine disappointment. "I hate to do this," he said, "but I'll have to take you in. Get up."

The very next day, Avila jumped bail and went into hiding. Starck now wondered if the smugglers had shot up the town. *Where is Avila?*

"It's the way of the heathen."

Police chief Connor continued reading from his notes: "They fired into Yturria's house at Washington and 15th Street, the Telegraph House, and the Ruby Saloon. Miller's Hotel had a bullet hole in the jamb of one of the windows on the alley side and was hit twice in the brickwork on the 13th Street side. There was a bullet hole in the door of Mr. Wells's office on 13th Street, and another bullet hole in Sam Wreford's office. A few lamp posts were blown out, and a building column or two got hit. Paulino Preciado says he was grazed by a bullet at the Ruby Saloon about the time Frank Natus was killed. That's about the extent of the damages and the casualties. Oh. And, of course, poor Old Gray." The chief folded his papers and stepped down from the podium.

Mayor Combe then stood and addressed the crowd. "My people, my good citizens, we've had a terrible night! But as the chief said, our God stood watch over us, except for one soul who was taken from us. The murderers took a young life, a boy of only twenty-three. God must have had a good reason for calling him home because He knows as well as the rest of us, Frank Natus didn't have an enemy in the world. And I want you to know: Frank is with the Lord! And our Lord is with us!" The mayor paused to gauge the crowd's reaction. Then he resumed:

> "But I need you to understand we don't have to go out and avenge his death. I know the fires that burn in your hearts, because they also burn in mine. But revenge is not the way. Revenge only incites men to take the law into their own hands. But citizens! That's not the American way. It's not the Christian way. It's the way of the heathen. And if we go that way, it'll be the ruination of Brownsville—your town!—my town!—God's town!"

Fred Combe paused and took a few sips of water from his jar. Then he lowered his voice and adopted a pleading tone: "Now, I agree with you that this hideous crime against God was committed by some outlaws at Fort Brown. But we cannot condemn all of the men. So far, most of them have acted respectably, just like you and me. However..."

Finally, the mayor uttered the only words the crowd wanted to hear: "I will demand that Washington remove the Black soldiers and their officers from Brownsville immediately."

Abruptly, the mayor emerged from behind the podium, and raising a balled fist he shouted, "I will go to the highest authority in Washington, to the president himself, my friend the great Theodore Roosevelt! He'll get these soldiers out of Brownsville and get them out of Texas. I promise you, by God, they will go—and never come back! And I solemnly vow to you that the guilty ones will be caught, brought to trial, and hanged at Fort Leavenworth! They will never walk upon this land again! Oh, God! If I lie…if I lie, strike me dead, right now! Strike me dead!"

Combe's passion ignited the crowd, and the people cheered wildly, captivated by the mayor's theatrics, mixing politics with old-time religious rapture. His fervor soothed them. They knew their mayor would keep his promise.

Combe by now was drenched in perspiration, and his sweaty shirt was pasted to his skin. He was emotionally exhausted, but he still had more to say. He pushed his hair back, took out a handkerchief, wiped his face, and addressed Captain Kelly: "Captain Kelly, I want you to select a committee of citizens to investigate the night of horrors. I am appointing you chairman. I will sit on the committee and also appoint the sheriff and the chief of police. You pick the rest. Select the best people you know and tell them I expect their full cooperation. Go on, now. We can't afford to wait."

Eleven

A Citizens' Committee *Investigates*

Captain Kelly liked to boast that there was less racial prejudice in Brownsville than any other place in Texas. Nevertheless, while choosing members for his committee, he selected mostly Northern Republicans, who he believed had no particular animus against Negroes. Among them were county judge Frank Kibbe, city attorney James A. Brown, and the editor of the *Herald*, Jesse O. Wheeler. Kelly also invited E.H. Goodrich, an alderman, and John G. Fernandez, a banker.

Major Penrose sat in his office with his elbows on his desk, chin resting in the palms of his hands. He was dumbfounded by the contradictory evidence that lay before him. He had just finished scrutinizing the sworn statements of the three noncommissioned officers in charge of quarters, the men who held the keys to the rifle racks. The officers were authorized to open them only upon orders or on hearing the call to arms. Each man had sworn he had given his keys to no one. *If my men shot up the town,* he wondered, *how did they get the rifles? Not only that, but I was there when the rolls were called. All were present or accounted for!*

Suddenly, a gust of wind whipped across Penrose's desk, scattering his papers as well as the empty cartridges, shells, and ammunition clips. He jumped up to close the window and started gathering the strewn items. As he picked up one of the empty shells, something caught his eye that he hadn't noticed before: The date of manufacture, which should have been printed on the base, was missing.

Having failed to reconcile the sworn statements with the physical evidence, he then turned to the affidavit of Tamayo, the post scavenger. Tamayo swore that the shooting began on the town side of the garrison wall, and that he hadn't seen any soldiers shooting.

A familiar three taps on his door startled him. "Come in, Scottie."

"Sir, Captain Kelly, Mayor Combe, and several other people are here to see you."

"Take them to the staff room; I'll be right in. Tell Captain Lyon and Lieutenant Grier to meet me there."

"I don't understand this at all."

The men wasted no time with introductions. Kelly slid some empty cartridge shells down the table toward Penrose and got straight to the point. "Well, Major Penrose, your men are guilty. And here's the evidence. No one else has that kind of ammunition."

"I know my men," Penrose said. "They could never have committed such an outrage."

Kelly raised an eyebrow. "Well then, you tell me who did it!"

Penrose replied with confidence. "I think the townsmen attacked the barracks."

With a raised voice and sarcastic tone, Kelly retorted, "Really! So *your* buildings were shot up?"

Penrose was forced to admit that none of the buildings at the fort showed any sign of damage by gunfire.

The room fell silent.

Holding the evidence he could not reconcile, in neither his mind nor his heart, Penrose said quietly, "Gentlemen, I tell you. I don't understand this at all. I don't see how my men could have done it."

"Well, they *could* do it and they *did do it!*" Kelly growled while all the other committee members remained stone faced.

Penrose was backed into a corner with what seemed to be overwhelming evidence. Finally, he conceded: "I'm afraid you must be right."

With that admission, Captain Kelly, Fred Combe, and the rest of the citizens' committee got up from the conference table and left without shaking hands or showing any other courtesies.

A despondent Penrose went back to his office and slumped into his chair. Then he picked up his pen and wrote the following telegram to the military secretary in San Antonio:

> Regret to report serious shooting in Brownsville last evening, in which one civilian was killed, and the lieutenant chief of police so seriously wounded that his right arm had to be amputated. Brownsville officials claim shooting was done by enlisted men of this command and borne out in their opinion by empty shells and clips picked up in the streets.

He handed the message to Lieutenant Grier, the acting adjutant. "Take this to the telegraph office immediately."

"Send a telegram to President Roosevelt."

After Kelly and his team had left the post, they walked back into town for lunch. But first, Kelly turned to the police chief and said, "We should get a lawyer on board. Go ask Wells if he'll meet with us."

That afternoon, the group gathered at the office of James B. Wells, Esq., the defense attorney who had saved Texas Ranger A.Y. Baker from the gallows. They closed the drapes and set up shop. The committee members took their seats in the heavy leather chairs surrounding an enormous mahogany conference table. Kelly sat calmly at the head. The orderly setting of the law office, with its scores of imposing law books neatly aligned in built-in mahogany bookshelves, stood in sharp contrast to the raucous mob that was gathering outside. Armed vigilante groups had begun patrolling the streets, getting ready for an old-fashioned lynching.

The police had no trouble finding people willing to talk to the committee. They pulled men in off the streets, lined them up at the door, ushered them in one by one, and started taking testimony. No one was put under oath or asked to swear on the Bible.

Captain Kelly, the chairman, greeted each man cordially before asking him to tell what he knew about "this attack by the Negroes on our town."

"You know the object of this meeting," said Kelly. "We know that this outrage was committed by the Negro soldiers. But we need all information we can get in order to find the particular ones who did it."

Charles S. Canada

Questioner: We are inquiring into the matter of last night with a view to ascertaining who the guilty parties are. We know they were Negro soldiers. If there is anything that throws any light on the subject, we would like to have it.
Witness: I was raised among them. I know their voices pretty well. I heard one of them Negroes say, "We got him."
Questioner: Did you see him?
Witness: No. But I recognized that coarse voice.

Miller Hotel Proprietor

Witness: I heard someone shout, "There goes the son of a bitch! Get him!"

The Brownsville Redemption

Questioner: Did you see him?
Witness: No. I just heard a voice coming from the alley in back of the hotel.

C.C. Madison

Witness: I heard someone say, "Halt!"
Questioner: Did you see any soldiers?
Witness: No.

Dr. Thorn

Witness: I heard two men's voices. One said, "There he goes, give him hell." Then the other man said, "God damn him!" I'm sure the last voice was a Negro's.

James P. McDonnel

Witness: I knew there was bitter feelings in town and thought that if they caught any Negro soldiers uptown, they might do them up. So I laid awake, never pulled off my shoes. When I heard the shooting, I ran down Elizabeth Street to the alley between Elizabeth and Washington. I heard more shots, just inside the garrison wall. I saw about twenty men assembled on the town side, near the telegraph office. I don't know where they came from.
Questioner: Did you see any soldiers jump the wall?
A: No.
Questioner: Were they Negro soldiers or white men?
A: I don't know, but they were soldiers.
Questioner: How do you know that?
A: Because they were wearing uniforms."

George W. Rendall

Witness: Where's the Bible?
Questioner: You don't need a Bible, George. Just tell the truth.
Witness: I want a Bible!
Questioner: George, you know the soldiers shot up the town, and our Lord Jesus Christ knows it, too. Just tell us what you saw or heard.
Witness: Well, pistol shots woke me up around 10 o'clock. They were fired close to my house, I'd say about 60 feet (18 meters) from inside the garrison wall. When my wife and I went to the window, I could see soldiers moving back and forth inside the fort, and they were shooting. I watched one man in particular. I saw his pistol fire straight up in the air. Then I heard someone shout, "There he goes!" Then the men moved toward the wall.

Genaro Padron

Witness: I knew they were soldiers because they were in their uniforms.
Questioner: Were they white or Black men?
Witness: I couldn't tell. They were firing at me.

The committee rushed through 15 more witnesses. Out of a total of 22, eight had said the raiders were Black. Five of the eight said they actually saw them; the other three said they had only heard the raiders but could tell from their voices that they were Black. The other witnesses had offered only confused and contradictory statements.

Some committee members began fidgeting in their chairs and cupping their mouths to suppress their persistent yawns, so Kelly called a recess. He went to a window, pulled back a corner of the heavy draperies, and saw a long line of impatient men still waiting to get in to tell their stories.

But Kelly decided they had heard enough. After recess, he congratulated himself and the committee: "Gentlemen, we have conducted a most diligent inquiry. I'll go outside and give the people our verdict. We must not wait any longer to send a telegram to President Roosevelt."

There was no dissent.

Kelly stepped outside the door: "Gentlemen! We have concluded our investigation." He waited for the crowd to quiet down. "We have found that the Black soldiers at the fort perpetrated this heinous crime, and we are sending a telegram to President Roosevelt to ask him to arrest and remove them from this town!"

Katie Leahy pushed her way to the head of the line. "You didn't talk to me."

"Now, Katie, you know this is a men's thing."

Having pacified the crowd, Kelly stepped back inside and said to his colleagues, "Y'all go home now. We'll meet again first thing tomorrow and write the president."

Physical Evidence, Testimony, and a Telegram

That same afternoon at the fort, Penrose began his own inquiry. He agonized over the physical evidence, going over it again and again. Something peculiar about the base of not one but two of the empty cartridge casings had caught his eye. He picked one up and studied it. It was marked U.M.C.30 S. Then he examined the other one. It was the same. Then he compared those two with other empty casings. *Aha! They're different!* The others were marked U.M.C. Co., followed by a date. He knew these markings identified the manufacture of the ammunition as Union Metallic Cartridge Company of Bridgeport, Connecticut. He was baffled. *Why the difference?*

Penrose decided to summon a few of the enlisted men to his office for interrogation. Corporal John H. Hill, who had been stationed in the rear of post, was the first soldier he questioned:

"Corporal, Captain Lyon tells me you witnessed some civilians near the wall last night. Tell me what you saw."

"Sir," said Corporal Hill, "I saw some civilians running toward town from a dark place near the stone wall in front of Company D quarters. I think they'd been hiding there."

At this, Penrose perked up and leaned closer to Hill. "How many do you think?"

"About five. Maybe a few more."

"Is that all you can tell me?"

"Yes, sir."

Next, Private William Mapp of Company C told Penrose, "I heard voices on the outside of the company barracks saying, 'Come out, you Black sons of bitches.'"

Finally, Private Charles E Rudy, artificer of Company C, came in and said, "I was sleeping on the back porch when I was awakened by a shot. Then I heard a number of shots. I saw flashes from guns from outside the wall toward Company B headquarters, but the fire was aimed high. I heard cursing and calls. 'Come out, you Black sons of bitches! We'll kill you all!'"

Penrose wanted desperately to believe his soldiers, but the physical evidence was overwhelming. Besides, he thought, *Who would take a Negro's word over that of a white man?*

He decided it was time to inform his superiors of his conclusion. He composed a telegram to the Department of Texas military secretary:

> After further investigation, I am convinced the killing of a citizen and wounding of the lieutenant chief of police at

Brownsville last night was done by from seven to ten men of this command, abetted by others in post.

If anyone else harbored any doubts as to who shot up the town, all they had to do that afternoon was scan the front page of the Brownsville *Daily Herald* to disabuse them.

Tuesday, August 14, 1906

DASTARDLY OUTRAGE BY NEGRO SOLDIERS
Fired on Private Residences and Other Places—Houses of L.R. Cowen and F.E. Stark Riddled with Bullets
MIDNIGHT ATTACK ON CITIZENS —VOLLEY UPON VOLLEY OF KRAG-JØRGENSEN BULLETS
Frank Natus, Bartender at Ruby Saloon, Killed Instantly by Murderous Fiends. Wounded Policeman Joe Dominguez and His Horse Killed under Him

The next day, the citizens' committee dispatched a telegram to President Roosevelt, with the news that about 20 to 30 Black soldiers armed with rifles and plenty of ammunition had broken out of Fort Brown just before midnight on August 13th and fired into the homes of citizens and buildings. They concluded the telegram with the following:

> "...we ask you to have the troops at once removed from Fort Brown and replaced by white soldiers."

Twelve

The Blocksom *Investigation*

What Katie Leahy Saw

William Howard Taft, the secretary of war, was on vacation, so the committee sent a telegram directly to President Roosevelt at his New York home in Oyster Bay. He responded immediately and ordered an inquiry, but he would not remove the soldiers until the investigation was concluded.

Major Augustus P. Blocksom, assistant inspector general (IG) of the Southwestern Division, was assigned by the commanding general in Texas, William S. MacCaskey, to review the situation in Brownsville. MacCaskey chose Blocksom, a northern native of Ohio, specifically because he was not a Southerner. He did not want to appear to be taking sides with a populace known to harbor severe racial prejudice.

MacCaskey knew Blocksom to be a careful, methodical man. He also knew him to be malleable and willing to accommodate any decision or outcome his superiors might suggest to him.

But there was something else about Blocksom not commonly known in military circles, though it was well known in Ohio: Blocksom was the son of an aggressive Copperhead—an extremely racially prejudiced Northern Democrat, who sympathized with the Confederate States. He had taken his son to many political rallies, where Copperhead white women carried signs expressing their fears of miscegenation: "SAVE US FROM NIGGER HUSBANDS!"

The Brownsville Redemption

Blocksom arrived in Brownsville on August 18th, 1906. The next day, he plunged headlong into the investigation, interviewing a string of willing witnesses. *He had to get something out quickly to headquarters.* He brushed aside all formalities. He took unsworn statements, speaking casually to people in bars and hotel lobbies and on the streets. He interviewed Judge Parks. The judge told him he saw the whole thing, although he failed to mention he thought the raiders had been Negroes.

Several people asked Blocksom if he had talked to Katie Leahy. They told him that she had been trying to contact him, and he could not leave town without speaking to her.

When he finally met with Katie Leahy, she had a lot to say:

"Mrs. Leahy," he instructed. "Just tell me all you know."

"Call me Katie. I have been trying to catch up with you," she admonished him. "They were shooting at random."

"Who, Katie? Who was doing the shooting?"

"The Negroes. I was out in the middle of Elizabeth Street, and bullets started flying all around me. I ran back inside and went up to look out my second-floor window. Sixteen men were standing where the alley meets 14th Street. It had been raining, and they paused to avoid a big mud hole. Then they went around it. One of the men had trouble with his gun, and another man stopped to help him. The second man looked up and saw me in the window. I heard him say,

'That's Mrs. Leahy. Keep straight to the front.' They were just shooting straight up in the air."

"You say they were Negroes?"

"Yeah, they were Negroes. The one who looked up at me was very dark. But the one who had trouble with his gun was lighter. I could see spots on his face."

"How far do you think they were from you?"

"About 35 feet."

"Was anybody else standing in the window with you?"

"Yes, Judge Parks."

Blocksom already knew this and was testing her. "Did Judge Parks see the Negroes?"

"Yes, I think he did, but he wasn't wearing his glasses."

Blocksom considered Katie Leahy's account the most compelling. The soldiers were guilty. He wished, however, that Judge Parks had confirmed Katie's opinion that the raiders were Black men.

Blocksom believed he had gathered enough evidence for the moment. He could see that Brownsville was an armed camp, and the situation was deteriorating quickly. Special armed deputies on the town side of Garrison Road were standing opposite 65 armed soldiers on the garrison side. He knew that one wild shot by a hastily deputized citizen would certainly lead to a rapid return of fire. In a "fire fight," these deputies would surely lose. *It'll be a massacre.* The potential of this unthinkable scenario horrified him. Not to mention the potential damage to his career.

On August 19th, Blocksom wired a preliminary report to headquarters: "The cause of the disturbance was racial. People did not desire Colored troops here. Showed they thought them inferior by slights, denial of privileges. Soldiers resented this." He concluded that the soldiers shot up the town. He also acknowledged there was a rumor circulating in the lower part of town that the citizens had fired first, but he believed that rumor was without foundation. He recommended the removal of the Black soldiers and their replacement by white soldiers.

Blocksom's preliminary report went through the chain of command to Taft, who was still on vacation in Canada. The military secretary kept the president informed by telegram.

The Brownsville Redemption

By the time Roosevelt received Blocksom's report, he had already received demands from both Texas senators to "transfer the disorderly troops." Senator Culberson had been among the first to warn the president not to station Negro soldiers in Brownsville.

The pressure was building up on Roosevelt. The citizens' committee had sent him another telegram. It read:

> "Our position is misunderstood. We cannot convince our women and children that another outbreak may not occur at any time...Many of our citizens have moved and are removing their families elsewhere. A Texas town should not be left unaided in this condition."

Roosevelt approved Blocksom's recommendation. He ordered the removal of all the Black soldiers and sent a contingent of white soldiers from the 26th Infantry to secure Fort Brown and close it down.

Thirteen

A Texas Ranger *Comes to Town*

Captain Bill McDonald, a Texas Ranger, was in Dallas when he first heard about the trouble in Brownsville and had since followed the situation closely. He had called the governor's office almost daily, interviewed Mayor Combe, and read every scrap of news he could find on the subject. When there were no immediate arrests, and none seemed forthcoming, he became impatient. *I guess it's gonna take me to go down and straighten this here thing out!*

When McDonald got word that Roosevelt had ordered the Black soldiers out of Texas but there still were no arrests, he traveled to Austin to speak to the adjutant general (AG) to ask for approval to take a contingent of militia troops to settle what he called "that Brownsville business."

The adjutant general, a big, beefy man, sat at his desk, reading through a stack of papers, when his aide-de-camp announced, "Sir, Captain Bill McDonald is here to speak to you."

"Let him in."

"McDonald, I've been expecting you," said the AG without looking up.

"Then you know what I want."

"I can't authorize any Texas militia troops for use at Brownsville. You don't have the authority to enter the fort and investigate federal troops."

The Brownsville Redemption

"Why?" yelled McDonald. "Them hellions have violated the laws of Texas, shooting into people's houses and committing murder!"

"McDonald! You cannot enter that fort! Stay out of Brownsville."

Captain W. J. ("Bill") McDonald Source: The Texas Rangers, by Walter Prescott Webb, University of Texas Press, 1965

McDonald started to leave but stopped at the door and turned around. "George, why don't you get off your big fat ass and do something for Texas?"

Even without the militia, McDonald knew that he must go to Brownsville. After all, he was a Texas Ranger lawman with a reputation to uphold. He was known for always "getting his man"—though "his man" would usually turn up dead.

McDonald was a small man with a big presence—a legendary fighter for law and order in Texas. A dead shot with a six-shooter, he packed two pistols. But his favorite weapon was his double-barreled shotgun. Most of the time, he wore it strapped across his chest, but he was known to wave it around to intimidate anyone who disagreed with him.

McDonald left the adjutant general's office, wondering who else might give him the authority to enter the fort. Eventually, he turned to the one Texas judge he knew would not defer to the niceties of federalism.

District Judge Stanley Welch, the highest legal authority in the county, was a blustering patriot who'd lost an arm firing a cannon one Fourth of July. He was an unabashed street fighter and, with little provocation, would rather fight than adjudicate. He certainly brooked no-nonsense in his court. When McDonald called him, Judge Welch agreed to work with him.

The two men caught a train for Brownsville and arrived Tuesday evening, August 23rd, at about six o'clock. McDonald hopped off the train first, looked around, and was surprised that there weren't any town officials there to meet them. "Stan, there's not a damn soul here to meet us! And them bastards knew we were coming, too."

"I don't care. I need to rest up a bit," said the judge, and he headed straight for the Miller Hotel. McDonald, however, went directly to the mayor's office, where he found Mayor Combe and Captain Kelly going over the citizens' committee report.

McDonald burst in unannounced, huffing and puffing, threatening to turn Fort Brown upside down. "Combe, just who in the hell is in charge down there at that damn fort?" Before Combe could answer, McDonald roared, "I'll shake 'em till them murderers come tumbling ass-first into my lap!"

"No, you won't, McDonald. We don't want any more trouble. We're handling it."

The Brownsville Redemption

"Really? You sodbusters been dillydallying for over a week now, wasting time, letting a bunch of niggers outsmart you."

Captain Kelly and Mayor Combe were taken aback by such insolence. Combe held up a copy of the message they'd sent to Roosevelt. "Look here! We sent the president a telegram."

"I don't wanna see that shit!" McDonald brushed the telegram away. "You keep it to wipe your ass." Then he left, kicking the door shut behind him with his bootheel.

McDonald went looking for the two rangers he'd sent ahead to Brownsville to help with the investigation. He found the men in the lobby of the Miller Hotel. "Let's get some privacy," he said in a low tone. One of the men, Blaze Dalling, offered up his room.

As soon as Dalling's door was closed, McDonald wasted no time. "What the hell have you found out?"

Dalling replied, "We discovered some important information, sir."

"Let me hear it," McDonald said.

"Well, there's this sodawater man who works for this Negro soldier who opened a saloon on the edge of town. The man told me that on the night of the shooting, the Negro saloon closed early."

McDonald rubbed his chin. "Downright suspicious."

"Also," Dalling continued, "the sheriff caught a Negro man out on the street that night and…"

McDonald interrupted. "Did they kill 'im?"

"No, he's in jail."

For once, McDonald was pleased. "Good! So, what are we waiting for? Let's go see what this nigger has to say!"

Lieutenant Colonel (Ret) William Baker

"What do you yellowbellies use around here for balls?"

The men arrived at the county jail, and the sheriff led them to the one Black prisoner, whom McDonald immediately began to cross examine.

"Who are you, and what do you know about this shooting?"

"Sir, my name's Mack Hamilton."

"Are you a soldier?"

"No, sir. I used to be in the cavalry, but I got out."

"Do you know any of them soldiers at Fort Brown?"

"Yes, sir."

"Then you know a damn lot more than you're telling!" McDonald grabbed him by the collar and pushed him against the bars. "You better tell me every goddamned thing you know. Stop stalling."

"Willie Miller—he's my cousin—he's the only soldier I know down there. I talked to him 'fore I went to bed. Shooting woke me up. Then I gone outside to see what's going on. Sheriff seen me, says to me, 'Mack, you gonna git killed.' So he puts me in jail. I been here ever since. I want to see my wife. I ain't done nothing."

McDonald figured he had gotten all the information he was going to get. He instructed the sheriff, "Keep his Black ass in jail. He's lying."

"Oh, don't worry, he ain't going nowhere!" the sheriff reassured him, then added, "Oh, Captain, I forgot to tell you that a company of soldiers came to the jail immediately after the shooting and wanted to know who I had locked up in here. They claimed that the citizens had fired on the post."

Unimpressed with this added bit of information, McDonald stood up and moved toward the door. "Got anything else?"

"Yes. Here's a soldier's cap. It was picked up in the street the morning after the shooting. Look, it has the initials C.W.A. I checked it out. There's a Private Charles W. Askew at the fort." The sheriff was obviously proud to have that piece of evidence to show McDonald. "I'm saving it for the grand jury."

"Grand jury, hell! Gimme that!" McDonald wasn't waiting for any grand jury. He snatched the cap, then looked around the room.

"Where's your telephone?"

McDonald called the governor and left a message to report his tremendous progress. "I got good evidence. Some of it's gonna be pretty hard for you to believe. I think the white officers were in on it up to their assholes! I believe they sent the nigger soldiers to attack and that a Captain Lyon and his company went out later to finish up the job." After he hung up, McDonald turned to the sheriff and said, "I'm going to the fort first thing tomorrow morning. If you've got any guts, you'll come with me."

"You will never come out alive," the sheriff said.

"What do you yellowbellies use around here for balls?" McDonald grumbled as he left, slamming the door behind him.

"I have a warrant for the arrest of twelve of your men."

The next morning McDonald marched on Fort Brown accompanied by his two subordinates, all of them armed with Winchester rifles. When they got within 10 feet (3 meters) of the gate, they heard a shout.

"Halt!" It was Mingo Sanders, standing at the gate with 20 soldiers brandishing new Springfield rifles.

"I'm Captain McDonald, and we're of the Texas Rangers. I'm down here to investigate a foul murder you scoundrels have committed. I'll show you niggers something you never been used to. Put up them guns!"

Sanders, fully aware of the situation, kept his cool. "This is federal property, mister. Advance, show your papers, and be recognized."

McDonald looked at the guns aimed at him and, for a moment, seemed slightly intimidated. He strapped his shotgun across his chest and approached Sanders. He reached into his pocket to take out the order from Judge Welch. But then he changed his mind. "I don't need any goddamned paper to get in here."

He started to move past Sanders but found himself blocked by two crossed rifles. Recognizing that he was outgunned, McDonald reached into his breast pocket and waved Judge Welch's order in Sanders's face. "See this, boy?" he barked. "I got an order from a judge."

Sanders snapped his heels together and said politely, "Yes, sir. Who do you want to see? How can I help you?"

The patronizing tone inflamed McDonald. "Yeah, you can get the hell outta my way!"

"Holoman!" Sanders ordered. "Escort these men to the administration building."

Once through the gate, McDonald barreled into the administration building. Sergeant Major Taliaferro was sitting at his desk. McDonald shouted at him, "Sergeant! Where is your commander?"

"He's in his office. I'll see if…"

McDonald saw the nameplate Battalion Commander on a closed door. "Never mind." He elbowed past the sergeant major and barged into Penrose's office, just as Penrose was holding a meeting with Captain Macklin.

"Where is Corporal Miller?" McDonald demanded.

"Captain McDonald," Penrose said as he rose and reached out to shake McDonald's hand. "Sergeant Sanders called from the gate and…"

"Major, I asked you a question. Where is that Miller nigger?" Penrose withdrew his hand, turned to Macklin, and said, "Bring Miller in."

"Get Private Askew, too," McDonald demanded.

Macklin stuck his head out of the door and told the sergeant major to bring the two men to headquarters.

McDonald sat down and started questioning Penrose. "Major, what have you found out?"

"We have the empty cartridge shells, nothing else," Penrose said.

"Tell me something new. I know your darkies did it. I just want to know which ones."

Penrose stared at McDonald but said nothing. McDonald turned to Macklin. "Captain, where were you during this here shooting?"

"Sleeping."

"Sleeping? Cracker! Don't you trifle with me. What the hell do you mean, sleeping!"

Macklin bristled. He looked at Penrose and asked, "Do I have to answer this man?"

Penrose placed his hand on Macklin's shoulder. "No, Ed, you don't. But go ahead. We have nothing to hide."

Macklin tightened his lips and said slowly, "Sleeping means sleeping, McDonald. I was in my quarters."

Within minutes, the sergeant major ushered Corporal Miller in for questioning. McDonald got straight to the point: "Miller, where were you on the night of this here shooting?"

"Sir. I was in Matamoros on a twenty-four-hour pass. When I got back, I stopped by to see my cousin, Mack Hamilton. After I left him, I went to a Mexican saloon. When I heard the shooting, I showed the bartender my pass. He'll tell ya."

"Damn right you did. You're the only son of a bitch telling the truth around here." McDonald got up from his chair, took out his pistol, walked over to Miller, and got in his face. "Boy, you're doing good so far. Now, admit you showed that bartender your pass because you knew your buddies was planning to get even with them crackers. Didn't ya? You're a good boy. You're not a murderer. You didn't want any part in this here killing." Then, raising his voice, McDonald thundered, "All right, now tell me who did it!"

"Sir, I don't know."

"Come, come, boy. Tell me."

"Sir, if I knowed, I would tell ya."

McDonald sensed his most promising lead slipping away. He raised his pistol and shouted, "You'd better give me names, boy! *Now, boy!*"

"I don't know!"

McDonald started to bring the pistol down on Miller's head. Macklin jumped to his feet and blocked his arm. "That's enough, McDonald! Miller, go back to your barracks. I believe you."

"Take your goddamned hands off me," McDonald growled. Macklin let go of McDonald's arm, took a step backward, and balled up his fists.

Penrose stepped between the two men and spread his arms like a referee. "Don't do this. We've got enough trouble."

Private C.W. Askew was the next soldier interrogated. McDonald, who had cooled off a bit, showed him the cap. "Tell me about this cap. Are these your initials, C.W.A?"

"Yes, sir," said Askew. "When we were at Fort Niobrara, we turned in our old caps for new ones. When we got down here, they put that box of old caps on the back porch. I suppose some *muchachos* must have found them and taken them away."

"So you think the Mexicans shot up the town?" McDonald said. "I don't know who did it," Askew replied.

Several other soldiers were interrogated, but they all denied knowing anything about the shooting. McDonald thought they were all lying. Still furious, McDonald rubbed his chin and peered intently at Macklin. "You know," he said threateningly. "I don't believe you were sleeping. I believe you were out with them coons, committing murder and trying to kill ladies and their children.

"And you, Penrose, when I came in here, you told me you couldn't find out anything. I've been here less than an hour, and I've found enough to warrant me charging a bunch of your men with murder. How do you explain that?"

"You haven't uncovered anything new," Penrose parried.

"You crackers down here are dumber than the niggers." McDonald shook his finger at Penrose and Macklin. "You officers ought to be the first to hunt them down instead of trying to hide them."

The next morning, Thursday, August 23rd, a beaming McDonald sauntered into Penrose's office. "Penrose! I have a warrant for the arrest of twelve of your men. I'm charging them with conspiracy to commit murder." He handed the major a bench warrant signed by Judge Welch.

"I will confine them to the guardhouse on post until I consult with my superiors," Penrose replied coldly.

"The hell you will. You're gonna turn them over to me now."

Penrose refused. McDonald stormed out, saying, "All right, big buddy, but I'll be back."

As McDonald exited the Fort Brown gate, he headed straight for the telegraph office. He went in, slammed the door, slid the bolt lock in place, and pushed through the swinging gate. The telegraph master reached down for his pistol. When he looked up, he came face to face with a double-barreled shotgun.

"Don't go for that. This is not a robbery. I am Captain McDonald of the Texas Rangers. From now on, you will deliver to me *every telegram* sent to that fort."

"But I can't do that! They're confidential."

McDonald jabbed him with the shotgun. "Got no time to argue with you. Do what I tell ya. Whenever one comes in, bring them telegrams to the sheriff's office."

"I propose to do my duty."

Penrose met with Texas's commanding general, William S. MacCaskey, to discuss the alarming developments. "These men will never get a fair trial here. And if I turn them over to the civil authorities, I'll be putting their lives in jeopardy."

MacCaskey agreed and sent a telegram to the War Department:

> We think it unsafe to leave the accused at Fort Brown with only one white company of forty-eight men to protect them. We also fear that turning them over to civil authorities now or in the immediate future would be disastrous to them. Train is now waiting at Fort Brown to take battalion, the 25th Infantry, to Fort Reno, Okla.

The telegram further recommended that the accused men be taken on the same train and dropped off at Fort Sam Houston in San Antonio, where they could be confined to the guardhouse until it was safe to turn them over to civil authorities. The rest of the battalion would continue on to Fort Reno.

The recommendation was hand delivered to President Roosevelt in Oyster Bay. He responded, "I entirely approve of the action you propose to take. Act immediately."

The Brownsville Redemption

Penrose received his orders by confidential telegram at five o'clock that evening. At about the same time, a man hurried into the sheriff's office, dropped an envelope on the sheriff's desk, and left. McDonald, who was there at the time, recognized the man as the telegraph master. The sheriff reached to pick up the missive, but McDonald slapped his hand down. "It's mine!" He stepped into an alcove, read the communication, and rushed out the door. He headed straight for the fort.

McDonald brushed past the sergeant major's desk into Penrose's office, yelling, "Penrose! I want custody of them prisoners!"

"I am directed by the president himself not to release these men," Penrose said evenly. And, with the knowledge he had the backing of the commander-in-chief, he bellowed, "Now get out of my office!"

"Let's see what Stan Welch got to say about this here shit," McDonald said as he left to find the judge.

As a courtesy to Judge Welch, Penrose went to his office that evening to inform him of the higher order from the president nullifying the warrant. He found McDonald already there and arguing with the judge.

Penrose showed Judge Welch the telegram. McDonald pretended that he had not already seen it and argued that he be allowed to read it. Penrose refused. When Judge Welch nodded his head in agreement, McDonald turned against him.

"Judge, nobody gonna move them niggers from here. They are my prisoners. I'm gonna hold them. I'll wire the governor."

McDonald took off for the telegraph office, where he wrote out a message and handed it to the clerk. "Send this!"

> Brownsville, Texas, August 24th
> To Gov. S.W.T. Lanham, and Gen. John A. Hulen.
> Austin, Texas—The Military authorities are trying to take our prisoners from here for the purpose of defeating

justice and will attempt to do so at once over my protest. Please send assistance to prevent this outrage. The officers are trying to cover up this diabolical crime that I am about to uncover and it will be a shame to allow this to be done. I turned warrants over to them in due form with the promise that they would hold prisoners in the guardhouse and then turn them over to me when called for. I propose to do my duty.

McDonald then sent a telegram to Penrose, again demanding the release of the prisoners. Again, Penrose refused, saying that the soldiers would be turned over to civil authorities when their safety had been assured. "After a most careful investigation, I am unable to find anyone or any party in any way connected with the crime of which you speak. I return to you herewith the warrants delivered to me yesterday."

Later that day, Governor Lanham replied to McDonald:

> Austin, Texas, August 24th – To Capt. W.J. McDonald, Brownsville, Texas.
>
> Have requested General MacCaskey to prevent removal of soldiers charged with recent murder. Consult district judge and sheriff and act under, through them. S.W.T. LANHAM, Gov.

McDonald went back to see Judge Welch and showed him the telegram from the governor. "You see, the governor agrees with me."

"I read no such thing in that telegram. You'll act under me."

"We got to hold that train!"

While Judge Welch firmly believed some of the soldiers had shot up the town, he began having doubts about the twelve men McDonald had fingered. It seemed to him that the twelve had been picked at random, so he pressed McDonald: "You've got to get me more evidence."

"Judge, the niggers did it."

"But which ones?"

"The ones we got."

Welch was losing patience with McDonald. "I want those warrants back."

"Judge, that means they'll take them murderers out of town!"

"I'm telling you, McDonald! Those warrants I gave you for the arrest of those men are abrogated. Get them back to me!"

McDonald turned on his heel and left Welch's office.

Within the next hour, Judge Welch followed up with McDonald by telegram, revoking the warrants:

> Brownsville, Texas, August 24th—Capt. W.J. McDonald—Sir. This is to direct you to immediately return to me without any further attempt at execution the three warrants of arrest placed in your hands by myself yesterday, wherein thirteen persons—twelve soldiers and one ex-soldier—were charged with murder and assault with intent to murder.
>
> Given under my official hand this 24th day of August, 1906.
>
> Stanley Welch, Judge 28th Jud. Dist of Texas.

McDonald examined the order, then reread the governor's telegram. The more he thought about it, the more furious he became. The governor seemed to be shilly-shallying, passing the buck down to Judge Welch and the sheriff. Worst of all, the governor had put him under the authority of those two men—the sheriff, for whom he had no respect, and Judge Welch, who he suspected was caving in and now personally moving against him. He now despised the judge. The nerve of him asking for those warrants. *I won't give them back,* he thought. *Got to be somebody around here to help me.*

McDonald was in and out of the mayor's office, the district attorney's office, and the sheriff's office—but no one agreed with his position to hold the prisoners. He went to the train station and pleaded with the railroad officials to hold the troop train, which was scheduled to depart at midnight. They flatly rejected what the station master called a "crazy idea." Exasperated, McDonald barged in on Congressman John Gardner in his hotel room to get the politician to use his influence. Gardner had come to Brownsville to check on "the mess" himself.

Gardner called Judge Welch. "We'd better call a meeting. McDonald's gone off his rocker."

"All right," the judge said. "We'll meet tonight. And if you see McDonald, tell him he damn sure better bring those warrants!"

McDonald was the last person to arrive at the meeting that night.

Mayor Combe, the district attorney, Congressman Gardner, Attorney James B. Wells, and Judge Welch were patiently waiting for him in the judge's office. He walked into the meeting, gripping his shotgun tightly. "That train ain't leaving here with them prisoners. I'll have a shoot-out with the whole damn army! I'll stop that train if I have to stand in the middle of the goddamned tracks!"

Wells tried to calm him down. "If you attempt to interfere with those soldiers, this matter will break out anew, and we will lose a great many lives here."

"You're all being lied to!" McDonald shouted. "We got to hold that train!"

Judge Welch stepped forward. "McDonald, put down that shotgun. You no longer have the authority to hold those men. Give me those warrants."

"You can't change 'em now," McDonald said. "Them warrants are still good."

"They are abrogated."

Welch rose from his chair, revealing a snub-nosed pistol in his hand. The two men stood face to face—McDonald with his shotgun and the judge, with his powerful derringer aimed at McDonald's gut.

"You'll return those bench warrants to me."

Fourteen

Departure from *Fort Brown*

"Sunrises are not for the walking dead."

It was early Saturday morning, August 25th. The soldiers of the 25th Infantry and their wives and children were packed and ready to leave Fort Brown. It was the first sad day of a long, bitter journey down the road of dishonor, disgrace, and shame. They were also burdened with the knowledge that there might be murderers among them, the phantom raiders who had robbed them of their good names, their honor, and their livelihoods. They must have been ghost soldiers. They had come out of nowhere, shot up a community, then vanished into the night, leaving no trace of who they were or where they had come from.

As the sun rose, so did the spirits of the townspeople. They had gotten what they wanted. But the soldiers saw no sunrise. Sunrises are not for the walking dead.

Everything was in place for the departure. The police deputized a force of 50 to 60 hand-picked civilians to stand guard along the route the soldiers would take to the depot. Unbeknownst to McDonald, Mayor Combe and Major Penrose were working together to devise a plan to ensure the safe and orderly departure of the soldiers.

It was widely circulated that the troops would leave at midnight, but the mayor advised Major Penrose against it. "Anyone who is unkindly disposed toward your command could easily commit an act of violence under the cover of darkness."

Penrose agreed.

The Brownsville Redemption

The three companies of the United States Twenty-Fifth Infantry making their way out of Brownsville after their expulsion from Fort Brown in August 1906. *Courtesy MHMA.*

An old news clipping of the soldiers and their families leaving Brownsville, August 25, 1906. Courtesy MHMA

The mayor issued instructions to the sheriff. "If any citizen makes any demonstration or interferes with the departure of the troops, arrest him. And if a citizen fires a shot or anything of that kind, shoot him." That morning, Penrose met Combe at the main gate, and the two men marched side by side, leading the troops out of Fort Brown toward the depot. All was silent except for the sound of the orderly, methodical thud of boots striking the dusty streets. As they marched, the soldiers heard a church bell ring in the distance as if it were mourning their fate. To Mingo Sanders, it was the death knell of justice.

The soldiers marched as if on parade while masking their grief. Heads were held high, shoulders snapped back—proud United States Army soldiers marching in unison. They carried their colors, Old Glory, along with battle streamers signifying their proud victories in Cuba, the Philippines, and the Indian campaigns. Their wives and children, who had refused to ride in carriages, walked in silence behind the men. Their heads were bent, some sobbed. A single soldier brought up the rear with the dog, Trooper, who trotted alongside him on a short leash.

McDonald watched for his twelve prisoners. He wondered where they could be. He stretched his neck forward and looked up and down the column. He couldn't see them.

When the column of soldiers reached the depot, Major Penrose turned around and faced his command. Then he marched backward about three or four steps, raised his hand, and stopped the column. The special troop train waited. The conductor shouted, "All aboard!" Mayor Combe extended his hand to Penrose, and the two men said their goodbyes.

The soldiers, company by company, boarded the train. Their wives and children followed. As the soldier with Trooper started to board the train, Trooper broke away and ran across the street to menace José Garza, the "special policeman" who, on the night of the shooting, had had whiskey on his breath and mud on his pants. The dog growled at the man and grabbed his pants' leg. Garza tried to kick the dog away, then pulled out his pistol. When the sheriff saw what was going on, he shouted, "Hold your fire, Garza!" The soldier retrieved the dog, pulled him back across the street, and boarded the train.

When the conductor shouted the final, "All aboard!" and took up the train steps, McDonald suddenly realized there were no guards and no prisoners—everyone was on the train!

The engineer yanked the cord, and a cloud of hot steam blew the whistle. As black smoke rose from the stack, the train advanced slowly, gradually picking up speed as it took the soldiers away from Brownsville to El Reno, Oklahoma.

McDonald turned on the sheriff: "Where in the hell are the armed guards with my prisoners? I didn't see them get on that train. Did Penrose turn them over to you?"

"No," the sheriff said.

McDonald flew into a rage. "You're lying!" he shouted in the sheriff's face. "You dirty rotten Mexican! You've been working with the niggers all along, haven't you!"

Major Penrose made an unusual decision from the outset after Judge Welch revoked the warrants. He had allowed the prisoners to march with their units to the depot without armed guards. They would also be allowed to move and associate freely aboard the train. This decision might lend an opportunity for someone to overhear loose talk that might give a clue as to who had shot up the town.

As the train departed, Mayor Combe, satisfied that the crisis had passed, calmed down as he walked slowly back to his office. But now, something new was nagging at him. Why had that dog attacked Garza? He thought back to the night of the shooting and his encounter with the man. What had he been doing with that jammed Winchester rifle? And now on reflection, Joe Crixell's explanation had not made much sense either. Why would Crixell's brother give Garza a rifle with a jammed bullet? When was it last fired? Could it have been fired that night before it jammed? And if so, by whom?

Major Blocksom felt triumphant on the carriage ride back to his hotel from the depot. The president had approved his recommendation, and the Black soldiers were on a train speeding away from Brownsville. He had averted a disaster. With that kind of success, the War Department would be undoubtedly pleased with him. *Maybe the president will invite me to the White House. Maybe I'll get a promotion for finding a peaceful resolution.* All he had to do now was find the evidence to support his recommendation. But that should be easy, for this was his area of strength. He was a red-tape officer and a consummate paper-pusher. He was the white-glove inspector the troops loved to hate. And he could justify any argument. But first, he had more work to do. His carriage pulled up in front of the Miller Hotel.

Blocksom stepped down and headed immediately to his room to plan his next moves.

Meanwhile, McDonald had gone back to his own hotel room. He had spent much of the day talking to various people, trying to figure out who had been involved in what he now considered a conspiracy against him personally. As the day wore on, he had just about given up. That evening, he read the *Daily Herald*, looking to see how he had been covered by the press. A subtitle caught his eye: "Prisoners Released and March Out with Their Comrades."

So that's how they done it! he seethed. *They done mixed up them prisoners with the rest of them niggers, knowing they all look alike.*

"Where is Holoman?"

The train trip to Fort Reno was uneventful but wearying for the soldiers and their loved ones. Their lives had been an emotional roller coaster ever since they had first arrived in Brownsville less than three weeks before. Now that it was over, they found themselves numbed by their experience.

The only excitement came when the train stopped in San Antonio, where the prisoners were to be turned over to the military authorities, who were waiting to take them to Fort Sam Houston. All of the prisoners came forward to disembark, except John Holoman.

"Where is Holoman?" Mingo Sanders asked his squad leader.

"He went back to the freight car a few minutes ago."

Holoman had entered the baggage car with his hand in his pocket, rattling his gold coins. A man there in hiding peeped around a stack of luggage. Holoman handed him a letter and a bag of money and whispered, "Mail this letter to my son and put the money in the bank. Goodbye, my friend." The man took the letter and the bag and disappeared into the dark.

"Holoman, let's go!" cried Sanders.

"I'm coming!"

"Get out here now!"

The prisoners said goodbye to their friends, saluted their officers, and were taken away to prison at Fort Sam Houston as the troop train continued north. The rest of the soldiers and their families arrived at Fort Reno just past midnight on August 27th.

FIFTEEN

Fort Reno: *Days of Forced March*

Mingo Sanders was up early that first morning at the fort. He poked around outside, looking over his new surroundings. *What a God-forsaken place this is,* he thought. In every direction, he saw disrepair and disorder—rundown buildings, peeling paint. Maybe it was good the place was in such a mess. There would be a lot of repair work to keep the men busy and keep their minds off visiting the town. Major Penrose had confined everyone to post: No soldier was permitted to enter El Reno for any reason whatsoever.

The officers ordered Sanders and the other sergeants to conduct daily training drills, hoping that a punishing routine would loosen someone's lips about the shoot-up of Brownsville. Day after day, the sergeants led the men on long, forced marches into the bleak area surrounding the fort. They trudged up "Misery Hill" and then descended into the salt flats on the far side. The next day it was up and down "Agony Hill."

There was no relief for the soldiers. The sergeants even conducted surprise shakedown inspections, usually in the middle of the night. They would rouse the men from their bunks to deprive them of sleep. Sanders hoped that sooner or later, the unremitting ill-treatment would break the soldiers' will, and somebody would talk.

There would be no reprieve. At dawn on a particularly raw and sodden morning, the sergeants assembled the soldiers on the parade field and announced the orders of the day: "There's a change in schedule because of the rain," said Sanders. "We are going to follow the inclement weather schedule. I see some of you got your raincoats on. Take 'em off! You don't want to get your raincoats wet, do you? The mud will be great for you today, nice and slippery. We're going back up Misery Hill again. Tomorrow it'll be hot, so we'll take a speed march up Agony Hill. Let's go!"

The exhausted troops marched into the downpour. They trod mile after mile along the road toward Misery Hill, carrying full packs on their backs. Streams of muddy water ran down the hill, settling into pools of gluey muck. Sanders gave the order to stack arms. The soldiers put their rifles in neat stacks in any place they could find free of mud. Sanders gave the orders. "Form a skirmish line! Go!" As they turned to climb the hill, they found their boots were stuck in the mud. When Sanders saw the men having trouble getting a foothold, he barked, "Get on your knees! Crawl!"

As they struggled and moved a little way up the hill, he shouted, "Fall on your bellies, slither up the hill! Now get on your backs, scrub your way up the hill!"

On their backs, the men scooched farther up the hill.

"Sit on your ass! Butt walk!" Sanders yelled. "Now get on your feet! Run!"

The men began slipping, sliding, and falling all over the hill. Some of the old soldiers had difficulty. When one fell, a young one helped him up. When another wanted to quit, someone grabbed him and pushed him forward. No man was allowed to give up.

Everyone reached the top of Misery Hill. They all sat down and watched as Mingo Sanders charged the hill as if he were in a real field action. Unlike the other soldiers who climbed the hill, Sanders carried his rifle. He darted here and there along the steep rise, falling to the kneeling position, then the prone. He rolled from side to side, all the time pointing his rifle at an unknown enemy. One time he fell and couldn't get up. He thought he wouldn't make it, but then he heard the men cheering. He got up slowly—and stumbled to the top of the hill.

After Sanders got his breath, all the soldiers ran down the hill together as fast as they could and started back to camp. It was late. They were worn out and filthy, but they were not broken. And their *esprit de corps* was intact. They marched at an easy gait with their flag and their battle streamers flying high.

Morale was so high after the Misery Hill march that the men felt they had earned the right to go into town. Dorsie Willis, an 18-year-old soldier from Mississippi, yelled, "Hey, Sarge, we did good! See if we can go into town."

All of the soldiers chimed in at once: "Yeah, Sarge! Go see Major Penrose!"

Penrose had set up an extended open-door policy for any soldier to come in and talk to him freely without going through the chain of command. He also tasked several particularly trustworthy soldiers to act as "listening posts." Thus, he hoped to gain information or at least some clues about the shooting. But weeks went by, and no soldier came to his office.

When Penrose learned that Sanders wanted to speak to him, he hoped the sergeant had finally found out something. As soon as he heard Sanders talking to the sergeant major in the outer office, he eagerly got up and met him at the door.

"Come in, Sergeant Sanders. What have you got for me?"

"Nothing yet, sir."

"Nothing?"

"We're still listening, sir. I want to talk to you about something else."

"About what?"

"We've been here for weeks. Nobody has been allowed in town. You know, sir, soldiers are soldiers. The young ones are not married. They need to get to town."

Penrose knew what Sanders was trying to tell him—he couldn't keep soldiers locked up in compulsory chastity for too long. Somebody would break out eventually.

"Tell them to bring me some information, and I will cancel the 'off limits' order."

"Suppose they don't have anything to tell us, sir? How can we make them tell us something they don't know?"

Penrose was startled by Sanders's logic and directness. He reflected for a moment, then said, "Well, Sanders, you've got a point. But how do you explain those empty cartridge shells in the streets?"

"I don't know, sir. But, sir, did you smell those empty shells?" Penrose was embarrassed that Sanders had hit upon something he and Captain Macklin had failed to check. They had not smelled the empty casings for the tell-tale smell of sulfur.

Penrose sighed. "Come to think of it, no, we didn't." He rested his chin in the palm of his hand with his elbow on the table and frowned. "How could we have missed doing that?"

"I don't know, sir, but it's too late now."

Sanders passed the word to the other sergeants that Major Penrose refused to lift the "off limits" restriction—and they, in turn, passed the bad news on to the men. That same night some men began to sneak into town. Five were caught, and charges were prepared against them.

Penrose offered each man the same deal. "If you will tell me of any man, or if you can find me any clue that will lead to the identity of the men connected with the deed in Brownsville, I will tear up these charges. They will not be proffered against you." Each man denied any knowledge about the shooting.

One man begged Penrose to save him from dismissal from the service. With tears streaming down his cheeks, he declared, "I swear before Almighty God, I don't know nothin' about this thing!" Shortly afterward, he was court-martialed with the other four men, and they were dishonorably discharged.

As time went by, the men grew suspicious of each other. They ate their meals almost in silence and talked only when necessary: "Pass the potatoes, the beans, the salt, the pepper." They glared at each other across the aged oak dining room tables.

Sanders sat alone at the noncommissioned officers' (NCO) dining room table. He did not go to his quarters to eat supper with his wife. To learn anything about the shooting, he felt he must eat with his men. But he found it getting harder to eat. He stared into space, his hands lying limp along the edge of the table. Then, his fingers began trembling. It disturbed him that the men seemed to be counting the notches. When he reflected on what the notches meant, it saddened him. They were carved by soldiers like him not too long ago. They indicated how many Indians they had killed as they drove the Red Man into Oklahoma and beyond.

He tried to stop the uncontrollable twitching of his fingers, but he couldn't. His thoughts troubled him. He was frightened for one of the few times in his life when he was not facing an enemy. He now faced one he couldn't see, couldn't shoot—one he knew nothing about. Soldiers needed something to shoot to keep them edgy and ready for battle.

His men told him nothing. The other first sergeants got nothing from their men either. He repeated to himself what he suggested to

The Brownsville Redemption

Penrose: *My men aren't telling me anything because they have nothing to tell me.*

Sixteen

Judge Parks Fails to Keep *His Appointment*

"He smelled like a busted whiskey keg."

Judge Parks had not felt well since the night he stood at his window at the Leahy Hotel and watched the raiders tear up the town of Brownsville. Something was eating at him. He couldn't put his finger on it, but it had something to do with Major Blocksom's investigation. He wanted to speak to Mayor Combe in confidence, so he called him and made an appointment to talk later that evening. The judge also mentioned to Combe that he was going to meet with Blocksom early the next morning to discuss a sensitive matter.

Hours before the meeting, Judge Parks decided that he had time to skip across the border to Matamoros and have a little fun. So he crossed over to Mexico, met some friends, had a good time—and completely forgot about his appointment.

Mayor Combe waited for Judge Parks for over an hour. He was worried. It was unusual for him to break an appointment.

Later that evening, Katie Leahy saw Judge Parks stumble up the stairs to his hotel room. "He smelled like a busted whiskey keg." The judge was last seen leaning his head out of his bedroom window, sucking in the night air, trying to shake it off.

The boarder in the next room said, "I heard the judge come in. Then a minute or so later, someone else entered his room. I heard, 'What do you want? God, can't a man get any peace, anywhere?' I fell asleep while they were still talking."

The Brownsville Redemption

The next morning Katie Leahy found Judge Parks lying dead outside on the ground, underneath his window. It was August 27th, the same night the troops arrived at Fort Reno.

Seventeen

A "Conspiracy of *Silence*"

Black over White Won't Go

Major Blocksom had just finished packing his bags and was about to go to the depot to catch a train for Fort Reno. He had given up on meeting with Judge Parks. He would complete his final report without whatever Parks wanted to see him about. He picked up his bags and was about to go out the door when Mayor Combe walked into his office at Fort Brown. "Major, Judge Parks is dead," Combe said softly. "Katie Leahy found him this morning lying on the ground beneath his window."

"Do you know what happened?"

"Sort of. I found out he went to Matamoros. Probably imbibed too much and fell out the window. That's all there is to it, I guess."

"Poor fellow. Thanks for letting me know. I've got to catch a train."

Blocksom settled into one of the hardbacked leather seats on the train. Ten days after he arrived in Brownsville, he was on his way to Fort Reno to finish his investigation. It was the 27th of August. He had to write his final report. He opened his rawhide case and searched for his notes on Judge Parks.

Who was Combe trying to fool, saying "That's all there is to it"?

There had to be more to Parks's death, but what was it? There was Parks's story of what he said he saw. He said he saw the whole thing from his window in the Leahy Hotel. He saw men shooting but never said he recognized them as Black soldiers. Did he tell anybody else this?

What else did he see? Katie Leahy stood in the same window and told Blocksom that Judge Parks couldn't have recognized them because he didn't have on his glasses. Well, whatever Parks had to tell him, he would carry it to his grave.

Blocksom had talked to many people who represented themselves as eyewitnesses, but most were gossipers, storytellers, barflies, politicians, and loafers. The saloon keepers, policemen, Miller Hotel residents, and many citizens also claimed the Black soldiers shot up the town. But which ones did the shooting? How could he explain the contradictory testimony between the civilians and the soldiers?

The soldiers denied that they had anything to do with the shooting or knew who did it. They denied that they held any animosity toward the citizens. Where is the motive? He was perplexed and conflicted. Who was lying?

He wanted to believe the soldiers. After all, he was a soldier. We all wear the same uniform. That's what connects us, he thought. The battalion had an excellent reputation up to the 13th of August. But this stain was the worst he ever saw in the army. How could the old soldiers not know? How could the sergeant of the guard not know? Or, harder to believe, how could the guards walking their posts in the barracks area not know? Worse yet, how could Company B's noncommissioned officer in charge of quarters not know?

He took out a pen and began to jot down some of his thoughts. They came rushing out on the paper, though the bumpy ride made it difficult for him to write:

> How could sixteen to twenty men jump the wall, break out of the fort, shoot up the town, and sneak back in undetected by the guards? And then, how could they fall into formation and answer to their names without some of the soldiers not knowing? Impossible! Surely somebody

must have seen them and have knowledge of the guilty parties. They had to be tacitly cooperating in a conspiracy of silence to protect their race. That was it! To protect their race, they lied, he thought. They had to be lying.

He concluded that if the old soldiers didn't disclose their knowledge, or if any of the Black soldiers didn't disclose what they knew, they should be made to suffer with others who were more guilty and suffer as far as the law will permit.

That thought was so powerful, he dropped his pen.

The men Captain McDonald fingered as the actual raiders were probably guilty, he concluded, but how could that be proven in a court of law or by military court-martial? He reasoned that there was little prospect of conviction on evidence produced so far.

Who was he kidding? He knew there was evidence on the other side in favor of the soldiers, which he must deal with if his final report was going to be accepted.

That post scavenger's story—he didn't see any soldiers shooting from the porch of Company B, and he didn't see any soldiers shooting at all—would be hard to controvert since he had been in the best position to see. He must have seen them. Why was he lying?

He might have known Wilbur Voshelle would lie to protect his job. He was the corral boss at the fort, a post employee. But he seemed to be an honest man with nothing to hide. Why did he tell him that fantastic story—that when he heard the shots, he was sleeping in town, got up, dressed hastily, and went down to the corral at the post? He didn't see a single soldier on the streets. He saw only two policemen and four citizens with arms talking about soldiers. When he got to the fort, he went to bed in the corral with the horses. Before he fell asleep, he heard about six shots fired in town again. That sounded like a big lie to

The Brownsville Redemption

Blocksom. Why was that white man lying to protect those Colored soldiers?

Blocksom had to admit to himself that he had uncovered a mixture of contradictory information. In addition to that evidence, both Mayor Combe and Major Penrose told him that the first shots heard were pistol shots, then high-powered rifles. Where did the soldiers get pistols? Only the officers had access to pistols.

Now that he thought more about it, doubts began to surface about the evidence. It was too late now, though, for him to change his first recommendation that the soldiers did it. He must go with it. He must make it stick. But only eight witnesses could qualify as actually having seen the raiders, and the soldiers denied it. It was a dark night, and the streets were poorly lit. That fact would not escape General McCaskey, old "Eagle Eyes." He needed to bury it somewhere in his report.

He stopped writing, shut his case, lay his head back, and closed his eyes. But he could not sleep. He agonized: *Who would the top generals believe? Who would the politicians believe? And, most important, who would the president believe?—eight white people or 167 Black soldiers?*

The answer became clear to him. He knew what it was even though it was buried deep in his subconscious, created by his teachings, his experience, and his upbringing. The answer was so deeply entrenched in his soul that it easily answered the question. No matter how hard he tried to believe the soldiers, no matter the evidence, something in him wouldn't let him go. And it wouldn't let him believe Black soldiers over white citizens.

Upon arriving at Fort Reno, he went directly to see Major Penrose to find out if he had uncovered any more information. The expression on Penrose's face spoke for itself: He had not.

Blocksom set himself up in a local office and wrote his final report on the 29th of August.

> "That the raiders were soldiers of the 25th Infantry cannot be doubted. The evidence of many witnesses of all classes is conclusive. Shattered bullets, shells, and clips are merely corroborative."

From all he had heard and seen of the evidence and from his analysis, Blocksom didn't believe the individual criminals ever would be identified. So he knew he must come up with something extraordinary. His second recommendation must be conclusive and final. All along, he was formulating his "conspiracy of silence" theory as the foundation upon which to base his final recommendation.

He finished his recommendation saying that if the Black soldiers didn't come forward with the evidence to convict somebody, then "All enlisted men of the three companies present on the night of the 13th of August be discharged from the service without [honor] and debarred from reenlistment in the Army, Navy, and Marine Corps." That included all the Black soldiers and the sick men in the hospital under the care of white hospital corpsmen.

He ended his report with these words:

> "It must be confessed that the Colored soldier is much more aggressive in his attitude on the social equality question than he used to be."

Taft, Roosevelt's secretary of war, accepted Blocksom's report even though he had doubts about it and thought it was sweeping, drastic, and excessively punitive. Nevertheless, he sent it directly to President Roosevelt, who approved it. But first, Taft thought the army should try the twelve soldiers being held in the guardhouse at Fort Sam Houston by military court-martial before they announced the decision. Military charges and specifications were promptly prepared. Lieutenant Colonel

The Brownsville Redemption

Leonard A. Lovering was sent to Fort Reno to collect evidence for the trial.

EIGHTEEN

The Grand Jury *Investigates*

"You don't know who in the hell did this."

When Judge Stanley Welch heard the news of the mysterious death of Judge Parks, he was in his chambers preparing to preside over the Cameron County Grand Jury investigation of the Brownsville raid. Welch wasn't a friend of Judge Parks. Parks was a bit too liberal for him—and worse than that, he was a Republican. But Welch considered him a fair judge and thought his death both tragic and somewhat puzzling. He could not believe that Parks simply got drunk and fell out of a window. He contacted the district attorney to investigate the circumstances.

As Welch was walking back to his hotel late one evening, he felt certain he was being followed. When he turned around to see who it was, a shadowy figure bent down behind a water barrel, and a muffled voice called out, "Stanley, let it go."

He didn't recognize the voice. Welch walked back toward the barrel, fumbling for his pistol in his sleeve, but the man darted into Cowen's Alley and disappeared. Welch decided to keep this incident quiet. He did not want anyone to think he could be intimidated.

Welch convened the grand jury in the early part of September without Parks, whom Welch had been counting on as a witness. But there were plenty of others. He also had the report from the tough-talking Texas Ranger Bill McDonald, although he had not found it very credible.

The Brownsville Redemption

Welch was in a sour mood the morning he opened the grand jury session and began with an excoriating speech about the soldiers:

> ...[the] unprovoked, murderous midnight assault committed by the Negro soldiers, their fiendish malice and hate-showing hearts blacker than their skins, was evidenced by their firing volley after volley from deadly rifles into and through the doors and windows of family residences, clearly with the brutish hope on their part of killing women and children, and thus make memorable their hatred of the white race.

Judge Welch put the witnesses under oath, subject to the penalty of perjury. Day after day, witness after witness, irate white citizens testified that the soldiers had shot up the town.

After weeks of hearing obviously rehearsed, identical stories, Judge Welch began to question his own judgment about the soldiers. *Why did I allow myself to be suckered in on such flimsy evidence?* He had always prided himself on his fairness and objectivity and was accustomed to saying, "Every dog, every Indian, every Mexican, every nigger, every Chinaman, gets justice in my court."

Welch finally said to the lawyers and jurors, "I haven't heard a damn thing that would indict a ham sandwich! You haven't uncovered any clues, and you're no closer to the truth now than when you started. I'm not going to let this thing go on any longer." Welch dismissed the grand jury, saying, "You don't know who in the hell did this. Let's wrap this up."

He issued an order notifying the military authorities that the soldiers now being held in jail were entitled to go free.

Overnight, Welch became a pariah.

In support of the judge, the district attorney later pointed out that the "evidence did not point with sufficient certainty to any individual or individuals to justify or warrant bringing in an indictment."

Later, Welch wondered why the War Department and President Roosevelt still insisted on keeping the soldiers locked up. Why were they violating his order? And why in the world did they still believe that the twelve soldiers McDonald had fingered were the actual raiders in the first place?

When Welch learned that the army was sending Lieutenant Colonel Leonard A. Lovering to Fort Reno to collect evidence for a court martial, he wondered whether the grand jury had missed something. Perhaps he had dismissed it too hastily.

Colonel Lovering arrived at Fort Reno in early October to collect more evidence for the court-martial of the twelve prisoners. He found none and wrote:

> The reasons for the selecting of these men, or the manner by which their names were procured, is a mystery. As far as is known, there is no evidence that the majority of them were in any way directly connected with the affair. It seems to have been a dragnet proceeding.

Welch felt vindicated by Lovering's report. The charges again were dropped—and yet, the twelve men were still behind bars. Why was the War Department keeping those soldiers locked up? *Must have something to do with politics,* he thought.

Welch's dismissal of the grand jury and dropping the charges against the twelve soldiers enraged McDonald. Back at his ranger station in Corpus Christi, he began plotting how he could get even with Welch and his Republican cronies. He was also incensed that the Texas authorities had given up so easily, just when he was on the verge of

The Brownsville Redemption

drawing a bigger conspiracy that involved the white officers. *This must have to do with politics.* A military jail was not good enough for McDonald. He wanted the soldiers behind bars in a Texas prison, waiting to be hanged by Texans. Welch was a turncoat. But Texas, he knew, had a way of taking care of turncoats.

In early November, Judge Welch traveled to nearby Rio Grande City to talk to the Brownsville district attorney to take care of some political business. Over dinner at the Casa de los Abogados, Welch told the DA the strange story about the muffled voice in Brownsville. "And, tonight, on my way here to meet you, I heard the same voice. I heard, 'Stanley, I told you to let it go. Now it's too late.' I demanded, Who the hell are you? What do you want? Then, whoever it was disappeared down a side street."

Welch asked the DA, "Who did you tell about our investigation into Parks's death?"

"Only the sheriff and the police chief," the DA replied.

Welch and the DA retired to their separate rooms at the Casa de los Abogados. The next day, when the judge did not appear by lunchtime, the innkeepers tried to rouse him. The door to his room was locked from the inside. So they broke it down, only to find that the judge had been murdered in his bed.

Judge Welch's murder shocked the citizens of Cameron County, and particularly Mayor Combe. He wondered, *Was it connected to the judge's dismissal of the grand jury?*

Attorney Wells wired the governor, asking that the Texas Rangers investigate the murder. He also advised him to send anybody but Bill McDonald. The governor ignored him—and sent McDonald.

NINETEEN

The Ultimatum

"So help me, God, I don't know."

Things were not looking good from a legal standpoint for the War Department and Roosevelt. The Cameron County Grand Jury returned no indictments. Colonel Lovering found no evidence to indict anyone, and the citizens' committee failed to identify the guilty parties. Worst of all, the lawyers in the judge advocate general's office privately considered Blocksom's report worthless since it contained no sworn statements and too many contradictory witnesses. But the president had already approved the report, and Lovering didn't want to go into it any deeper.

But Roosevelt wasn't finished with the matter. On October 4, 1906, he ordered General Ernest A. Garlington, the inspector general (IG) of the army, to go to Fort Reno and Fort Sam Houston to conduct still another investigation.

Roosevelt never doubted Blocksom's report that some of the soldiers were guilty, but he wanted to know which ones. Yes, he had approved it. And he knew it prescribed drastic punishment if the guilty ones were not discovered. But he needed to have a valid justification for such a harsh decision. So he went one step further and directed Garlington to issue an ultimatum that unless the enlisted men who had knowledge of the incident came forward and identified the guilty parties, "every Black soldier stationed at Fort Brown would be discharged 'without honor' and would be forever debarred from reenlistment as well as from employment in any civil capacity under government."[5]

General Garlington was a native of South Carolina, the home state of "Pitchfork" Ben Tillman. Tillman was the fiery senator from South Carolina who blasted Roosevelt for inviting Booker T. Washington to the White House for dinner in 1901. "The action of President Roosevelt in entertaining that nigger," he predicted, "will necessitate our killing a thousand niggers in the South before they will learn their place again."

Garlington welcomed the task Roosevelt assigned him. In fact, he thought he was uniquely qualified to identify the culprits. "I lived with them, played with them as a child, was brought up on a large plantation with them."

He arrived in Oklahoma City on October 8, 1906. He immediately consulted Major Blocksom, who he considered had made an "exhaustive investigation." He was briefed by Blocksom, listened to the talk about the "niggers" breaking out of the fort, absorbed all of the "evidence" McDonald collected on the twelve prisoners, and agreed with it absolutely. He reviewed the personnel records of the twelve prisoners and went over them again and again until he felt that he knew everything about them.

He obtained a copy of Colonel Lovering's report and reviewed the sworn testimony Lovering took. He was disappointed that Lovering gained no evidence from the soldiers. All he got were denials that they participated in the raid or knew who the raiders were.

Garlington got back on the train and headed for Fort Sam Houston to interview the twelve soldiers McDonald accused. For more than a month, the twelve men languished in the guardhouse, wasting away

---

[5]Earlier, Roosevelt had softened his order by allowing each soldier to apply for reinstatement provided he could prove his innocence.

and not understanding why they were still being held behind barbed wire after Judge Welch had urged their release.

Military escorts met Garlington at the San Antonio depot and carried him away in the commanding general's carriage to Fort Sam Houston. As was customary for an IG visit, Garlington was shown great deference—and even more so than usual for this man from Washington. He was greeted with much saluting, bowing, and heel clicking, and a lot of "Yes, sir!"s.

Every soldier knew he could go directly to the IG, without going through the chain of command, to get his grievances redressed without fear of reprisal. So the twelve Brownsville prisoners looked forward to meeting General Garlington. They believed he would be fair. He would get them out of jail and back to their unit, where they would be reunited with their friends, wives, and children. And for Holoman, get him back to his business interests.

The carriage reached the entrance to the guardhouse grounds and stopped at the foot of the hill. Garlington stuck his head out and looked up the hill. He saw the guardhouse, a low, bubble-like building with thick adobe walls, squatting on a low hill. It was protected by a barbed-wire fence, which began at the bottom of the hill and encircled it with concentric rings of wire. Each ring became smaller and smaller as the fences went up the hillside, until a small ring at the top choked the neck of the hill.

The guardhouse was all that was left of an old fortress with heavy masonry fortifications. These were embedded with old guns, which used to provide 360 degrees of coverage. Narrow windows at the top, now reinforced with short iron bars, provided observation but discouraged any escape plans.

Two guards standing at the door of the guardhouse came to attention and saluted. The commandant greeted Garlington and led him

The Brownsville Redemption

inside the guardhouse. The inside walls were bare, rough slabs of crumbling sandstone, reaching up to the ceiling like giant tombstones.

Each cell was a square cage formed by zigzagging barbed wire.

Garlington met the twelve men as a group. First, he tried the friendly approach, a folksy manner, the southern gentleman's approach:

"Where are y'all from, boys? I am here to get you out of this mess. Ain't this place horrible? This is the ugliest place I ever laid my eyes on. Are they treating you all right here? Are you getting enough to eat? "I know that some of your buddies got all liquored up and jumped that wall, went into town, and did a little shooting. Now they really didn't mean to hurt anybody, but wild shooting sometimes can kill folks. Somebody is guilty. Not all of you, but some of you know who the rascals are. You got to tell me who these criminals are. Now you just tell me, and everythang gonna be alright. I'm gonna talk to y'all in private.

Who's from South Carolina?"

"I am," Private James Newton answered.

"I'll talk to you first." Garlington turned to the commandant. "Let these here other boys out in the yard to get some fresh air. It's stuffy in here."

Having said that, Garlington and Newton went into the visitors' room and continued the interview.

"Oh, so you're from South Carolina? What part?"

"Greenville."

"Oh, Greenville. Mighty fine town. Now that's some coincidence." Garlington grabbed Newton's hand and shook it vigorously, pumping it like a politician looking for votes. "I'm from South Carolina, Greenville! I know you are a good boy. You don't belong in here. Who are your folks? I may know them."

"The Newtons."

"Why, yes, I know 'em. Mighty fine family." Garlington was pleased with this discovery.

But Newton noticed the general's hand was cold. It felt like a fish freshly caught from Greenville Creek. *His hand should be warm from all this handshaking,* Newton thought, *but it's icy.* He remembered what his mother used to tell him, "Deceit in a man's heart chills the blood flowing to his hand."

"Now that man that knocked you in the head with his pistol, he was wrong, shouldn't have done it. Didn't you wanna git back at 'im?" Garlington said.

"Yes, sir, but after a day or so, and a few beers, I forgot about it."

"You forgot about it!"

"Yes, sir."

"You didn't feel any animosity against him and the people in Brownsville?"

"No, sir."

"Now, Newton, tell me what you have heard about this shooting."

"I don't know nothing about it. I didn't do it."

"Newton, I have the power to get you out of here if you tell me who did it."

"I told you, sir," Newton said, shaking his head. "So help me, God, I don't know."

A "Conspiracy of Silence"

John Holoman, the moneylender, was of special interest to Garlington. "Send John Holoman in here!"

Garlington had read McDonald's report before he left Washington. McDonald speculated that Holoman was the ringleader of the raiders and the real leader of the enlisted men. After all, Holoman was captain of the Company B's baseball team and ran the saloon. Everybody owed him money, and nothing could be planned or done without Holoman knowing about it. McDonald wrote that Holoman held a business grudge against John Tillman, the owner of the Ruby Saloon, and wanted to run him out of business.

Holoman walked in with his hands buried deep in his pockets, eyes fixed, defiant, distrustful. He had lost weight and looked almost emaciated. His uniform hung on his body like a sheet. His once bulging baseball arms were shriveled, his once broad chest shrunken. His face was hollow.

Garlington was unnerved by the appearance of this soldier. He looked like a ghost. Garlington reached out to shake his hand. Holoman looked down at the stars on the general's shoulders, removed his hands from his pockets, snapped to attention, saluted, and said, "Private Holoman, reporting, sir! I have a complaint to make."

Garlington withdrew his hand and returned the salute. "At ease, soldier. Sit down."

"I have a complaint to make," Holoman repeated.

"You're damned right you gotta complaint. Haven't they been feeding you?

"No, sir."

"Well, they're gonna feed ya!"

"Yes, sir, there's plenty of food."

"Boy, I don't understand you. You say, 'No, sir.' when I asked you if they've been feeding ya, and you say, 'Yes, sir, there's plenty of food.' Which is it?"

"Sir, I don't wanna talk about eating. I want to get out of here. I got a son to take care of. I got to get hold of him."

Garlington thought he had better get straight to the point with Holoman. "You are a good businessman, I hear."

"I'm a better soldier, sir."

"You ran the Holoman Saloon?"

"It was called Allison's Saloon, but I owned it."

"What time did you close the saloon on the night of the shooting?"

"About 7:30 that evening."

"That was early, wasn't it.?"

"Yes, sir. We had a curfew. We had orders to be in by eight o'clock."

"Were the troops liquored up?"

"I didn't sell whiskey. I sold beer."

"Well, were they juiced up?"

"I didn't see anybody drunk."

"Okay. Do you know a saloon keeper called John Tillman? He runs the Ruby Saloon."

"I met him when we first came to Brownsville."

"The Ruby Saloon was competition with your saloon, now, wasn't it?

"I wouldn't say it like that. Most of the men never went to the Ruby Saloon. My saloon had most of the soldier business."

"Boy, you had a grudge against the Ruby Saloon, now, didn't ya? You know a soldier named John Brown, don't ya? You, John Brown, and your buddy Allison planned the whole damn thing. You did, didn't ya? You got whiskey from San Antonio, you fed a few boys liquor, you went into town to put the Ruby out of business, to scare 'em. Didn't ya? You figured a little shooting wouldn't hurt anybody, but it got out of hand, didn't it? You fed 'em too much whiskey. Didn't ya? You did it, didn't ya?"

Holoman appeared amused. He tried to compose himself. A faint smile broke out around his lips and he looked the general dead in the eyes. He started to snicker, chuckled a little—and tried to hold it back.

The Brownsville Redemption

Finally, he couldn't hold it back any longer. He placed his hand over his mouth and burst out laughing.

"What's so funny? What're you laughing at? Don't you disrespect me."

"I'm not disrespecting you, sir. You asked if I knew John Brown. I know 'im."

"He was absent when the roll was called, wasn't he?"

"He was over at the bake shop, baking bread, when the shooting was going on."

"He was in on it with you, wasn't he?"

"Sir, if I had any notion of committing a crime," Holoman said, "John Brown would have been one of the last men in the world I would have carry out a deed like that."

"Why?"

"Because he's the dumbest man I ever met. That guy put in about six years without learning to right shoulder arms. He's dumb and stupid. You couldn't learn him anything."

"Is John Brown too dumb to bake bread?"

"That's about all he can do."

There was a knock at the door that interrupted the interview. The commandant came in and handed Garlington a note that read:

> This prisoner puts himself on bread and water for days, some days on, some days off. Some kinda protest.

Garlington realized that he wasn't dealing with the average soldier, but a shrewd manipulator. He thought he had better make a deal, a money deal, if he were to get anything out of Holoman. "Son, did you leave any money in the bank in Brownsville?"

"No, sir, I got it out before we left."

"Oh?"

"Yes, sir. I got it all out."

"Well, maybe you weren't in on it, but you must know who was. You tell me and I'll see what I can do to get a transfer for you to the Ninth Cavalry or Tenth Cavalry. You can still open a saloon and carry on your business. You can still make money. How's about that? You just tell me, son."

Holoman hesitated as all kinds of thoughts ran through his head. Money was uppermost in his mind. He also thought of his money-lending business, opening up another saloon, his son, his army career, and even an escape from the gallows, if they somehow managed to pin this crime on him. This angle was his way out. He could lie, but he never liked lying. Lying was like cheating, and he never cheated on anybody except his wife.

He hesitated so long that it encouraged Garlington. "Come on now, son, tell me. It'll be all right. Leave it to me. I'll take care of it." Finally, Holoman said, "Sir, if I had any previous knowledge of any crime contemplated by the soldiers, I would have done everything in my power to stop it."

"Why would you do that?"

"If for no other reason, to protect my financial interest. And I have another reason, my son Robert. He's nine years old and lives in Macon, Georgia, with my wife. My marriage is in the shithouse, it's over. I want my son with me. I had planned to bring him to Brownsville. I haven't seen him in a long time. I just rented a house across the street from my saloon, on Garrison Road."

Holoman reached in his pocket, pulled out a receipt, handed it to Garlington, and said, "See? I paid three dollars for one month's rent for the house. I shipped my household goods to Brownsville. I bought a dining room set on the same day of the shooting. I planned to set up a home for my son."

"How were you gonna do that?"

"I had a housekeeper in Valentine, Nebraska. I was going to bring her to Brownsville to care for my son."

"What was the woman's name?"

"Stella Harris."

"Well, maybe we can still work it out."

"I don't think so, sir."

"Why not?"

"You want me to lie."

"You're lying now!"

"I want a court martial. They will know I didn't do it. I want my day in court, sir. I don't know who did it."

"You're dismissed."

In succession, Garlington interviewed the rest of the twelve prisoners without success. He assembled them in a group again and said, "You all have until 5 o'clock to tell me who did it. I know beyond a reasonable doubt that somebody in the 25th Infantry fired into the houses of Brownsville. I told you the president sent me here to give you all a last chance to identify the guilty culprits. You all didn't tell me anything, and if you all don't by 5 o'clock, you will all be kicked out of this army without honor." Garlington waited until 5 o'clock rolled around. No soldier showed up. He departed for Fort Reno, Oklahoma, empty handed.

When Garlington reached Fort Reno, to his chagrin he learned that Penrose and his officers had not found out anything new from the soldiers either. Thus far, Penrose had failed. And so had he. He didn't know what else to do.

Garlington rationalized the reasons why he did not get anything from the men in the guardhouse. They had to have known who was guilty. They must have been in on it. They were the real guilty ones.

No soldier could have jumped that wall, shot up the town, and returned without those key people knowing about it, seeing it—and perhaps participating in it. They were hardened criminals, not amenable to reason.

Some of the old soldiers who had a lot to lose still might be induced to talk. He would remove some formality. He would examine some of the men under oath, others he would not.

He questioned about 28 men, restricting them to answering a narrow range of questions:

Who was engaged in the shooting? Didn't you participate in the riot? Wasn't Holoman the ringleader?

Garlington refused to listen to any answers explaining where they were or to conditions which made it impossible for them to have knowledge of the rioters' identities or any details. When a soldier tried to explain that he was sick in the hospital or that there was some other situation which could exonerate him, Garlington refused to hear it. He would interrupt, "I didn't ask you that."

Every man insisted that he had no knowledge, that he had not taken part in any shooting and that he didn't know anybody who had. As each man denied the accusations, Garlington became more and more convinced that Blocksom was right—all of the soldiers had entered into a "conspiracy of silence."

Garlington became so exasperated that his true feelings began to surface during the interviews. "Now, Sergeant, don't you know that your people are always sticking themselves into some place where they are not wanted?" he asked Sergeant Walker McCurdy.

"Sir, I don't know anything about it. I only follow orders."

After Garlington asked Sergeant Luther T. Thornton a few questions, he said:

Now, Sergeant, I am a Southern man myself, and naturally, what I speak I speak from experience. Have you noticed that in the South, when the Colored people get into trouble with white people, a class of Colored people place themselves in a position of authority where they had no business to be, and when a Colored man commits a crime, he is protected by all the rest of his people?

Luther responded:

Sir, I was born in the North. The only experience I had with Southern white people was while in the army. Their attitude toward Colored soldiers was one of disrespect for the men in uniform and not a charitable feeling for the man of color.

"He might even lie about the weather."

On Friday morning, Garlington and Penrose walked along a small trail in the back of the officers' quarters, heads down in deep conversation. Since nothing had worked to get the soldiers to produce any information about who shot up the town, Garlington decided to use his last, most powerful, and most draconian tactic. He would issue an ultimatum which had been recommended by Blocksom and directed by Teddy Roosevelt.

"Major," he said to Penrose. "Your men are lying to me. They are telling me that they have not heard any barracks' talk about taking revenge against the white people in town. That was their motive. Revenge. God dammit! Somebody heard something and I'm gonna get it out of 'em!"

"Yes, sir." Penrose racked his brain, trying to think of something to add. He looked around and saw that it was a beautiful autumn day without a cloud in the sky. "Sir, I have heard you say many times that you are a Southern man. Do Southern white people believe Colored people are truthful?"

Garlington bristled at Penrose's question. "I don't know about all Southern white people."

"What about you, sir?" Penrose asked. "Do you believe Colored folks tell the truth?"

Garlington moved closer to Penrose and faced him squarely. "No! I don't believe Colored folks are generally truthful."

"That's why you don't believe that any of my men—even the ones you put under oath—are telling you the truth."

"I told you, Penrose, Colored folks just don't tell the truth."

The two men began walking slowly, heads down. "You think a Colored man might tell the truth about the weather, but not about a crime, sir?"

"He might even lie about the weather," Garlington replied. Penrose was devastated by Garlington's cynical admission. He was still conflicted. He knew his soldiers had been truthful with him before the shooting. Why would all of them be lying now? What was he to believe? Whom was he to believe? He was deeply saddened. He felt that no white officer, not even his commander in chief, the president, would take his soldiers' word over that of a white Brownsville citizen. But why did he want to believe his men?

"Major Penrose, tomorrow morning at ten o'clock, assemble all of your men and officers on the parade field in an informal horseshoe formation. I'm gonna make one more appeal, then I'm gonna give 'em the president's ultimatum."

"White officers too?" Penrose asked. "No, Penrose, just the Colored men."

"What about the men in the hospital?"

The Brownsville Redemption

"All of 'em, Penrose!"

"You have until nine o'clock tomorrow morning."

It was Saturday morning. By ten o'clock the fog should have lifted, but a heavy cloud still hugged the ground. Garlington stood in the center of a horseshoe formation. He noticed that Penrose had assembled his men without the flag or battalion colors. He yelled at Penrose, "Major, get the flag and battalion colors out here!"

The request was soon fulfilled, and Garlington addressed the troops:

> It has been established by investigation that certain men of your battalion have committed the crime of killing one man, wounding another, and shooting into houses containing women and children. I have been sent here by the president of the United States to endeavor to discover the guilty men. You men have fought for that flag.

He pointed to the flag behind him.

> I appeal to your pride in your regiment and your individual service to this Army to come forward and take this stain from your regiment. Keep it out of your personal records. It will be a blot on your records, a blot on your race. You must come forward now. Tell me who did this horrible thing.

No soldier stepped forward. No soldier said anything.

> Many of you old timers have long service. You have too much to lose. Think of your pensions. You are too close to retirement. Don't throw it all away. Don't let the criminals among you damage your good service. Throw

them up! Cast them out from among you! Step forward! Tell me who did it!

No soldier moved forward. There was not even a cough. No one even cleared his throat.

Men, think of your families, your women, your wives, and your children. Don't let this hurt them.

When no one came forward, Garlington issued the president's ultimatum:

Unless you men with guilty knowledge come forward and identify the guilty parties, you all will be discharged 'without honor' and will be forever debarred from reenlistment, as well as from employment in any civil capacity under government. There, you got it! Do you understand? Do you hear me? You better come on up here this very minute!

There was a long silence and a seemingly longer wait. Garlington continued:

I'm gonna give you one last chance. You have until nine o'clock tomorrow morning. I'll be accessible until then for any man who desires to give me information.

By Sunday morning, no one had shown up. Then Mingo Sanders walked through the door, stood ramrod straight, and saluted the general. He then laid his military records out on the desk and said, "Sir, I have talked to every man, and…"

"Wait a minute there, Sergeant. You mean to say you talked to every man in this outfit?"

"Yes, sir! Not all last night. I started talking with them in Brownsville, on the train up here, and since we been here in Oklahoma. I spent

The Brownsville Redemption

all last night talking. I finished talking to the last ones early this morning. That's why I got here the last minute."

"Well, I hope you got something to tell me."

"All the men deny it. I'm convinced that no man in the 25th Infantry did this. Sir, I believe that they don't know anything to tell you. That's why they are not telling."

Garlington pounded the table with his fist. "You're a liar. You are lying, Sergeant!"

"I beg your pardon, sir. Why would I lie to protect a criminal? Why would any of the men lie to protect a murderer?"

"You people lie to protect your race."

"Sir, I'm telling you the truth. I believe the men told me the truth."

"So, Sergeant, you are speaking for all those liars. Yeah, I believe you're talking for 'em all. Sergeant, you are part of this 'conspiracy of silence!'"

"Sir, I don't understand what you're saying. Are you saying I'm part of some kind of gang?"

"Yeah. And more to the point, Sergeant, a silent gang."

"I'm not part of any gang. I brought my enlistment records. My records show, 'Character excellent, a faithful and reliable soldier.' I'm fifty years old. I have served twenty-five years, six months, and seven days. I fought in Cuba and the Philippines and I was continually on the firing line. On June 25, about nine or ten miles from Siboney in Cuba, Theodore Roosevelt himself came to me, and at my special request, my company shared our supply of hardtack with his command."

Garlington became uneasy and shifted around in his chair. "Hold on there, Sergeant," he said. "You're talking about the president of the United States. That's a serious accusation you're making. Do you know what you're saying? Do you understand you're slandering President

Roosevelt? You're telling me he outran his supply lines? And you had to give them some of your biscuits?"

"I don't mean any disrespect. President Roosevelt knows me and some of the old-timers who fought with him in Cuba. He knows we are honorable soldiers. Tell 'im you talked to me. He'll know. We captured El Caney and San Juan Hill, then helped him and the Rough Riders at Kettle Hill. We are in a tight spot now. We need his help."

"You have anything else to say?"

"Yes, sir. You know many of us don't have much longer to serve to get our pension. We don't want to lose that."

"I told you that."

"I only have two-and-a-half years to go. Now, I am a poor man. I served honest and faithful for the government."

"I understand, Sergeant, but you all are standing together to resist the detection of the guilty. Therefore, you all should stand together when the penalty falls."

Garlington completed his investigation on October 19, 1906, and agreed with Blocksom's theory that the men had joined a conspiracy of silence. His recommendation: All of them must be punished and discharged without honor.

Mingo Sanders still had faith in Colonel Roosevelt. "He will not let us down," he told Sergeant McCurdy. "We shared our rations with him. We helped him. Now he will remember, and he will help us."

"Will he?" said McCurdy.

TWENTY

President Roosevelt *Makes His Decision*

Turkey Hunting in Virginia

By October 22, 1906, Garlington's report had passed through the military chain of command and reached the War Department. It immediately caused a stir among the department's lawyers. Judge Advocate General George B. Davis opposed it and went directly to William Howard Taft to lobby against it. Davis had hoped that Garlington would bring back a tighter legal case. He told Taft he was disappointed in the report and considered it just a warmed-over version of Blocksom's report. It had no hard evidence or even a factual basis for its conclusive findings that, beyond a reasonable doubt, the men of the 25th Infantry committed a crime. Davis laid the report on Taft's desk directly in front of him.

"Mr. Secretary," Davis said. "You can't let this report get to the president without more evidence."

"Hold on a minute," Taft said. "I'll get my copy."

His secretary brought the report to him. Taft said he had been studying it and flipped to a page that he said had been giving him a headache. "This part faults all of the soldiers for refusing to tell something that nobody has shown they knew anything about in the first place."

"If this thing is ever implemented," Davis said, picking up his copy, "it will ruin them all. And Mr. Secretary, look at this paragraph. It prevents future employment in any capacity with the government, even as garbage collectors." He paused for a second. "Mr. Secretary, I don't believe the president has the power to bar them from future employment."

"Well, he may not have the power, but he'll demand we find a way to get it done," Taft said.

"Just think about this," Davis said. "This paper would punish everybody, even the men who were in the hospital during the shooting. But the thing I object to the most is that it punishes all of them without due process. There is no constitutional basis for such a drastic recommendation without giving those boys a trial."

"I'll talk to the president about it before I send the report," Taft said.

Taft sat in his private dining room nibbling at his food, distracted by the troublesome legal issues Davis had raised. Taft knew no one could change Roosevelt's mind once he had made a decision. Still, he must find a way to get Roosevelt to pull back on this thing or at least delay it until after the midterm elections in November.

By the time Garlington's report reached the president's desk, Roosevelt had gone turkey hunting in Virginia, until after the elections. The report sat on his desk for days.

Mingo Sanders waited patiently for his former brother-in-arms to support him and proclaim his belief in Sanders's innocence. He hoped he would not forget him. Sanders felt that Roosevelt was still their best hope for getting out of "this mess."

"...a crime 'blacker than black'"

It was Monday, November 5, 1906. Roosevelt was ready to make his decision. He sent for Taft. They met briefly and discussed Garlington's report. Roosevelt accused the soldiers of shooting up the town, perpe-

The Brownsville Redemption

trating a crime "blacker than black," calling them murderers, midnight assassins, criminals. He further accused all of them of engaging in a conspiracy of silence to shield the guilty.

Taft, a lawyer by profession, made a legal argument against it. Roosevelt, not a lawyer, didn't want to hear the legal details. He pointed to the paragraph in the report, which obviously impressed him, and perhaps was the overriding reason for his decision. Garlington had emphasized that his recommendation was designed as a deterrent, "a forceful lesson" for other soldiers, and a vow to the citizens of Brownsville and other citizens that "men wearing the uniform of the U.S. Army are their protectors, and not midnight assassins."

Roosevelt had made his decision. He directed Taft to implement Garlington's recommendations but to delay public announcement until the next day.

President Theodore Roosevelt Source: American History Illus-trated, Volume xxi, Number 6, 1986, Historical Times, Inc. Harrisburg, PA. Culver Pictures, New York City

Roosevelt did not hang around Washington for long after he made his decision public. He went aboard the presidential yacht and headed for the Panama Canal Zone to see how construction was progressing. The next day, Friday, November 9, 1906, the War Department issued Special Order 266.

TWENTY-ONE

A Public *Outcry*

A New Hope

It was late Tuesday evening, November 6, 1906, after the off-year elections, when Roosevelt's decision was publicly announced. Almost simultaneously with the public announcement of that decision, there was a huge public outcry against the decision. Having secured overwhelming Black support for the Republicans, the election of Charles Evans Hughes, and a Republican Congress, which included the reelection of his son-in-law, Nicholas Longworth, from Ohio, Roosevelt could now make his decision known to key Black leaders. This, he did. But Roosevelt gave his loyal Republican friend, Dr. Booker T. Washington, the founder of Tuskegee Institute in Alabama, advance notice of his decision before it was made public that day. It was still a *fait accompli*, and he was not about to change his decision, notwithstanding Dr. Washington's best efforts to talk him out of it. Washington pleaded with him, urging his good friend and the best white friend of the Negro race (in Washington's opinion) to change his mind. When Roosevelt refused, Washington candidly characterized the decision as a "blunder."

But the other influential Black leader—educator, sociologist, and activist, Dr. W.E.B. Du Bois—got no advance warning from Roosevelt. When he got word of the decision, he was less charitable in his characterization of Roosevelt's decision. "It was a cowardly act," he said, and he denounced Roosevelt as a "coward." Du Bois even went further. He threatened to break ranks with the Republican Party and support the Northern Democrats. He began to openly court William Jennings Bryan for president, even though the presidential election of 1908 was two years away.

Like Du Bois, some of the Black press was not charitable in its depiction of Roosevelt's decision and the timing of its announcement. *The Washington Bee*, a Black-owned newspaper, made this observation: "Negroes are not fools, at least not all of them, and this after election order is well understood by them."

The *Waterville Maine Sentinel* made a direct challenge to Roosevelt's bravery, just as Du Bois had done:

> The picture of the president, whose chief merit is supposed to lie in his fearless bravery, dodging an issue like this one until after the votes are counted, is not pleasant to look upon, even though it stamps him as a clever politician.

The Black press was not alone in its criticism of Roosevelt. White newspapers, notably the *New York Times* and the *Washington Post*, joined in the public outcry against the president. While the press railed against Roosevelt and Black ministers excoriated him from their pulpits, all without any effect, the Constitutional League swung into action to offer direct help to the soldiers.

The Constitutional League (the League) was a civil rights organization financed by John Milholland, a white millionaire. He was sitting in his office, reading the *Wall Street Journal* and checking his stocks and bonds, when his telephone rang. The caller was Gilchrist Stewart. A tall and leathery-faced man, Stewart was a Black lawyer who was active in the League's pursuit of justice. "John, did you see what our friend Roosevelt did to the Colored soldiers? If these were white soldiers, he wouldn't have done it."

"Wait a minute, Gil," Milholland said, "you're jumping to conclusions. He hasn't done anything yet. This is just a political thing right now. Taft put the order out. He wants to be president. There are a lot of Black voters in Ohio. He needs Ohio in the presidential election in 1908, and he's starting early. He is out on the campaign trail right now. He'll change that order. If Roosevelt is serious about actual implementation of that fatuous order, and I don't think he is, we'll stop him. We've got the U.S. Constitution on our side. Believe me, it won't be a problem—he'll change that order. We should not be too quick to bring race into it. We'll do better without using race. Let's just get facts."

"Now, John, you know race prejudice is pervasive throughout the Army. I tell you, it's ripe with racial bigotry, just as the French Army is with anti-Semitism. You know what the French Generals did to Captain Dreyfus just a few years ago," Gil responded.

"You know I know. Dreyfus was set up just because he was a Jew. They framed him."

"That's exactly what the army is doing to these soldiers, except it is doing it 167 times over. There are 167 Dreyfuses. Nobody is helping them. There is going to be a lot of hand-wringing and talk, but nobody is going to do anything about it except talk it to death. We must get involved."

"So, you want to be Émile Zola? All right, why don't you go to Texas and talk to the soldiers?"

Time was running out, and Stewart knew it. He packed his bags and took the next train to Oklahoma City, where he continued by hack to Fort Reno, about 23 miles away. There he found the soldiers in a desperate situation. They were still cooped up in virtual house arrest. Dispirited, they were now feeling the full impact of the public announcement of the order. They were overwhelmed by a heavy sense of helplessness, abandonment, and betrayal by their commander in chief.

Stewart asked Penrose to get the men together in one group. Penrose assembled the Black soldiers in the same horseshoe formation used by Garlington. When all the men were assembled, Stewart addressed them as a group. "My name is Gilchrist Stewart. I'm a lawyer from New York representing the United States Constitutional League. The League, as we lawyers call it, is a civil rights organization. It sent me here to help you secure your constitutional rights to due process and to get a fair hearing and a fair trial.

"At this time, this moment, this day, you should know that our Constitution considers all of you innocent until proven guilty in a court of law. I'm going to hear your side of the story. All you have to do is tell the truth."

Private Conyers raised his hand and got Stewart's attention. "Sir, that's what we've been doing. Nobody will listen to us. Major Blocksom and the general from Washington wouldn't let us tell our side of the story. They tried to force us to tell who did it. We don't know who did the shooting. If we don't know who did it in the first place, how can we tell anybody who did it? We can't tell what we don't know, even if we wanted to."

"That's a good point. You can't tell me or anybody else anything you don't know. But you can say what you want to say or say nothing. I'm going to ask all of you to make sworn statements. I can't tell you what to say because I wasn't there the night of the shooting, and I am not allowed to tell you what to say anyway. You don't have to make any statement if you don't want to, but I strongly encourage each and every one of you to do so."

The League formed a "commission of inquiry" and hired George H. White, a prominent lawyer, as counsel. The League sent more lawyers to Fort Reno in Oklahoma, and to forts Sam Houston and Brown in Texas. In the days that followed, morale among the soldiers began to rise as they saw visible activity of the League lawyers, counseling them on their rights, taking affidavits, talking to Major Penrose and the others officers.

"We don't have much time."

It was Saturday morning, November 17, 1906. Mary Church Terell, a Black woman, civil rights activist, and president of the National Association of Colored Women, had just returned to her home in Washington, D.C., from a trip to Boston. Her telephone rang, and on the line in New York City was John Milholland, the white financial sponsor of the Constitutional League.

"Mary, I want you to go over to the War Department and talk to Taft about that order. Get him to delay it till we get the facts. The League has a lot of lawyers running around in Texas and Oklahoma, trying to make sense of this thing."

"I heard the rumors floating around Washington for several days before I left for Boston," Mary said, her voice shaking. "I didn't believe our friend Roosevelt would take such drastic action. In fact, few of the people I talked to believed he would do so. All right, I will go see Secretary Taft."

"See him today. He's supposed to be back in Washington. We don't have much time."

Secretary Taft was sitting at his desk at the War Department, elbow deep in a pile of letters, petitions, resolutions, telegrams, and newspaper articles, all concerning Roosevelt's Brownsville decision. Most of them blamed him, and he didn't like it.

A military aide to the secretary stepped into Taft's office and saw that Taft was extremely busy. He turned around and started to leave when Taft raised his head. "What is it? I hope there are no more papers on this subject today."

"There's a Colored woman outside. She stopped me as I was walking through the lobby and asked me to tell you she's been waiting all day to see you. Says she knows you. Your secretary says the woman doesn't have an appointment."

"What's her name?"

"Mrs. Mary Church Terrell."

"Tell my secretary to show her in right now." Taft was concerned that a powerful, influential Black Republican like Mary Church Terrell, who could influence so many Black voters across the country, had been kept waiting outside his door like a servant.

Pushing down on both arms of his chair, Taft slowly lifted his massive bulk and moved from behind his desk. He was standing when his secretary ushered Mrs. Terrell into his office. "Mary, have a seat over here," he stretched out his beefy hand toward a leather couch along the mahogany wall under an oil painting of General Ulysses S. Grant. "Sorry they kept you waiting." He sat down again.

"Mr. Secretary, I've come on behalf of the Colored soldiers."

"What do you want me to do about it? President Roosevelt has already dismissed them, and he has gone to Panama. There is nothing I can do."

"All I want you to do, Mr. Secretary, is to suspend the order dismissing the soldiers until an investigation can be made."

"Is that all you want me to do, Mary?" Taft said with a patronizing smile.

"For now, yes. I'll always ask for more til we get the same rights."

"So, all you want me to do for now is suspend an order issued by the president of the United States during his absence from the country?"

"I want you to do what's morally right and what's politically right, and they are the same in this situation, Mr. Secretary."

Taft understood well what Mary Church Terrell was talking about. The political cost might be high. It might mean the difference between winning the 1908 presidential election and losing to William Jennings Bryan or any other Democrat. Taft stood up, indicating that he had gotten the message. "All right, Mary, no promises. I'll think about it."

"Thank you, Mr. Secretary."

Political pressure was building against Roosevelt's decision, and Taft felt it. On Sunday morning, November 18, 1906, Black ministers shouted from their pulpits that the Republican Party had sold out to the Southern Democrats—that the United States Constitution was being lynched in Texas along with the Black soldiers. They cried that Roosevelt had betrayed the Black race and that Taft would pay in '08 if the order was not suspended.

Taft Has Cold Feet

Taft was on the train to New Haven, Connecticut, reading the Sunday morning newspapers, when the pressure became so overwhelming that he stopped first in Baltimore and again in Philadelphia's West Philadelphia station to call his private secretary. Taft instructed him to cable the president that the implementation of the order had hardly begun and that the order could be suspended. But Roosevelt had left Panama and hadn't received either of the messages.

By Sunday's end, the pressure had become too great to ignore. Taft suspended the president's order, an act unthinkable to him before Mary Church Terrell's visit.

Two days passed, and Taft had heard nothing from Roosevelt about his decision. Taft grew uneasy, worrying that perhaps he had done the wrong thing and that Roosevelt would think he had crossed him. It was not like Roosevelt to keep quiet about the suspension. He should have gotten at least one of the messages sent to him by now. Furthermore, several newspapers had carried the story in bold headlines on their front pages.

Anxiety finally got the better of him, and he lifted the suspension of the order, directing the discharges without honor to be executed.

It was a good thing he did because when Roosevelt got news of the suspension in Ponce, Puerto Rico, he fired back at Taft on Wednesday, November 21, 1906:

> Discharge is not to be suspended unless there are new facts of such importance as to warrant your cabling me. I care nothing whatsoever for the yelling of either politicians or the sentimentalists. The offense was most heinous, and the punishment I inflicted was imposed after due deliberation.

After Taft read Roosevelt's telegram characterizing the alleged offense as most heinous, the fear that the Black soldiers would mutiny troubled him. He feared that they might cause a nasty incident at Fort Reno that would get beyond the control of their white officers. To prevent such an occurrence, which was indeed probable in his mind, he secretly ordered a battalion of white soldiers to Fort Reno to quell any revolt. And considering the potential consequences of his actions, which could be perilous, he decided to make all the evidence public. He released the essential elements of facts contained in the two reports by Major Blocksom and General Garlington, the inspector generals. The newspapers had a field day criticizing the reports.

When the news of Taft's cancellation of the suspension of the order reached Fort Reno, hope began to fade. The Constitutional League had not finished its investigation, and Stewart had not finished taking sworn statements from the soldiers. However, he had gathered sufficient facts to reach two significant conclusions: 1) The soldiers were not in a conspiracy, and 2) The soldiers had not been allowed to present their side of the story to General Garlington. Stewart wired Taft and told him of these important and possibly game-changing findings.

But it was too late.

Lieutenant Colonel (Ret) William Baker

Twenty-Two

Without Honor: The Drumming Out

"...collect the rifles and secure them..."

Winter seemed to be coming early to Fort Reno. A few snowflakes had been dropping all night, and in the middle of the afternoon, a light snow had begun to fall. In the back of the narrow dining room kitchen, Dorsie Willis sat outside on the back steps, peeling potatoes. The falling snow made that simple task difficult. His fingers were growing stiff, but never mind that—he would get the job done.

Using a sharp knife an Indian friend gave him when he was growing up in Oklahoma, he peeled them quickly, cutting off long strips of skin. When they were peeled, he tossed them into several buckets of water. Why so many today? He soon got his answer.

Along the road leading into Fort Reno, Willis saw a long line of soldiers marching through the main gate of the fort. Through the falling snow, he couldn't quite make out who they were. He stood up and gazed intently at the line of soldiers. It was Company A! He sure was glad to see them. The soldiers of Company A, their sister company, had been left in Montana to protect the settlers. They were supposed to join them later in Brownsville. Now they were coming to Fort Reno. He could see them.

But there were too many soldiers coming through the gate to be Company A. It looked like a battalion of soldiers—three times the number of men in Company A. He looked at the battalion colors and streamers as the column came closer. Then he made out the unit designation. It was the 26th Infantry. That's not our regiment, he thought. As they marched closer and closer, he could see that they were white soldiers.

He dropped his knife, and he took off running as fast he could, telling everybody he met, "White soldiers are coming! White soldiers are coming! They're going to drum us out!"

Mingo Sanders stood at a window and watched as the new troops marched onto the parade field. It was an unhappy sight for him. Other Black soldiers stopped what they were doing and glared at the newcomers as if they were foreign soldiers who had no business at the fort.

Penrose went out on the parade field to meet the new troops and their commander. He knew they were coming, but he was caught by surprise when he saw their commander. "So they sent you, C.T."

"My orders were secret. Glad to see you, but I've got to say, not like this."

Major C.T. Clarke, the commander of the white troops, was an old friend of Major Penrose. They had attended high school in Detroit and hadn't seen each other since graduation.

"Been an ugly job for me," Penrose said. "Now it's an ugly one for you."

Major Clarke hastily moved his troops into their quarters and prepared to supervise the unpleasant business to come.

Starting at the noon assembly formation, the Black troops were ordered to assemble with their rifles. All the Black soldiers of companies B, C, and D, without any exceptions, were to attend—sergeants, corporals, privates, cooks, mechanics, musicians, corral masters, and orderlies. After all the men were in formation, the ceremony of surrender arms began. The battalion of white soldiers with loaded guns marched onto the parade ground and surrounded them.

The commands were given by Major Penrose to his company commanders. "Have your musicians, buglers, and drummers come front and center and surrender their instruments!"

Each company musician marched to the center of his company with his musical instrument and laid it down on the ground in front of his company commander, never to be raised again by that musician to blow reveille, assembly, retreat, tattoo, or sound taps or call to arms. "Have your men take two steps backward and surrender," Penrose ordered.

This came as a terrible shock to Mingo Sanders. He believed that such a dishonor would not come to him. Somehow he believed Roosevelt would not let it happen to him. After all, he had helped Roosevelt when he came begging him for bread for himself and his Rough Riders when they first met in Cuba. He realized he had not faced the harsh possibility that the unthinkable could actually happen. Sanders stepped forward two steps and laid his rifle on the ground. Unlike Sanders, the other soldiers took two steps backward and came to "port arms," a position that made it easy for the officers to take their rifles.

Lieutenant Lawrason strode up to Mingo Sanders. "Sergeant Sanders, what's the matter with you? Didn't you hear the command?"

"Yes, sir. I heard the order to surrender arms. To me, surrender arms means to lay down your rifle. I've done that. I cannot shoot anybody because I don't have a gun in my hands, and I can't hit anybody with the butt of my rifle because it is not in my hands."

"Lieutenant Lawrason!" Penrose shouted. "Don't push Sergeant Sanders! He's doing the best he can. Get out of his face. Go back to your position!"

Lawrason didn't move. Penrose knew Lawrason had a temper. Penrose also knew Sanders was a natural leader. He might lead a revolt, and

The Brownsville Redemption

the men might follow him. Penrose could have a mutiny on his hands and a lot of bloodshed. Why didn't he do more to get an exception for Sanders from Calingor? He reflected on the raid. Were the rifles really unloaded? Had the officers checked?

Major Clarke, sensing the mounting crisis, rushed over to Major Penrose and whispered something in his ear. Penrose nodded, the two men exchanged salutes, and Major Clarke returned to his command.

Speaking in a normal tone to Lieutenant Lawrason, Penrose seemed somewhat relieved. "Lieutenant, return to your position. Sergeant Sanders is right. The correct command is, 'Take two steps forward and lay down your rifles, then take two steps backward to return to your position.'"

When Lieutenant Lawrason returned to his position in front of Company B, the company commanders repeated the new, correct command. Having heard it, the soldiers took two steps forward, laid down their rifles, and took two steps backward to their original positions.

Lieutenant Leckie, a white officer, was standing on the parade field observing the ceremony. He whispered to Lieutenant Grier. "Looks like they're taking it awful hard. Look! The old soldiers have tears in their eyes, even Mingo Sanders. You know, giving up their rifles today means giving up their pensions later. I feel sorry for them from the bottom of my heart. I know they are innocent of any wrongdoing, and it looks pretty hard on them. I'll do whatever I can to prove they didn't do it."

"You're a little late, aren't you?" Lieutenant Grier said.

"No! It's never too late to stand up for justice," Leckie whispered back.

When the Black soldiers had cleared the parade ground, Major Clarke walked over to Major Penrose and said, "That was no ragtag group of soldiers. They were very neat, orderly, and soldierly. How is it that they could have shot up Brownsville?"

"I don't know. It's still a mystery to me. Please have your soldiers collect the rifles and secure them in the armory."

The Day the World Changed

Mingo Sanders hadn't slept at all that night. Now it was early in the morning on November 20. It was his last day in his beloved army and the day the drumming out of the soldiers was to begin. It was a gray morning, and with low hanging clouds already in the sky, no one would see the sun. It looked like it might snow. The wind was sweeping low along the ground across the parade field like a giant broom. Little corkscrew-like whirlwinds followed the sweep of the wind, jumping across the field like spinning tops, picking up little balls of weeds and spinning them round and round. As a small boy growing up in South Carolina, Sanders had been fascinated by the little dust devils churning across the dirt yard. He chased them about the yard and wondered what made them spin.

Today was a day he never dreamed would come for him. He had seen soldiers drummed out of the regiment before. He had heard the reading of the orders, the charges, heard the roll of the drum. He had seen buttons cut off the uniforms. He had watched as regimental coats of arms, crests, and insignias of rank were ripped off. But anticipating the image of the final humiliation disturbed him most. At the roll of the drum, the soldiers would be marched across the center of the parade field, followed by a lone drummer beating a slow, mournful drumbeat. Then they would march to the main gate and be booted off the post.

He could understand those cases where the men were guilty of some serious infraction. He had never seen this happen to an innocent man.

The Brownsville Redemption

And he still found it hard to believe that his friend, President Roosevelt, would let this happen to him.

A little before noon, company commanders marched the Black soldiers onto the parade field. They stood at attention in their usual positions and were ordered by their company commanders to stand at parade rest, a semi-relaxed position. Each soldier stood with his arms behind his back, and his hands clasped together at the small of his back.

From four directions, white soldiers simultaneously marched onto the field, encircling the entire formation. Everything was ready, except that Major Penrose and Major Clarke hadn't come onto the field. They hadn't left Penrose's office. Everybody was waiting for them.

Lieutenant Grier was concerned. He was the battalion adjutant. It was his responsibility to read the order, get the men paid, and handle the discharge paperwork. It seemed strange to him that Major Penrose would hold up the discharge ceremony. Penrose was always prompt, never late. Grier looked toward the administration building, and through the window, he could see the two men talking. Penrose appeared to be making defiant gestures.

From the Black soldiers' perspective, with their backs to the administration building, the delay took on a hopeful sign. Maybe the whole thing was going to be called off. Maybe a last-minute reprieve had come through.

But the reality was different. The two officers were standing in Penrose's office in a heated discussion. An argument had broken out between the two friends about the use of the drums in the discharge ceremony and the interpretation of Clarke's instruction from the Military Department at Fort Sam Houston, Texas. Penrose was animated, anxious, and angry. "We don't have to use the drums," he said.

"My orders were to go to Fort Reno, prevent any disturbance, and drum 'em out," Clarke growled. "Penrose, why are you resisting this? The authorities in Texas want these soldiers out. And I've got the power to do it."

"Where are your written orders? I want to see them."

"They were verbal and secret. Somebody at headquarters thought you might not be up to the task of carrying this thing to conclusion. I am empowered to do it. You can witness it, or you can leave the fort now. Don't make this harder than it is, my friend. Believe me. It'll come back to hurt you. Don't blame me. Let's get this over with." Having said that, Major Clarke turned on his heels, walked out, down the steps, and onto the parade field. At the same time, he raised his saber, giving the signal for his drummers to play a drum roll and then take their positions.

Two drummers from the white battalion gave a drum roll standing in place. Then they marched onto the field to a drum beat, crossing in front of the formation and stepping separately to opposite ends of the field.

By the time the drums stopped, Major Penrose had regained his composure and mustered up enough nerve to take charge of his command. He walked out of the administration building, took his command position, and called his battalion to attention for what he knew would be the last time.

"Battalion attention!"

The soldiers snapped to attention smartly, as always. "Adjutant, publish the orders," Penrose said softly.

After a brief drum roll, Lieutenant Grier stepped forward with a sheaf of papers in his hand.

"Attention to orders!" he said. Then he read the order:

The Brownsville Redemption

Special Orders No. 266, War Department. Washington, November 9, 1906.

By direction of the president, the following named enlisted men who, on August 13, 1906, were members of Companies B, C, and D, 25th Infantry, certain members of which organizations participated in the riotous disturbance which occurred in Brownsville, Texas, on the night of August 13, 1906, will be discharged without honor from the Army by their respective commanding officers and forever barred from reenlisting in the Army or Navy of the United States, as well as from employment in any civil capacity under the Government.

The adjutant paused and looked up at the sky. It had been threatening snow all morning but had not begun yet. It was so heavily overcast that the clouds appeared to be descending to the ground, threatening to engulf the parade field in darkness even though it was just past noon. The adjutant continued reading, calling off the name of the first company to be dismissed.

"Company B, 25th Infantry." Then he read the name of the first soldier on the list.

"First Sergeant Mingo Sanders. Discharged without honor. Quartermaster Sergeant Walker McCurdy; Sergeants James R. Reid, George Jackson, and Luther T. Thornton."

Hearing the sound of his name called out for dishonor jolted Sanders. He stiffened and stared straight ahead. He showed no outward signs of emotion, but the words "without honor" tore him apart inside. Feelings of shame and sadness overwhelmed him. They caused him to question his heroic exploits in battle. He had experienced the cruelty of war. And now a moral uncertainty crept into his soul. Were all the killings he had seen in war with—or without—honor?

Images of past battles now pained him. He felt as if he were fighting fragments of those battles again. But this time, the battles seemed to be collisions between right and wrong. With honor? Without honor?

The image of Colonel Roosevelt came floating into his mind and sat on the front steps of his memory. It was June 25, 1898. Colonel Roosevelt was no longer a supplicant, begging for food for himself and his men. His countenance had changed inexplicably from friendly to unfriendly, his eyes from kind to cold and his lips from a smile to a smirk. Like the portrait of Dorian Gray, he had evolved into something darkly unsavory. Roosevelt had a scowl on his face and was aggressively belligerent. He was not asking for food; he was taking it.

Why did soldiers end up killing so many people in battle like the Sioux Indian campaigns of 1890 and 1891? He recalled sadly the battle at the Pine Ridge Reservation, later known as Wounded Knee. The ground had been littered with scores of dead Sioux. Why did he care now?

Memories of the Battle for San Juan Heights, Cuba, July 1, 1898

The assault on the blockhouse perched on top of San Juan Hill was dreamlike. It was nine o'clock in the morning, and he was fighting that battle all over again. The 25th Infantry was ordered into the fight to protect the flanks of the Second Massachusetts Volunteers as they moved up the hill to capture the blockhouse. Sporadic exchanges of gunfire between the Spaniards, the Second Massachusetts Volunteers, and the 25th Infantry signaled a standoff.

The Brownsville Redemption

Colonel Roosevelt and his Rough Riders were bogged down at the base of Kettle Hill. They couldn't advance until the blockhouse was captured.

It was now about two o'clock in the afternoon. The Second Massachusetts Volunteers were ordered to make a frontal assault and take the blockhouse. As they began the final assault, the Spaniards laid down a hail of heavy fire against them. Second, Massachusetts collapsed under the barrage and executed a full-scale retreat back down the hill.

"Move up! Advance!" The 25th got the order to continue the frontal assault abandoned by the Volunteers.

"You might as well turn back," shouted a bloodied straggler as he staggered down the hill.

"If anybody can take the blockhouse, we can," Sanders shouted back.

Taking advantage of the lush vegetation, Sanders and his men concealed themselves as much as they could. They moved closer and closer toward the blockhouse, holding their fire as they went. When they were within 100 yards (91 meters) of their objective, a bugler blew the charge. Bayonets fixed and guns blazing, the Black soldiers of the 25th Infantry caught the Spaniards by surprise. They overwhelmed them and continued the attack. They went on to take the town of El Caney and pulled down the Spanish flag in celebration.

The sounds of dead men moaning, groaning, and begging for mercy passed through Sanders's mind as he half-listened to the drone of the adjutant's voice. The names of the other discharged soldiers were being called. "Boyd Conyers, John Amos Holoman, Carolina De Saussure, and Winter Washington."

He heard a woman's voice coming from the edge of the field where the wives of the soldiers and the officers had quietly gathered. It was a soft voice, sobbing, weeping. "No! No! No! Don't do this. Don't do this," she cried. Sanders recognized that voice. The sobbing and weeping were the sounds that always accompanied his being shipped off to war—Cuba, Philippines, India campaigns. It was the voice of his wife.

A powerful urge gripped him. He wanted to break ranks, go to her and take her in his arms, and comfort her. That he could not do. Military discipline would not let him go. He could not break ranks and leave the rest of his men standing there alone. That would break the bonds of unity, allow fear to creep in, and ultimately crush the goals of discipline he had worked so hard to achieve. No, he could not go to her. He was still a soldier. Even though he was being dishonored and his status as a soldier had just been taken from him, he felt he must still maintain discipline.

The adjutant continued down the list until he reached the name of the last man in Company D—Dorsie Willis. There were three other names on the list from other units who just happened to be on temporary duty at Fort Brown.

Having completed publishing the orders, the adjutant completed the instructions:

> Now listen up! You are not out of the army yet! You must come to the administration building. You will be given your discharge without honor certificates and your pay. You must remove all rank of insignia, buttons, and units' crests from your uniforms. If you don't, they will be ripped off, and then, and only then, will you be paid. You must leave immediately. You will be escorted out the gate in small groups beginning today and continuing until all of you are gone.

The adjutant did an about-face and saluted Major Penrose. "Sir, it's your command."

The Brownsville Redemption

Major Penrose wanted to say something to his troops, but he didn't know what to say. He couldn't praise them, and he couldn't condemn them. He was still unsure of their guilt or innocence. He was choking on indecision.

Their innocence had been impossible for him to prove. Had he tried hard enough? Then he remembered something about the empty shell casings. Yes, he thought, two of the empty cartridges that Mayor Combe gave him seemed peculiar. What was it about them that didn't ring true? Of course! *The markings imprinted on them didn't carry the date of manufacture!* His heart started racing, and he had to steady himself.

That was it! All bullets made by Union Metallic for the government by contract had to have the date of manufacture imprinted on them. Bullets made for the civilian market didn't have those markings. His men didn't have access to that kind of bullet. What did it mean? It could mean that some of the citizens of Brownsville fired those shots.

Maybe his men were innocent after all. Was that enough proof? Should he suspend the discharge of his soldiers until the new evidence could be investigated, or was it too late?

His stomach was churning. He felt sick and nervous. He felt the urge to move his bowels. The old dysentery was coming back. He started to speak but couldn't. The right words would not come. His resolve to say something of importance relevant to the plight of the men began to weaken. Then he looked straight ahead and saw Mingo standing there like a ramrod. His face belied his military posture. It was washed with sadness. His eyes spoke of betrayal, Penrose's betrayal, the army's betrayal, President Roosevelt's betrayal. There was no one who would speak for him or them.

Finally, Penrose said, "Company commanders, take charge of your companies." He turned to Major Clarke and said, "There go the best men, the best soldiers, and the best battalion, in the Army." Desperate to be alone, he rushed from the field.

Some of the soldiers didn't even have enough money to buy a suit of clothes. Later, John Holoman wired some of them money to buy clothes, and when he got into town from San Antonio, he arranged credit for others.

They were already packed. They left Fort Reno and the Army with their wives and children. While they were leaving, they were orderly, peaceful, and soldierly. Their carriage was one of silent dignity. When they arrived in El Reno, they didn't cause any disturbances or trouble of any kind. No one was arrested for drunkenness or lawlessness. They refreshed their long, three-month drought with beer and then slipped away quietly and separately into their new world.

The Brownsville Redemption

TWENTY-THREE

The Gridiron Club *Dinner Debate*

A New Investigation

When President Roosevelt returned to the White House on Tuesday morning, November 27, he declared the Brownsville matter closed to Booker T. Washington's emissary, Emmett J. Scott.

But it wasn't closed. After reading the president's 1907 message along with its attached investigative reports, Ohio Senator Joseph Benson Foraker found them legally insufficient for the action Roosevelt had taken. On the Senate floor, Foraker criticized Roosevelt's order dismissing the soldiers and introduced a Senate resolution calling for a full investigation into the Brownsville affair.

All along, the lawyers in Roosevelt's cabinet, as well as the Judge Advocate General (JAG) in the War Department, were unhappy with Blocksom's report. In response to Foraker's criticism, they advised Roosevelt to send Milton D. Purdy, an assistant attorney general, and Blocksom to Brownsville to take sworn testimony to refute Foraker. Purdy and Blocksom arrived in Brownsville the day after Christmas and started another after-the-fact investigation.

Purdy and Blocksom took 63 affidavits. They collected a host of items that had been picked up in the streets of Brownsville—33 empty shell casings, seven ball cartridges, a bandoleer, and four clips. Roosevelt then rushed the resulting report to the Senate in mid-January 1907, still confident that the Black soldiers were guilty. He made a point of saying so and challenged anyone who took a contrary view.

The additional evidence, he said, "renders it impossible to question the conclusion on which my order was based."

Foraker wasn't buying it. He took to the Senate floor and verbally ripped Purdy's report apart, saying that it was taken behind closed doors and the soldiers had had no opportunity to meet their accusers. He called again for the adoption of his resolution for a Senate investigation of the "Brownsville Affray."

"I want these men who have been accused of murder, mutiny, and treason to have their day in court, where they will have a chance to defend themselves," Foraker said.

A running debate ensued between Roosevelt and Foraker. Roosevelt defended his action as if he were acting on the divine right of kings, while Foraker hammered him with eloquent, scholarly legal speeches from the Senate floor.

"The men have been condemned without a hearing, and that is contrary to the spirit of our institutions," declared Foraker. "It is our duty to undo the wrong by giving them a chance to face their accusers."

On January 22, 1907, the Senate adopted Foraker's resolution to authorize a senate investigation. An outraged Roosevelt began plotting his revenge. Working behind the scenes, he set up surrogates in the Senate to attack Foraker. In this volatile political climate, Roosevelt and Foraker were destined to collide at the famous annual Gridiron Club dinner hosted by the Washington newspapermen.

A Fine Speech

Wet snow had been falling most of that day in Washington, and the accumulation was getting deep and mushy as Senator Foraker made his way toward the Willard Hotel where the dinner was being held. It was Saturday night, January 26, 1907, just a week or so after the Senate's adoption of his resolution to hold the Brownsville hearings. He hadn't expected anything serious at the dinner—nothing but a good old-fashioned stag party, a lot of fun, ribald humor, and good food.

Foraker didn't know the president was to attend until he saw him sitting at the head table next to Samuel G. Blythe, the club president. Tables were arranged to form the gridiron, and the banquet room was packed with the powerful and the elite—businessmen, senators, congressmen, cabinet officers, and federal judges. Reporters were there in force, too. Foraker took his seat at the first table on the immediate left of President Roosevelt. Foraker glanced over at Roosevelt and thought he appeared tense, grim, and worried.

A minstrel clown in blackface shuffled onto center stage. "I wants to see de president. I'se an old nigger from down Tuskegee way. I was up here and heard the president was here, so I came in here to see him. I'se surely interested in dat man. I had a boy in dem Colored troops down in Brownsville, but I 'spect he's own his way home now."

Roosevelt smiled.

By protocol, the president always spoke last. At this dinner, however, Roosevelt asked to speak first. He was called to the podium. The president of the Gridiron Club introduced Roosevelt.

Before he began his speech, he opened the souvenir booklet and saw a spoof attributed to him, which read in part, "All coons look alike to me."

Roosevelt frowned. Then he launched into his speech:

> I want to set a few things straight here tonight. The domination of this nation by big business is over. The time when a few plutocrats could get together behind closed corporate doors, set the policies of this government, rule this government, and fleece the people ended with my administration. Some of you sitting right

here in this room tonight better get used to it. You should be thankful that my railroad and corporate reforms were put in place by my conservative Republican administration. If not for this administration, you plutocrats would have had to swallow more drastic, punitive, and distasteful measures forced on you by the spirit of the mob. The Mob! The Mob! The Mob!

The government ought not to conduct the business of the country, but it ought to regulate it so that it shall be conducted in the interest of the public. You can bet on it. I'll damn sure do that.

Then he leaned over the podium. He made his remarks personal. He shook his fist at J.P. Morgan, the Wall Street financier, and at Henry Rogers, the vice president of Standard Oil. "You boys better correct your ways," he warned them. "You better not try to block my reforms. Your time is thoroughly over."

Then he raised his head, looked around the banquet room, and said softly, "No man in this country is so high or so low that I would not punish him, if I could, for violating the law. No man is so high or so low that I would not give him the full protection of the law if innocent of offense against the law."

The guests at the dinner couldn't believe it. Mouths fell open, and eyebrows were raised. People squirmed in their seats and looked around at each other as Roosevelt continued to pour it on. They had expected friendly banter, not an hour-long sermon, and certainly not a self-righteous diatribe. J.P. Morgan sat there stone-faced, angrily glaring back at Roosevelt.

Foraker was not mentioned by name. Nonetheless, he was attacked. Roosevelt chastised the opponents of his railroad regulations and dismissed the Senate debate on Brownsville, characterizing it as an "academic discussion." It just happened that Foraker was the chief opponent of Roosevelt's railroad regulations and his nemesis on Brownsville. As to his constitutional power to dismiss the soldiers, he said it was not subject to review by the legislative branch of government.

Roosevelt seemed to be in the same frame of mind he was in just before Christmas when he said he would even refuse to obey the law if Congress passed legislation over his veto reinstating the black soldiers. "I would invite impeachment," he said.

Roosevelt ended his speech with words he probably thought wouldn't get reported by the press. "There may have been but two companies of that regiment engaged in that unwholesome business, but all coons look alike to me."

The *Washington Post* reported that "All coons look alike to the president" on the front page, Monday, January 28, 1907.

No one usually was allowed to speak after the president, but in this case, Roosevelt had opted to speak first, leaving the toastmaster no choice but to allow Foraker to speak since he had been the main target of Roosevelt's speech. After being called to the podium, Foraker hesitated. His first thought was to refuse. He had not expected to speak, had not prepared a speech, and didn't feel equal to the occasion.

Calls came from the floor. "Speech! Speech!"

The toastmaster shouted, "Let the bloody sarcasm begin!"

Hearing those words, Foraker knew he could not refuse. He took the floor, making a striking appearance. He was tall, over six feet, slim, with a shock of iron-gray hair and a well-trimmed gray mustache. He was a patrician-looking, handsome man who now looked like he had been wounded. His face was ashen white, and he didn't appear ready to do verbal combat with Roosevelt.

After looking directly at the president for what seemed like a long, reflective moment, Foraker began slowly. "I, too, like you, Mr. President, favor governmental supervision and regulation of railroads and corporations. The only difference between us is the character of the legislation that should be enacted to accomplish it. My opposition to the rate bill had been because I thought it unconstitutional."

As to his votes, he said he was only responsible to his constituency and nobody else, and he denied the right of anybody there or anywhere else to tell him how he should vote on great constitutional issues.

Not lingering long on esoteric corporate law, anti-trust law, and regulations, he moved on to the Brownsville debate. It was his favorite passion, and he challenged Roosevelt's assertion that it was merely "academic" because all power was vested in him. Then Foraker quoted from one of his earlier speeches.

"Where a soldier is charged with a crime and denies it and stands upon his rights, he has the right to a trial, and without it, there is no power lodged anywhere to say he is guilty and order him dismissed; there is no power lodged anywhere to indict a man by order; convict a man by order, and then punish him by order."

Foraker continued to lecture the president. "That, Mr. President, has been the law of the world since civilization…No man shall be convicted of a crime until he has been permitted to face his accusers and cross-examine the witnesses."

When Roosevelt made that eloquent remark in his speech about his policy toward corporations—"No man is too high or low to be punished or to receive justice"—Foraker saw in that statement the ultimate contradiction when that standard was applied to the Black soldiers, and he stated this view to the president.

"Mr. President, you have failed to apply that standard in the Brownsville case, where, according to your own statement of it, there were doubtless many men with splendid records as soldiers, absolutely innocent, yet you branded them as criminals and dismissed them without honor."

"That's not so," Roosevelt said in a low voice but loud enough for some of the guests to hear.

Foraker started to speak about the illustrious record of Sergeant Mingo Sanders and how badly he was treated. "Sergeant Mingo Sanders had twenty-six years of service and a record of bravery in battle."

"That's not so." The President gritted his teeth while shaking his head.

"He was turned out when he was nearing the time when he would have had a right to retire," Foraker said.

"I'm going to answer that!" Roosevelt balled up his fist and started to rise from his seat. Supreme Court Justice Harlan reached over and laid his hand on Roosevelt's shoulder. "No, please."

Foraker felt the pressure from the interruptions of Roosevelt. He struggled to continue his speech. "He would have a right to retire on pay, but he was stripped of all his valuable rights and disgraced."

"I'm not going to stand for it." Roosevelt started to get up again but was restrained by the justice again.

Foraker came to the end of his speech. "When legal and human rights are involved, all persons look alike to me." Foraker completed his speech with a brave assertion of his high duty as a senator. "I didn't come to the Senate to take orders from anybody, either at this line or the other. Whenever I fall so low that I cannot express my opinion on a great question freely, and without mental reservation, I will resign and leave my place to some man who has the courage to discharge his duties."

Those words brought thunderous applause from the guests. Foraker finished his speech and was about to return to his seat, but he hesitated and appeared to reflect for a moment. Then he addressed Roosevelt directly with outstretched arms, as if he were welcoming him into his embrace in respect for some great occasion.

"Mr. President, there was a time, which you well know, when I loved you as though you were one of my own family. There was nothing legitimate or honorable that I wouldn't do for you. I supported many of your programs—not all. Yet I didn't feel that my love stood in the way or that I had any right to allow it to stand in the way of my differing from you when in my judgment you were in error. So, as it was in the past, so it will continue in the future."

The crowd rushed the podium before Foraker could take his seat. He was mobbed by cheering guests and reporters, wishing him well and telling him what a great speech that was.

Roosevelt stood up and tried to quiet the crowd, saying that he was entitled to have the last say. And he was, by club protocol. He made it back to the podium and said, "Some of those men were bloody butchers. They ought to be hung. The only reason that I didn't have them hung was because I couldn't find out which ones did the shooting."

The Brownsville Redemption

THE WHITE HOUSE,
WASHINGTON.

November 27, 1906.

My dear Mr. Secretary:

The President directs me to call your attention to the enclosed clipping of an interview with Major Penrose appearing in this evening's Star. The President directs that you wire Major Penrose this evening asking what explanation he has for giving out such an interview or any publication whatever in reference to the dismissal of the three Companies of the 25th Infantry. The President desires an immediate and full explanation of what he has said and his reasons for saying it. If this interview was authentic the President wishes by wire an immediate and full statement in justification or explanation of it.

Very truly yours,

[signature]
Secretary to the President.

Hon. Wm. H. Taft,
Secretary of War.

Letter from President Roosevelt's secretary to William Howard Taft, 11/27/06. The President demands an explanation from Major Penrose for making laudatory comments to the *Evening Star* about the discharged soldiers.

TWENTY-FOUR

The Last *Investigations*

The Con Artist

The Senate began its investigation on February 4, 1907, just a few days after the Gridiron dinner debate. Roosevelt had vigorously opposed the investigation. After that debate and the start of the Senate probe, the social and political relations between the president and Foraker were, for all practical purposes, broken. Foraker had hoped the wounds inflicted in that debate would heal with the passage of time, but Roosevelt began maneuvering socially and politically against him. He never invited him again to the White House for social or political events. Roosevelt also denied federal judgeship appointments and other patronage jobs to Foraker's recommended candidates.

Secret Service agents stood near Foraker's home and watched the comings and goings of guests to such an extent that old friends and political allies, fearing Roosevelt's political retribution, virtually stopped visiting him and his wife. Their mail was opened and tampered with. It got so bad that Foraker felt that Roosevelt wanted to oust him from political life altogether.

As Roosevelt mounted the political pressure against him, Foraker became more and more passionate in his defense of the soldiers. He pounded Roosevelt in speeches on the Senate floor at every opportunity he could get.

Then, one Saturday night in April, Herbert J. Browne, a former newspaper editor, came to Foraker's home and gave him some startling information. He said he had it on good authority that seven white civilians had shot up the town. Four of the raiders were willing to talk if offered immunity from prosecution. The other three men, however, had left town without a word. Browne volunteered to go to Brownsville, take the testimony of the four men who were willing to talk, and make it available to the Senate. All he wanted were expenses and a small fee for his services. Foraker gave Browne $500 of his own money to get the venture started.

Browne arrived in Brownsville by train on Wednesday, April 24, 1907. Arriving at a quick conclusion after interviewing several citizens, he wrote Foraker on April 29 that Louis Cowen was the "head devil" in the whole business. He also noted that Cowen was really a renegade Russian Jew who had changed his name from Cowajiian to Cowen. To get additional information from Cowen and "his gang," he was going out hunting with them.

By early May, however, Browne had completely flip-flopped. He reported to Foraker that he had discovered the true answer. "The Negro troop had shot up the town. I can name four of them."

How could he have let himself be fooled? Foraker realized that he had been victimized by a con artist.

But the unfortunate con was just the beginning of a series of setbacks for Foraker and his ardent support of the soldiers. The Senate committee ended its investigation a little over a year later, in March 1908. Its finding was a bitter disappointment for Foraker. A majority of the committee members voted against the soldiers, confirming Roosevelt's position that some of the soldiers had shot up and terrorized the town. They still couldn't identify which ones, though.

After having bilked Foraker out of $500, Browne must have thought there must be other suckers out there waiting for him to lift their wallets. So about a year later, Browne wrote Taft a letter bragging,

"I spent three weeks in Brownsville last April and became thoroughly satisfied that, following a conspiracy, fourteen or more soldiers of Company B shot up the town."

Taft wanted to see him right away and did. Browne brought William J. Baldwin with him to the meeting. Baldwin was a detective from Roanoke, Virginia. The two men presented their credentials, which impressed Taft so much that he immediately offered them a $5,000 contract to find and identify the Brownsville terrorists. He wouldn't sign it, however, until he had a chance to consult with Roosevelt and check out their credentials.

Taft didn't have to do much to convince Roosevelt, even though he had won some sort of a victory when the Senate investigation agreed with him. However, Foraker had written a strong dissent backed up by several senators, and there was a bill before Congress to reinstate any of the soldiers who could prove their innocence.

After Taft satisfied himself that Browne and Baldwin were "competent, earnest, and reputable men," Browne and Baldwin formed a team, hired eight other agents, and began working for the War Department on April 28, 1908. They had a deadline of June 15 to finish their investigation.

Browne went undercover as a newspaper reporter, pretending he was interested in writing a sympathetic story about the injustice meted out to the Brownsville boys. Using this ruse, he obtained the home addresses of many of the men from a black lawyer who was a staunch supporter of the soldiers. Browne hid the fact that he was now a part of the Browne & Baldwin Detective Agency.

Browne & Baldwin detectives spread out across the country, hunting down the soldiers, interrogating, bribing, and threatening the former soldiers to try to extract confessions from them.

The Brownsville Redemption

Browne missed his deadline but sent in several progress reports over eight months to the JAG in the War Department. Finally, on December 5, 1908, Browne reported the good news that ex-private Boyd Conyers of Company B, living now in Monroe, Georgia, had confessed that he, John Holoman, John Brown, and Carolina De Saussure were the leaders in the raid and that they had shot Police Lieutenant Joe Dominguez and the bartender. Conyers's confession was supposedly made to William Lawson, one of Baldwin's detectives. When Conyers found out that he had made his statement to a detective, he tried to commit suicide.

Browne continued. "We have located over 130 of these ex-soldiers and have been in thirty states in quest for information." He concluded that there was a "general knowledge on the part of the ex-soldiers that the raid came from inside the fort," and he fastened the guilt on Company B. Browne claimed Conyers identified 14 of the raiders by name. "I have...sufficient evidence, circumstantial and direct, to indict, convict, and hang under the laws of Texas four ex-soldiers...for the murder of Frank Natus," Browne reported.

Upon receipt of Browne's good-news report, Roosevelt quickly got out a Special Message to the Senate on December 14, 1908:

> This report enables us to fix with tolerable definiteness at least some of the criminals who took the lead in the murderous shooting of private citizens at Brownsville...

Roosevelt, however, reminded the Senate that the detectives' work had not been completed and would continue until all the criminals were brought to justice.

When Senator Foraker read the Browne & Baldwin report in Roosevelt's Special Message, he was more than skeptical. He was horrified.

He didn't believe a word of it and set out to prove on the Senate floor that Conyers's alleged confession was an out-and-out fabrication.

Unknown to Browne & Baldwin and to Roosevelt, Conyers kept Foraker informed in detail of all the contacts the detectives had with him. Foraker had a stack of letters from Conyers detailing the interrogations, bribes, and threats made by Browne & Baldwin agents. Those letters would be crucial for Conyers. For if that confession couldn't be proven false, he was headed straight for the gallows in Texas.

Again, Foraker defended the ex-soldiers. On January 12, 1909, he took to the Senate floor, and based on Conyers's letters, he gutted Browne's report, laying bare the elements of its fiction starting with Lawson, Baldwin, and Browne. Detective Lawson had traveled to Monroe, Georgia, the hometown of Boyd Conyers. There he took a room in Ester Crews's boarding house, posing as a traveling salesman, and struck up a friendship with another roomer named Parker. As the friendship grew closer, Lawson asked Parker if he would write his detective reports for him about Brownsville, confiding to him that he couldn't read or write.

Later, the friendship soured when Lawson accused Parker of stealing a suit of clothes from him. Parker didn't want to tangle with a Washington detective, so he fled. But on his way out of town, he sent a warning to Mrs. Conyers, urging her to tell her husband that Will Lawson was not the person he claimed to be. He was a detective gathering information about the Brownsville shooting. At that time, Conyers was out of town, working at the National Guard Armory in nearby Chickamauga.

As Conyers related the story, when he got off the train, returning home from Chickamauga, his mother-in-law was at the station waiting for him. She told him that Will Lawson was a detective and that the word was out that he, Conyers, had confessed to shooting a white man in Brownsville.

When Conyers spotted Will Lawson on the street the next morning, he went to Sheriff Arnold and asked him to find out what Lawson was up to. Sheriff Arnold called Lawson in and demanded to see his papers. Lawson produced a letter satisfying the sheriff that he was indeed a detective working for Browne & Baldwin.

Sheriff Arnold later swore that Conyers denied that he had ever spoken to Lawson about Brownsville in his presence and said Conyers called Lawson a liar to his face. As Conyers related the story in his letters to Foraker, he had only a brief encounter with Lawson before he confronted him in Sheriff Arnold's office and that Will Lawson had said nothing about Brownsville. "I am just as innocent of taking any part in that trouble that night as God is on high."

A few weeks later, a white businessman calling himself Wallace L. Gray turned up in Monroe, Georgia, from Roanoke, Virginia. Several months ago, this same man had written Conyers a letter offering him a job paying $60 to $70 a month if he would move to Virginia. Conyers had declined the offer because he said his wife was too sick to move.

Sheriff Arnold asked Conyers to meet Mr. Gray and him in his office that night for an agenda not made known to Conyers. When Conyers stepped into the sheriff's office, to his surprise, he learned that Mr. Gray was a detective named William G. Baldwin and that Will Lawson worked for him. Baldwin interrogated Conyers, but Conyers denied any participation in the shooting. Baldwin asked Conyers, "Now what about that Negro Lawson I sent down here to talk to you. What did you tell him?"

"Sir, I didn't even have any private talk with him."

Baldwin returned to Washington and told Browne that Conyers denied having a private talk with Lawson and that the alleged confession was shaky.

Realizing that he had a weak case with a confession produced by an illiterate detective who signed his name with an X on an affidavit attesting to the authenticity of the confession, Browne decided he had better go talk to Conyers himself. So, several weeks later, another white man, a stranger to Conyers, arrived in Monroe and conducted a full press interrogation of Conyers in Sheriff Arnold's office.

Sheriff Arnold joined the interrogation, all the time hoping to collect the reward money. He had always believed that some of the soldiers shot up the town, and for that reason, he was happy to have an opportunity to be able to help solve the mystery.

Again, Conyers denied any part in the shooting.

Browne said, "We have been able to prove Company B men did the shooting, and what I want you to tell me is just the men that did the shooting. I know you can if you will. We already know three men that did it, but we want the whole gang. The three are you, John Holoman, and John Brown. Now suppose you dream on it and come back here in the morning and tell Sheriff Arnold and me about it. We will see that nobody hurts you if you were in on it."

"Mr. Browne, what do you want me to do—tell a lie?" Conyers said. "Pick out this man and that man and say they were in on it? It's impossible for me to do that."

Browne caught a train to Washington the next morning and didn't return to Monroe until October 6. He really tore into Conyers that time. Again, Sheriff Arnold participated, locking his door so they wouldn't be disturbed.

Browne and Sheriff Arnold kept Conyers under "the most severe" cross-examination until 11 o'clock that night but failed to get anything out of him. Browne asked Conyers if he had a picture of the Company B baseball team. Conyers retrieved his copy from home and showed it to Browne, who quickly copied down the names of the players. Except for the names of the baseball players, Browne went back to Washington empty-handed.

Browne returned to Monroe on October 11, feeling desperate. Again, Browne and Sheriff Arnold put Conyers under another rigid interrogation but this time they promised him monetary inducements and pardons. Then they threatened him with death by hanging in Texas. Conyers said, "Let God's will be done." He would not lie to save himself from the scaffold.

Sheriff Arnold read Herbert J. Browne's version of what happened in his presence with Conyers and swore, "It's the most absolutely false, the most willful misrepresentation of the truth, and the most shameful perversion of what really did take place between them that I have ever seen over the signature of any person."

So, after paying Browne & Baldwin thousands of dollars from a military contingency fund, Roosevelt and Taft got nothing for the government's money except a worthless, fabricated report.

The last government investigation during that time came at the urging of Senator Foraker in December 1908, near the end of his Senate term. Roosevelt had crushed the Ohio senator's political underpinnings, and he lost his re-election bid. But even though he was a lame duck, Foraker introduced a bill that, if passed, would have created a tribunal. The tribunal would have allowed the men to face their accusers, testify on their own behalf, and present witnesses and evidence—all under the presumption of innocence. He proposed that all the ex-soldiers should be allowed to reenlist if the government didn't show positively that they were guilty of the charges. In other words, his bill would place the burden of proof on the government.

Company B's Baseball Team: 1. Harry Carmichael 2. James Johnson 3. Edward Daniels 4. Henry Jones 5. George Mitchell 6. C. E. Cooper 7. Mingo Sanders 8. Isaiah Raynor 9. Wade Harris 10. John Holoman 11. J. Allen 12. Joseph Wilson

Roosevelt campaigned against Foraker's bill, stating in a personal letter to Senator Warren, "Senator Foraker's bill amounts simply to a proposal to condone murder, and perjury in the past [and] puts a premium upon perjury in the future…"

Foraker's bill failed. Senator Nelson W. Aldrich submitted a substitute bill designed in favor of Roosevelt and Taft. It was signed into law by President Roosevelt on March 3, 1909, creating a military court of inquiry—not to be confused with a military court-martial or any other duly constituted judicial court. Under the court of inquiry, the ex-soldiers were presumed guilty and required to prove their innocence.

The court of inquiry, composed of retired generals, met from 1909 to 1910 and heard 82 of the ex-soldiers. They allowed them to appear and testify but denied the other 85 who wanted to be heard. They were denied for no apparent reason except that the old generals were probably tired and worn out from the tedious proceedings of witnesses testifying, presentations of technical evidence, and arguments by lawyers over such a long period of time.

The court adjourned on March 28, 1910. It concluded that the soldiers shot up the town as charged, but it allowed 14 men to reenlist without giving any reasons why.

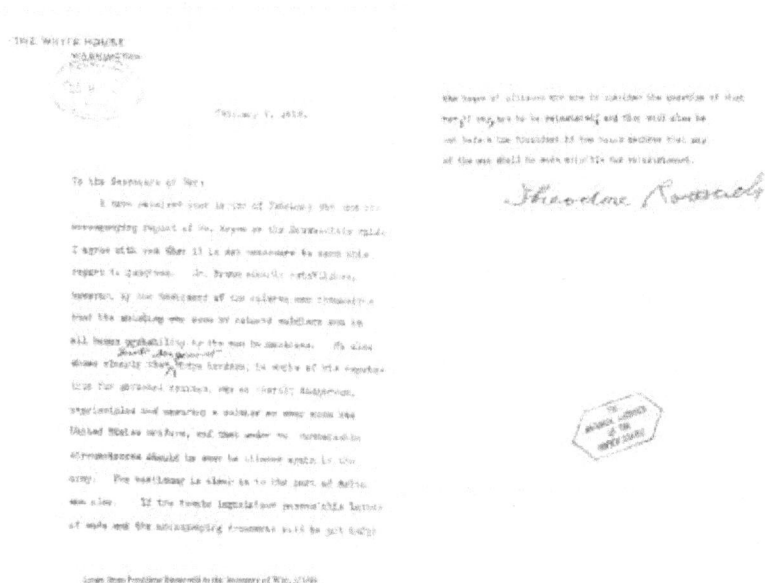

Letter from President Roosevelt to Secretary of War, 02/07/1909. This letter shows that the President believed the fraudulent report of detective Herbert Browne. It also shows Roosevelt's animus toward Sergeant Mingo Sanders.

BOOK II

Years Later

My Quest to Exonerate the Innocent

Twenty-Five

The Pentagon, *June 1972*

The Odyssey Begins

How strange, yet fortunate, that so many years after I had witnessed the tragic death of the old man with the wide-brimmed hat I should find myself as a staff officer at the Pentagon with the opportunity to reinvestigate the Brownsville Incident. I had not forgotten how fervently my grandfather had believed in the innocence of those soldiers! The assignment from Colonel Harry Brooks that had sent me scrambling all over my office looking for the Brownsville file grew into a personal odyssey.

"Now, what in the hell do you want from me?"

That journey began early on the Thursday morning of June 1, 1972. Augustus Hawkins, a Black congressman, had introduced a bill that, if passed, would require the secretary of defense to overturn the Brownsville ruling. However, the Judge Advocate General (JAG) opposed the bill. And, not only had the army general staff refused to intervene—it had concurred with JAG! Previous overtures to get JAG to change its position had been fruitless. Perhaps it was because Hawkins was a liberal from California and a member of the Congressional Black Caucus. He was also a close associate of Congressman Ron Dellums, who was a notorious persona non grata in the Pentagon because of his open opposition to the Vietnam War.

My job was to write a nonconcurrence position paper to fight JAG's opposition. But before I did that, I decided to make one last appeal to Colonel Wade Williamson, the lawyer leading the JAG charge against the proposed legislation.

As we were leaving Brooks's office, Bob Dews, the senior staff officer in our department, cautioned me, "Williamson is a good man. He has the reputation of being the most brilliant lawyer in the JAG's office. He's no bigot. But he's very religious, and sometimes he mixes his religion with the law. He's always saying, he 'believes in the right as God has given him the wisdom to do.'"

On my way over to Williamson's office, I began to wonder why he had agreed to see me. Was it just out of courtesy to Brooks, his friend? Or was he afraid of the formal nonconcurrence? If so, why? Did JAG have something to hide?

As I walked into a wide, spacious office, there was no doubt that I was in the domain of the legal profession. Heavy leather chairs were everywhere, law books lined the shelves, and a heavy rug carpeted the floor. A woman sat at a typewriter off in a corner of the room, tapping away. Two white men stood in the middle of the room. One was a military officer. He had broad shoulders, a square jaw, and close-cropped hair, and his green uniform was covered in ribbons. He was talking to a tall man with sandy hair, wearing an expensive-looking blue pinstripe suit and black wingtip shoes. A Star of David medallion indicated he was Jewish. I heard him say, "I'm not sure General Bowers will support you. Who in our office agreed to this?"

"Jessie Wheeler," answered Williamson.

The man in the suit grew agitated. "Jessie Wheeler doesn't work for General Bowers. He works for General Kerwin." Bowers was the adjutant general of the army; Kerwin was a four-star general and the deputy chief of staff for personnel in charge of all army personnel.

The Brownsville Redemption

The pair did not notice my presence until another man came through the door and said, "You must be Major Baker. I'm Captain Jim Murdoch, chief of the legislative team. I work for Colonel Williamson."

"Glad to meet you," I replied, pretending I had not been eavesdropping.

"Oh, Major Baker, you're here," said Williamson. "I'd like to introduce Mr. Richard Belnap, the special legal advisor to the adjutant general. I see you have already met Captain Murdoch. He's a fine lawyer—as one must be to work for General Bowers in the Pentagon."

Murdoch seemed somewhat embarrassed by the praise. He handed the colonel a manila folder. "All the papers are in here, sir. I'll be in my office if you need me."

Belnap seemed surprised to see me there. Maybe he was surprised that I was Black. Black officers were a rarity in the Pentagon. His nervous expression implied, *You've been listening. How long have you been standing there? How much did you hear?* However, when we shook hands in greeting, I felt a genuine warmth flow between us. Blacks and Jews have long recognized the other's history of slavery and persecution. We understood and had shared each other's struggles. During the Civil Rights Movement, Jews had stood with Blacks. *But where had they gone?* I wondered. *Had Affirmative Action chased them away?*

Belnap announced, "General Verne Bowers asked me to sit in on this meeting if I thought it necessary. But, after talking with Colonel Williamson, I don't think it is." As he left, I hoped he would not forget our common enemies and do what was right.

Williamson welcomed me into his office. "Come into my office, Major Baker. Do you take coffee or tea?" But before I could answer, he stepped to the door and asked his secretary to bring both coffee and tea. Once we were seated around a long mahogany conference table in the colonel's inner office, he asked me bluntly, "What do you want, Major?"

His question caught me by surprise. Colonel Williamson had made a complete metamorphosis from the friendly "Wade" to this stern-looking man, a hanging judge. He made me feel as if I were guilty of some crime. But then I realized who and what I was dealing with—a superior officer who was using his rank to intimidate me and scare me out of his office.

I stood my ground as respectfully as I could and reverted to military formality. "Colonel Williamson, sir, I want to know why the JAG is opposing Congressman Hawkins's bill."

"What do you mean by the JAG? Don't you mean the office of the JAG?

"No, sir, I mean the judge advocate general himself, Major General Prugh, not the office, sir. Why is he opposing it?"

What I really wanted to know, however, *was Was General Prugh aware that his staff had sent a letter to the Nixon administration? Did he know that his name had been used to oppose a major piece of legislation?*

Williamson stared at me, bit his bottom lip, and turned his head away as if in contempt. He picked up his telephone, held it for a second or two, then put it down and turned back to me in anger. "Major, you have made it clear that you know the difference between the JAG and the office of the JAG," he said. "Now, what in the hell do you want from me?"

"All right, sir, with all due respect to you: Can you tell me why you are opposing this bill?"

"Harry Brooks sent you over here to talk with me about the non-concurrence, didn't he? That's JAG's position, and we're not about to change. Dews told me yesterday he was going to write a nonconcurrence, and I told him that we were opposing that legislation. So, is Dews writing it now or are you?"

"Sir, the rules require us to try to resolve the matter first."

"Don't you lecture me. I know the goddamned rules. There's nothing for you to do but drop that stupid idea about writing a nonconcurrence."

"Sir, I don't think we are at loggerheads yet. The way I see it, we don't have a basis to write anything until we find out why you are objecting to this bill."

The colonel glared at me across the table. "All right, you want to know? I'll tell you." He shuffled through a stack of papers on the table in front of him until he came to Hawkins's bill. He picked it out and threw it across the table at me. "It's crap, that's why! It's a worthless piece of shit! Have you read it?"

Then he launched into an attack, ripping apart Hawkins's bill with such vehemence he seemed to hate the very paper on which it was written. Pointing to a copy of the bill, he bellowed, "It was sent over here *naked*, stark *naked*, without any legal arguments attached to it, *no new facts*, *no reinvestigation*, *no nothing. Just assertions.*" He also did not believe that Congress had the authority to reverse the discharges from "without honor" to "honor." He quoted Teddy Roosevelt: "President Roosevelt said, 'The order was within my discretion under the Constitution and *the laws and cannot be reviewed or reversed save by another executive order.*'"

"Just a minute, sir," I paused. "Are you saying that Congress doesn't have the power to reverse President Roosevelt's decision?"

"That's exactly what I'm saying."

"Then, sir, would you agree with me that President Nixon has the power to reverse that decision?"

"Well...well, I don't know. I'm not a constitutional lawyer," Williamson stammered. "By the way, where did you get your law degree?"

"I didn't go to law school."

"What!" Williamson raised himself halfway up from his chair. He leaned over the table toward me, obviously annoyed that he had been discussing law with a novice.

"That's right, sir. I'm not a lawyer."

"Well, that explains your goddamned ignorance." He looked me over, as if he had never seen me before, and grumbled, "I hope you're not one of those left-wing shithead sociologists."

"I'm a technical service officer, sir, Signal Corps."

I neglected to tell him I had been a ballistic research and development coordinator at the United States Ballistic Research Laboratories (BRL) as well as an operations research systems analyst in the Weapons Systems Laboratory. I had learned and practiced war game theory and was familiar with the techniques of winning and losing. But telling him wouldn't have made any difference. It was better that he continue to think of me as nothing more than a lowly staff officer.

"Well, I figure you've got half a brain, just like me. I got some respect for you."

Watch out, I thought. *He's trying another tactic. He's trying to soften me up.*

"Are you a poker player?"

What in the name of heaven was he getting at? What's poker playing got to do with this?

"I never played poker, sir. I grew up a Missionary Baptist. Gambling was forbidden. Why do you ask?"

"Well," he replied, "I grew up a Southern Baptist, and I still go to prayer meetings on Thursday nights when I can. But hell, I don't think a little poker game will keep me out of Heaven. Anyway, what will be, will be. That's what the Good Book says." Then, lowering his voice, he added, "You're holding a losing hand."

The colonel looked at his watch and said he had another meeting scheduled. Then he began rummaging through his papers and found the letter he had approved to George Shultz, the director of the Office of Management and Budget (OMB). He skipped through most of it until he came to the part about the "conspiracy of silence."

"You know," said Williamson, "those Black soldiers committed an atrocious crime, and all of them covered it up with their cowardly 'conspiracy of silence.' There were several investigations, and all of them concluded that the Black soldiers did it."

"What investigations, sir?" Of course, I was aware of them all, but I wanted to hear what he had to say. Maybe he knew some things that I hadn't read about.

"Don't you know? You mean you came over here unprepared, wasting my time? And don't tell me what your grandfather told you; I've heard that story from Dews."

He began reading aloud from the letter: *"It was the president's opinion that a heinous crime had been committed...and that another crime only of slightly lesser magnitude supplemented it in the shape of a successful conspiracy of silence, and the duty to come forward, that in fact was the basis for discharge of all of the participants. There was overwhelming evidence to support that conclusion by the inspector general."*

"That's my reason for opposing that bill," he said, "and I won't change. I told that to Dews, now I've told it to you, and I'll tell Harry, too. There is nothing for your office to do except join me in opposing that bill. You should drop this nonconcurrence nonsense."

"May I read the JAG's legal opinions on the case, sir?"

"You may not," Williamson said.

"You have them in that folder, don't you, sir?"

"Yes, but you can't see them."

"Where can I get information on the case, sir?"

"You can start with the law library."

"Thank you, sir. When can I talk with you again?"

"When you are ready to go along with my position. Anything else?"

"Yes, sir. May I have a copy of the letter from Attorney General Kleindienst?"

"Yeah." He rustled through the file folder, looking for it, then he looked up. "Can't find it. I'll have Murdoch get you a copy."

It seemed incredible that Colonel Williamson would not let me see JAG's legal opinions on the Brownsville case while admitting that he had them. Something was wrong here. I suspected that Wade Williamson was bluffing—and that JAG wasn't holding the winning cards at all.

TWENTY-SIX

The Search for Evidence of a "Conspiracy of Silence"

Fighting the Alligators

After thanking the secretary for copying the list of military investigations for me, I hurried to the Law Library on the A corridor. I skipped the card catalog and went directly to the reference librarian. When I showed her the list of military investigations I wanted, she did not need to check the card catalog. "Come with me," she said. She got up and headed for the reference stacks. She acted as if she had been expecting me. Had someone called her and told her that I was coming?

She opened up her arms in an expansive gesture as if she were going to fly off a hilltop. She said, "You see all of these books here? They are reference books on the Brownsville Affray. The red and yellow-bound volumes are the Senate documents, which include reports of the Senate Committee on Military Affairs investigation. The red-bound volumes are Court of Inquiry. Some of the smaller volumes are messages from the president, reports from the secretary of war, and some other documents."

My heart sank as I surveyed the overwhelming volume of reference materials—daunting for any reader to take in over a long period of time, and I didn't have much time. "Can I check out some of these materials?" I knew full well the answer would probably be "no," and that is what I got, a polite "no." Then, she reminded me that the library was open all night and went back to her desk.

After thumbing through a few pages of the neatly bound Senate reports, I saw that there were more than 3,000 pages of testimony, numerous exhibits, maps, pictures, and charts. I quickly moved along the shelves to the red volumes, the reports of the Court of Inquiry investigation. I looked at the first and last volumes. They were even more lengthy, with more than 13,000 pages of testimony and exhibits. And then there were the Congressional Records. These thick tomes stood all by themselves, taking up a lot of shelf space. I had a tortuous path in front of me.

"That's not what I want to hear."

I went back to the librarian and said, "Ma'am, I want the specific reports of these officials—Major Blocksom, Colonel Lovering, General Garlington, Assistant Attorney General Purdy, and the messages from President Roosevelt." Then she went somewhere in the back and came out with five military investigative reports. She spread them out on her desk and asked if those were the books I was looking for. I saw that they were indeed the ones I wanted, and I took them to a corner table to set up shop.

I spread the official reports out in front of me. I leafed through them all quickly, looking for the same keywords and phrases I had found in JAG's letter to George Shultz at the OMB— "conspiracy of silence," "due process," "presidential authority," "without honor," "evidence," and so on.

I knew that I had to set up a conceptual framework or a methodology to guide me, but I did not know where to begin. I was sitting with my elbow on the table and my chin in hand when a maxim from the poet and writer Edgar Allan Poe came to mind. *"Eliminate the impossibilities, and what remains must be the truth."* I wrote it down. Then

The Brownsville Redemption

I remembered what Dr. Holmes, my philosophy professor at Howard University, used to hammer into us when quoting the French philosopher René Descartes: "Reexamine your assumptions." So, I wrote down *"Reexamine their assumptions."* Finally, I wrote down another saying I had seen inscribed on a little sign that Colonel Brooks kept on his desk: *"Remember the mission is to drain the swamp—not to fight the alligators."*

I started my review with the reports from Major Blocksom, the racist Copperhead Democrat from Ohio. I learned from reading the panic-stricken telegrams that he sent to Washington that he had been afflicted by the same fear that had gripped Brownsville. On August 20, 1906, a mere two days after his arrival, he recommended that the soldiers be moved out of the town.

Based upon that recommendation, President Roosevelt ordered the soldiers removed from Fort Brown. They had arrived on July 25, 1906, and were removed on August 25, 1906. *My goodness,* I thought. *All of this happened in just one month, from arrival to kick out!*

I examined Blocksom's major conclusions—that nine to fifteen soldiers, possibly more, had jumped the garrison wall and attacked the town. He also concluded that all the soldiers who had not joined the attack must have known who had. He had based his conclusions on flimsy evidence, and some of the stories were complete fabrications.

What bedeviled me most of all were the empty cartridge casings and empty magazine clips found in the streets of Brownsville. How was I going to deal with that seemingly incontrovertible evidence? I decided to revisit that problem later.

As I continued to analyze Blocksom's report, I found references to Captain Bill McDonald of the Texas Rangers and to the twelve soldiers and one civilian he had arrested. Incredibly, Blocksom admitted to not having any evidence—he said he had only repeated what Bill McDonald had told him. He admitted as much in his report: *"Almost no evidence against men arrested, though believe majority more or less guilty."*

Blocksom's "conspiracy of silence" theory was the linchpin of JAG's opposition to the bill. I attributed the theory to Blocksom because it was he who first assumed the old soldiers must know something but were not telling. I searched his report for verifiable facts—but I found none. He used assumed facts to support his conclusion.

I moved on to the next military report, the investigation conducted by Lieutenant Colonel Leonard A. Lovering—the chief inspector general from the Southwestern Division, the superior headquarters for Fort Reno. I subjected it to the same tests and found the results amazingly revealing.

In his report, Lovering called attention to the soldiers' testimony that the town had been shot up by parties other than themselves. He did not mention anything about a "conspiracy of silence." Instead, he simply presented sworn testimony of the soldiers who denied participating in the shooting or knowing who had.

The results of Lovering's fact-finding mission clearly supported the innocence of the soldiers. In fact, embedded in his report was evidence debunking the whole "conspiracy of silence" theory, even though he must have known it could spell the death of his career. And so, he left whatever evidence there was raw and unexamined. He never even wrote an interpretation of it in his report. And I knew why.

It is common knowledge among military officers that when an inspector general finds evidence contrary to what his superiors want him to find, he will be implicitly advised, "That's not what I want to hear." Nevertheless, Lovering's investigation completely supported the innocence of at least eight of the twelve men implicated by Captain McDonald, including John Holoman. His report clearly stated, *"The* following men of the 25th Infantry, now prisoners at Fort Sam Houston, can apparently prove an alibi."

I was not at all surprised to find rebuttal notes attached to the report to discredit Lovering's conclusion. They were written by Major Blocksom, who was subordinate to Lovering. First, Blocksom flagrantly discounted sworn statements by a number of soldiers who had said they were certain that shots had been fired toward the post. Then he wrongly concluded that because he could find no evidence of bullets striking the post, none had been fired toward it. Did it not occur to him that the raiders might have intended to fire high? Perhaps they had really been manufacturing a crisis in order to disguise the frameup.

I then turned to the report of the inspector general of the army, General Ernest A. Garlington. It did not take me long to understand that Roosevelt had sent Garlington to Texas and Oklahoma *specifically* to break through the so-called "conspiracy of silence."

The president directs that you proceed to the places named...and endeavor to secure information that will lead to the apprehension and punishment of men of the 25th Infantry believed to have participated in the riotous disturbance which occurred in Brownsville, Texas...

Roosevelt's orders to Garlington were front-end loaded with assumptions of guilt, and Roosevelt was determined the soldiers be found guilty. And, whether or not he actually believed Major Blocksom's specious "conspiracy of silence" theory, he was resolved to punish the lot.

A Search for Evidence

In order to get Colonel Williamson and JAG to drop their opposition to Hawkins's bill, I would have to persuade them that a "conspiracy of silence" had never existed. So I looked for unbiased, hard evidence in

Garlington's report. What I found both shocked and delighted me. Garlington admitted that he had found *no evidence* of a "conspiracy of silence."

First, he admitted that he had read Judge Stanley Welch's decision, dated September 28, 1906, which stated that the Cameron County Grand Jury had found no evidence against any of the twelve soldiers, had not indicted any of them, and "therefore [they] are entitled to release." And yet, when he arrived at Fort Sam Houston, Garlington still found the men incarcerated there. When he questioned them about the raid, they denied participating or having any knowledge of it.

From Fort Sam Houston, he went to Fort Reno, where he encountered failure again and again as he questioned all the officers:

> I found that absolutely nothing had been discovered; that they had found no enlisted men who would admit any knowledge of the shooting or any circumstance, immediate or remote, connected with the same.

Garlington questioned the men at the post but uncovered nothing, not even a motive.

> ...[I] could discover absolutely nothing that would throw any light on the affair; and received the same denial that any feeling of animosity or spirit of revenge existed among the enlisted men of the 25th Infantry against the citizens of Brownsville on account of discrimination against them in the way of equal privileges in saloons or on account of the two acts of violence against their comrades.
>
> The uniform denial on the part of the enlisted men concerning the "barrack talk" in regard to these acts of hostility upon the part of certain citizens of Brownsville

indicated a possible [mutual] understanding among the enlisted men...but I could find no evidence of such understanding.

THE WHITE HOUSE,
WASHINGTON.

December 1, 1906.

My dear Mr. Secretary:

The President would like to have you look up any precedents (Lee's or others) for the action taken in discharging the battalion of the Twenty-fifth Infantry, and if there exist any such, send them to the President.

Very truly yours,

Secretary to the President.

Hon. William H. Taft,
    Secretary of War.

Letter from President Roosevelt's secretary to Secretary of War William Howard Taft, 12/01/1906

However, instead of saying there was no evidence, Garlington fell back on the "conspiracy of silence" theory to cover his "failure" to find real evidence. He blamed not only the soldiers but went so far as to evoke the hateful stereotype of the "secretive nature" of the Black race: *The secretive nature of the race, where crimes charged to members of their color are made, is well known. Under such circumstances, self-protection or self-interest is the only lever by which the casket of their minds can be pried open.*

Probing the Mind of a President

By this time, I had spent three days and two nights in the law library, and time was running out. I had barely scratched the surface of the materials lined up on the shelves. Starting with the Senate documents, I pulled out volume after volume, skimmed the tables of contents, and slid them back on the shelves again. There were over three thousand pages of testimony and numerous exhibits, maps, charts, affidavits, and so on. The books were thick and heavy, so I began just piling them up on the table and sat down.

After 15 minutes spent skimming the tables of contents, I soon found myself drawn hopelessly into the details of the books. I found the information, stories, testimony, and analyses so interesting and riveting that I deviated many times from my original plan. Skimming turned to scan, scanning to reading, and reading to methodical study.

I found it hard to believe that President Roosevelt would take such drastic action based only on the reports of Blocksom and Garlington. How could the president, the attorney general, and the secretary of war have scrutinized these investigations without concluding that the soldiers' guilt could not have been reached based upon the evidence thus far presented? Surely there must be more, something that so far, I had missed. Maybe President Roosevelt found more in the reports than I did.

My answer came when I read the reply of President Roosevelt to a Senate resolution dated December 6, 1906. The document concerned the discharge of the three companies offered by Senator Joseph Benson Foraker, Republican from Ohio, directing the secretary of war to send to the Senate all information in his possession on the subject.

President Roosevelt responded quickly, vigorously, and intemperately on December 19, 1906. To my immense disappointment, he had not only accepted completely and without questions the reports of Blocksom and Garlington (including copies of those reports in his reply), but to my amazement, he had not added anything new, nothing from the investigations of the Secret Service he dispatched to Brownsville and nothing from the assistant attorney generals in Texas.

Included in his reply to the Senate were memoranda citing "plenty of precedents for the action taken" to support his decision. After reading those precedents, they appeared to be powerful arguments, and I made a note to search the historical records for each precedent to determine the facts and circumstances involved. Where in the world would I find any facts on those precedents? It sounded like a master's thesis in history to me, and I was no historian.

Curiously, in an apparent contradiction, Roosevelt accepted Colonel Lovering's report, which did not support Blocksom's findings, but tended to support the innocence of the soldiers.

Even though the president said that he was "glad to avail" himself of the opportunity to answer the resolution, his whole response was one of righteous indignation. His constitutional authority was being questioned. His fairness to the soldiers and, yes, to the Colored race was being questioned. And the objectivity of General Garlington was being questioned because he was a Southerner.

Here are some of his characterizations:

> [I] lay before the Senate the following facts as to the murderous conduct of certain members of the companies in question and as to the conspiracy by which many of the other members of these companies saved the criminals from justice to the disgrace of the United States uniform.
>
> ...the evidence proves conclusively that a number of soldiers engaged in a deliberate and concerted attack as coldblooded as it was cowardly, the purpose being to terrorize the community and kill men, women, and children, in their homes, in their beds, and on the streets.

He spoke so confidently and with so much praise for Major Blocksom's investigation that I realized that something else must have been operating in Roosevelt's psyche. There must have been something deep-rooted and, in particular, race-driven, driving his thinking. It was the base notion of the dispensability of the Black soldiers. It appeared to me that this throwaway attitude operated just below his subconscious, surfacing under certain conditions of conflict (real or imagined) when it came to certain perceived God-given rights.

Roosevelt, who was such a brilliant man, a Harvard University graduate and a man who had read many books, had to know that neither Blocksom's nor Garlington's reports offered any evidence of a "conspiracy of silence." He had to know that General Garlington admitted as much. He knew the "conspiracy of silence" was, in fact, a lie. But Roosevelt embraced it. Why? My speculations will come later, but first, here is how Roosevelt praised Blocksom's report:

> ...most careful, is based upon the testimony of scores of eyewitnesses—testimony which conflicted only in

nonessentials, and which established the essential facts beyond the chance of successful contradiction.

If I could find the fallacies in Garlington's reports as well as Roosevelt's apparent complicity in embracing them (for Roosevelt was not a gullible or easily deceived man), then other objective observers must have found the holes, too. And certainly, some of the newspaper pundits must have as well. But it was not enough evidence to give me the confidence to return to JAG and confront them with what I believed they already knew. For some unknown reason, JAG continued perpetuating this myth of a "conspiracy of silence." But did not one of the soldiers shoot up the town? My objectivity required me to withhold judgment until I did more research and analyzed more evidence.

From the Law Library at the Pentagon, I called the Library of Congress and learned that there were many old newspaper articles about the Brownsville Affray. I spent all day Saturday at the Library of Congress, researching and reading old newspaper accounts about the incident. To my comfort, several newspapers arrived at much the same conclusion that I reached some 66 years later—that the reports of both Blocksom's and Garlington's investigations, and Roosevelt's curious use of them in his reply to the Senate, adduced no evidence of a "'conspiracy of silence."

Most comforting to me was the conclusion of the New York Times, November 22, 1906, which was just what I was looking for. "Their contents proved surprising. It was found that no evidence had been gathered to prove a 'conspiracy of silence' on the part of the members of the battalion. The whole proceeding, in fact, was based on the assumption of the officers who made the inquiry that those who did not take part in the riot at Brownsville 'must know' who did."

Speaking less charitably of Garlington's report, the *New York Times* characterized it as:

Lieutenant Colonel (Ret) William Baker

> "Extraordinary... Not a particle of evidence is given in the 112 pages of the document to prove that any enlisted man had certain knowledge of the identity of any participants in the riot."

I had found enough evidence that I believed would persuade JAG to drop its opposition to Hawkins's bill.

TWENTY-SEVEN

Writing the *Nonconcurrence*

"When I say get out, I mean get the hell out"

I was ready to confront JAG with a written nonconcurrence. I had found enough evidence to prove that the "conspiracy of silence" theory was unsupportable by Roosevelt back then and would certainly be intolerable for JAG to support now. I went back to my office and typed out a draft.

Just as I was leaving to discuss my draft with Colonel Williamson, the secretary called out to me. "Major Baker, you have a call from the White House. Mr. Paul Lavarkis wants to speak to you."

"Tell him to call me in five minutes at extension 53614," I replied. I walked into Colonel Williamson's outer office and asked his secretary to tell him that I needed to speak with him right away. Hearing my voice, he said, "Where have you been all of this time, Major? You've had enough time to educate yourself. Don't you think you should agree with our position now?"

"With all due respect, sir, I have to tell you that JAG's position is wrong, and it has been wrong for 67 years. There's no evidence of a "conspiracy of silence," and I think you know it. Nowhere in General Garlington's report does he say that he found conclusive evidence of a 'conspiracy of silence.' To the contrary, he said just the opposite, that there was no testimony whatsoever. You know what I think? You folks've been hiding this for years. Something like a historic cover-up."

Williamson flew into a rage. "What do you mean? What are you talking about? You get out of my office. Now!"

"Sir, I think you ought to hear me out," I cautioned. "When I say get out, I mean *get the hell out!*"

His secretary came to the door and said quietly, almost in a whisper, "Major Baker, there is a call from the White House. Mr. Larvarkis is waiting on the phone for you." I thanked the secretary and picked up the phone in the outer office. I answered a few routine questions from Larvarkis, then went back to my office, stopping along the way to make copies of my draft of nonconcurrence.

No sooner had I sat down at my desk than I received a call from Colonel Williamson's secretary. The colonel wanted to see me. I needed a little time to think, so I told her I would be there in about 15 minutes.

I began to reexamine my strategy, arguing with myself as to whether I had adopted the right game plan for winning. Where had I made my mistake in dealing with Colonel Williamson? Had I been too direct with him? Maybe I should not have said he knew that there was no conspiracy. Maybe he really did not know. But somebody in JAG had to know.

What did I know about the colonel? I knew that he was a brilliant lawyer. Sometimes he mixes his religion with the law. I needed to get into his head and determine what he was thinking, but that was impossible. But wait! He's a poker player. What did I know about poker? Not much. But I did know that it was a zero-sum game. All of this was classic Von Neumann theory. When the value +1 is assigned to one player and –1 to the other, the sum will always equal zero. One player must win, and one player must lose.

It was likely that in Williamson's mind, he considered himself in a zero-sum poker game with me and was determined not to lose, even if he had to end the game by throwing me out of his office. I had to change the paradigm to a cooperative game to engineer a win-win outcome for both of us.

Throwing me out was supposed to be a power move. Instead, it showed me his irascibility—a weakness. He had gotten rid of me before hearing what else I had to say.

I hurried back to Williamson's office and found him standing at a stand-up desk, writing out something on a yellow pad and rapidly turning the pages of General Garlington's report. Raising his head briefly to acknowledge me, he motioned to me to sit. "Be with you in a second, Baker."

The time spent waiting for him to finish what he was doing gave me a chance to reexamine my own assumption. Possibly, he did not know that Garlington had found no evidence of a conspiracy.

Williamson continued to flip back and forth through the documents he was reading. Then the rustling sound of the turning pages stopped. He sat down with an air of resignation and looked at me in disbelief: "I think I know now what you found out."

What else should I have found out? Did I miss something? I did not know what he was talking about. So, I deflected his question.

"What does it matter what I know if we proceed with the assumption that you and I are in a poker game where one of us has to lose?" I replied. "But first, I want to admit that I made a mistake in saying you knew that there was no evidence of a 'conspiracy of silence,' and I apologize to you for that. However, I am not backing away from the assumption that some of your staff lawyers knew it. Before I go further, I want to say that I want to start all over."

"Start over?"

"Yes," I said. "I've already apologized for my impertinence. I meant no disrespect. However, for whatever reasons we want to ascribe to it, we have been in a non-cooperative posture, and if we continue in that vein, it will lead to disaster for one of us and a Pyrrhic victory for the other. We should move to a cooperative mode so we can obtain the best solution for the army. If we do this, we will arrive at a cooperative solution that will put us in a win-win situation. It's the path that will lead us to an outcome, so we both will be better off, or at least neither one of us will be any worse off. We've got to cooperate."

"Baker, drop the abstract bullshit. Come to the point. I know what you are talking about. I guess I have been a little rough on you."

Having reached a truce, I addressed several delicate points. I brought up the specter of a "perceived cover-up" in JAG, a cover-up of the truth now and over many years. I brought to his attention that JAG had already sent a letter to OMB with half-truths and historical lies and had shamefully withheld evidence that would have cleared the soldiers from blame. And now JAG was about to send another letter with false information to OMB. I cautioned him that the Justice Department would unveil the cover-up and discover the truth. And if the attorney general found it, surely Congress would, if JAG persisted in its opposition to H.R. 6866.

"Have you written a nonconcurrence?"

"Yes, sir, I wrote a draft." I handed him my yellow notepad, which he started to read:

> For the reasons summarized in the following discussion, the Deputy Chief of Staff for Personnel non concurs with the Judge Advocate General's position opposing H.R. 6866, Congressman Hawkins's bill to 'rectify certain official action taken, as a result of the Brownsville Raid, 1906.'
> 1. JAG erred in stating that its opposition to Hawkins's bill was not controversial within the Department of

the Army. JAG made that statement in its transmittal memorandum, which was signed by Captain James W. Murdoch for Major General George S. Prugh, the judge advocate general. This memo was submitted to the Office of Congressional Liaison (OCL). See Exhibit "A" attached hereto. Attached to this memo was a proposed letter, written by JAG, to the Honorable F. Edward Hebert, Chairman, Committee on Armed Services, which has been further submitted to the Office of Management and Budget (OMB) for the Nixon administration's approval, which is required before it can be submitted to the Congress. JAG assumed facts relative to the so-called "conspiracy of silence" which were not found by any of the military investigators and which were not included in their reports.

2. JAG erred in assuming there would be no objection from the Nixon administration in presenting its opposition letter to the Congress when it advised Congressman Hebert that there would be no objection. As was clearly stated by OMB, the Justice Department objected to JAG's opposition report.

3. JAG's proposed letter to the Honorable George P. Shultz, Office of Management and Budget, contains factual errors with respect to the "conspiracy of silence" theory. But more egregious is the fact that JAG's staff lawyers should have known when they prepared the letter that the military investigators had found no evidence of such a theory. And, if they didn't know it when they prepared the letter, they

surely know it now, for Major Baker has presented the evidence to them. Nevertheless, JAG persists in submitting false evidence to OMB, which might eventually end up at the Congress, and if it does, the falsity of that letter will certainly be discovered, and it will be to the total embarrassment of the secretary of defense, Mr. Melvin R. Laird, and to the chief of staff of the army, General Creighton W. Abrams.
4. It is recommended that the army drop its opposition to H.R.
5. 6866.

"Don't ruin your career, son."

"Have you shown this to anybody else?"

"No, sir. And I haven't discussed it with anyone."

"Why? Why haven't you shown it to Harry if you are so sure of yourself?"

"I wanted to talk with you about it first. I want you to drop your opposition to the H.R. 6866. That's my job, to get you to change your mind."

"Baker, what makes you so sure General Kerwin will back you?"

"When I lay out the lack of evidence of a 'conspiracy of silence,' if I can show that JAG might be perpetuating a historic cover-up and that the Justice Department is bound to find out, I have confidence that Colonel Brooks and General Kerwin will back me," I said. "They might even take the issue to the chief of staff. But I don't believe General Prugh would let it go that far if he knew the truth."

"You're talking pretty high and mighty, aren't you, Baker? You think you're holding the winning hand, don't you?"

"Sir, we are back at zero-sum, where we started. We're repeating ourselves."

The Brownsville Redemption

"Son," he said. Colonel Williamson called me "son." *What the devil was he getting at now?*

He looked me straight in the eye and said, "Baker, you are naive. You're putting your career on the line, and for what? That bill hasn't got a snowball's chance in hell of getting out of committee, let alone passing in the House. If it's lucky enough to get passed in the House, it will be defeated in the Senate. And don't forget, there are powerful forces in this building that you don't want to cross.

"Don't ruin your career, son. You have a great career ahead of you. Look at where you are and where you have been. Look at all those ribbons on your chest, two bronze stars and three commendation medals. Look at your war campaign ribbons. You are on the promotion list for lieutenant colonel. You are going places. Don't throw all of this away for a bill that's doomed to fail. Tear up this nonconcurrence."

This time I didn't believe that Colonel Williamson was bluffing. He was clearly warning me there were forces in the Pentagon that could derail my career if I threatened the power of the establishment—especially if I called into question historical precedents, which the army deemed sacrosanct.

But, of all the things he said or hinted at, the most worrisome to me was his certainty that Hawkins's bill would not pass.

"Well, Baker," Williamson said. "I see you're undecided. Why don't you sleep on it and we'll talk again in the morning. It's Saturday. It'll be quiet in the building. You said you hadn't shown or talked about this thing with anyone. Is that true?"

"That's right, sir."

"Good!" He smiled as he ripped up my yellow pad notes with relish and threw the scraps in the wastepaper basket.

Lieutenant Colonel (Ret) William Baker

For a moment, I felt as if the truth had been shredded. But it would not be lost forever. The truth would always be there—waiting to be uncovered and for someone to speak it.

When I got back to my office, I found my regular staff work had piled up. Amid the paperwork, I found the letter from the Justice Department that Captain Murdoch had copied for me. I noted it was signed by the new U.S. attorney general, Richard G. Kleindienst. I knew from reading JAG's letter to the OMB that the Justice Department had opposed the army's report. But it did not say why. Probably to get Black votes in the upcoming election or to get more Blacks to take sub-cabinet posts in the Nixon administration. Nixon had had difficulty getting minorities to serve in his first administration.

I was tired and could no longer think clearly. So I packed my briefcase, went to the Pentagon parking lot, got into my car, and drove toward I-95 south.

Traffic flow down I-95 wasn't that bad for a Friday night, but for some reason, driving was difficult for me that night. I didn't feel well and had more than just a headache. I found I was driving too slowly and in the wrong lane, holding up traffic. The honking started and continued until I pulled into the extreme right lane. One motorist rolled down his window and gave me the finger. I felt a little dizzy. Cars in front of me seemed to be getting smaller and smaller and at a greater distance from me than they really were. When little stars began blinking and twinkling before my eyes, I realized that I had to pull off.

Since I was getting home unusually late for a Friday night, I thought I would stop at the supermarket and get flowers for my wife, Bettye. I chose a vase of flowers that I considered to be spectacularly beautiful and started through the checkout line. I asked the cashier, who was of Chinese descent, what she thought about the flowers. In broken English, she said something to me that I didn't quite understand.

Seeing that I wasn't catching on, she rubbed her hand delicately over the flowers, saying, "feke, feke." I still wasn't getting it.

When I got home, I handed the vase to Bettye. She said, "Oh, Bill, thanks for the beautiful silk flowers."

"Glad you like 'em. I thought they were real."

The sound of my voice upset me. But the thought that I had bought artificial flowers, thinking they were real, upset me even more. Artificial flowers? That cashier had read something in my eyes. She knew I intended to buy real flowers. She was trying to tell me the flowers were "fake."

I needed to settle my nerves. I fixed myself a bourbon and ginger, went out on the brick patio, and took a sip. It was bitter, so I spat it out. I lit a cigarette and took a draw, but it tasted nasty. I threw it down and ground it out under the heel of my shoe. *I must be firm when I meet with Williamson tomorrow, or he will crush me like I crushed that cigarette.*

When I came back into the house, Bettye looked me over. "Bill," she said, "you look awful. You're losing weight. Let's eat dinner, and then you should go to bed."

I barely touched my food. I took my wife's advice and went to bed, but I had difficulty falling asleep. I was hypersensitive to sound that night, even to the usual noises about the room—the ticking of the grandfather clock down the hall and the traffic on Old Keene Mill Road roaring like a diesel engine.

I turned over in the bed and then over again. I lay on my stomach for a while, then rolled over on my back. My heart pounded furiously. I started to wake my wife, but I knew she would call 911. I would feel foolish if I got to the emergency room and the doctors found nothing physically wrong with me except a bad case of the jitters.

What I needed was a good shot of Jack Daniel's. I got up, went to the kitchen, changed my mind—and drank a glass of water instead. It made me thirstier. So, I drank another glass of water, and another, and another. A strange uneasiness came over me.

I was afraid, but why? And of what? Certainly not of the harmless noises I was hearing. I went back to bed. Still unable to sleep, I began thinking about what Williamson had said about my career. That was one thing I was sure was not bothering me, for I had always been a risk-taker. I was confident in my skills as a technical officer, and there was a shortage of officers in my specialty. I could always go back to that—and moreover, I'd had several job offers in the corporate world. Some of my civilian friends thought that I was stupid to stay in the service when I could make more money outside. But the reason I stayed was simple: I loved the army.

No, it wasn't the perceived career threats. It was something else, real or imagined, that gave me pure hell that night. But it wasn't going to stop me from submitting that nonconcurrence. I resolved to take it to the end, wherever that might lead. I just had to get over these damn jitters. Why should I be afraid to disclose the truth to rational men? Military men were supposed to be rational. But what if these men weren't?

All of that water I drank forced me to get up and go to the bathroom, where I caught a glimpse of my face in the cabinet mirror. Looking back at me was the face of a frightened man.

Where did I go wrong? I felt uncomfortably warm. I opened the medicine cabinet, took out the thermometer, put it under my tongue, and took it out after a minute or so. My temperature was in the normal range. Knowing that brought me back to reality. Moving closer to the mirror, I looked into my eyes. Fear was still there, but it had become definable. Simply put, I was afraid of failure, afraid that even if JAG dropped its opposition to the bill, it still might fail in Congress.

That's what Williamson was trying to tell me. In fact, he was telling me he was certain it would fail. But what upset me most was the probable defeat of justice for the soldiers that was eating me up. It wasn't the possible damage to my career or the wasted time on a lost cause—but this was perhaps the last chance for those men to be exonerated, while some of them might still be alive. Blocking JAG alone should not be my goal. I needed to do something else, *but what?*

There was something I wasn't seeing. JAG knew what it was, but they were hiding it. Williamson had refused to allow me to see JAG's past opinions on the incident. I had a hunch that there was something in those documents that would show that JAG was suppressing evidence.

I began to feel better. I sat down at the kitchen table. My thoughts jumped from one thing to another. Assuming the nonconcurrence would accomplish my goal had been a mistake. Finding the missing link, a pointer to the solution—that was my problem.

I began to think more methodically. I had to be careful when trying to predict how Williamson might behave tomorrow morning when I met with him. First of all, I didn't believe he gave a damn about anything in connection with Brownsville, except protecting the honor of the JAG— and his own.

I wished I could call on God to help me and point the way. Like a sinner in his hour of distress, I needed Him to rescue me from my delirium of irrationality, but that was impossible. Earlier in my youth and throughout my life, I had sought Him through rationality and found nothing but contradictions.

I often saw people doing good and trying to do good, and some doing evil and trying to do evil, all without God's intervention. But goodness seemed to be winning out. Empirically, there seemed to be an evolution of goodness and a diminution of evil. Thus, by my calculations, goodness was a trend line moving upward.

My observations allowed me to further surmise that since goodness comes from people, goodness must be buried somewhere in people and that goodness must be God. But that God is imprisoned and must be freed. When He is released, He takes the form of goodness, and that is the only way good can happen—by the God within.

I realized that my notion—that God is passive and His goodness is released through people's actions—might not be an acceptable belief to Williamson. I had to approach him carefully if I were to persuade him to release the goodness I believed he possessed. What if he thinks it was God's will that President Roosevelt punished the soldiers and that it was his duty to uphold the decision. Thus, I hoped to convince Williamson that he should cooperate with me to rectify the injustice of Brownsville because it was the good and godly thing to do.

That was a tricky strategy, trying to get a religious man to do good by convincing him that God was within him. No, I wasn't going to try to play a religious trick on him, for I truly believed there is a God within us all.

The Letter from the Justice Department

Feeling much better now that I had determined what was wrong with me, I had enough energy to do some reading. I reached for my briefcase and took out the letter from the Justice Department. In the first paragraph, the Justice Department opposed the draft report or letter prepared by JAG. After briefly summarizing what the attorney general called the most significant facts, while also stating that the army's report misconceived the purpose of the bill, the attorney general took what I felt was a most remarkable and intriguing position. He recommended that the Department of Defense take action under existing law to set aside the dishonorable discharges of 1906. He went on to say, "If that is done, enactment of H.R. 6866 would be unnecessary." My pulse quickened. I had found the potential solution in the Justice Department's letter. Do it within the Department of the Army. Don't wait for the enactment of Hawkins's bill. That was the missing link in my own analysis—and I chastised myself for not arriving at that potential solution on my own.

The morning came. With the sunrise came rays of light through our small kitchen window, which spread across the papers on the kitchen table. With those rays came a new spark of hope. Even though I hadn't gotten much sleep, I felt invigorated. I just knew it was going to be a beautiful day.

My thoughts were filled with possibilities that the Justice Department's letter invoked in me—the possibility of reversing President Roosevelt's decision by revoking Special Order 266 and doing it "inhouse." That would, in effect, exonerate the soldiers, activate the search for old soldier survivors, allow the actual granting of honorable discharge certificates, and finally grant compensation. The clever strategy sought to achieve administratively what probably could not be attained through the Congress. What impressed me most was that Richard G. Kleindienst, the acting attorney general himself, he signed it and not left it to an assistant attorney general or a low-level staff lawyer.

I suspected JAG had not mentioned the Department of Justice's position in its reply, so I reread JAG's letter to George Shultz at the OMB to find out if JAG had mentioned the Justice's "do it from within'" strategy. They had not. They simply ignored the suggestion "to direct them to rectify certain official action taken as the result of the 'Brownsville Raid,' 1906." Now, why hadn't JAG mentioned the Department of Justice's position? Was it being hidden from the rest of the army general staff? If the rest of the staff knew of Justice's position, they might agree with Justice and ask, "Why not do it within?" Armed with this new information, I was ready to see Colonel Williamson again.

When we met in his office on Saturday morning, Williamson's face was pale and he looked bedraggled. The old gusto had disappeared overnight. And he did something unusual after I sat down at his conference table—he reached across the table and gave me the feeble, congratulatory handshake of a coach whose team had just lost the game. "Well, Major, it's your nickel. You go first. Did you think about your career last night?"

I wanted to tell him, "No, sir, but I did think about yours," but controlled the urge to use sarcasm. I waited a few seconds before speaking. I speculated that he was now ready for the cooperative strategy that I tried to talk him into the day before. I began speaking again about the expected benefits of cooperation with both sides winning and nobody losing.

"To be honest, sir, I was miserable last night, didn't sleep much at all. But after reading the letter from Justice this morning, I felt better. I'm firmly convinced that the only honorable and God-sanctioned thing for us to do is to cooperate and expose to the world the lack of evidence in this case. I am ready for that goodness to be freed. And I believe there is goodness in you that needs to be freed—and only you can do that. The God within you demands it! He demands the truth as you and I both know it. We must speak together, and as officers, we have a duty to speak the truth. Our honor expects it, demands it, and will never let us rest without speaking it."

Each time I mentioned the word "God," he trembled, and the word "honor" seemed to lift him up. When I finished, he said, "All right, Baker, let's make a deal. You drop the nonconcurrence, and I will see that JAG drops the opposition to the bill. But—you are never to mention the fact that there was no evidence of a "conspiracy of silence" as long as you and I are on active duty. Is it a deal?"

"No, not yet, sir. Will JAG write a legal brief for the secretary of the army to exonerate the soldiers? That's what Justice recommended."

"Baker, I don't have the authority to promise that, and I would be kidding you if I did. You must be aware that there are powerful forces in this building—and not all of them are in JAG—who will oppose reversing Roosevelt's decision without proving some of the men didn't shoot up that town. Well, I can tell you, JAG won't tackle it. The proof is too conclusive that some of the soldiers did it. We just don't know which ones. Of necessity, the brief would have to be conclusive before Secretary of the Army Froehlke would even consider reversing Roosevelt's decision.

"Justice's letter recommended that we do it from within, but they didn't volunteer to prepare the brief. They skirted around it. They don't want the Nixon administration to be on record opposing it, and they also want to avoid a nasty fight in Congress. I haven't changed my mind about Hawkins's bill. It's worthless without additional facts—and it has provided none."

"If JAG refuses to write the brief, then who will?" I asked. "Only JAG is staffed with lawyers."

"That's not exactly true. There are civilian lawyers in the secretary of the army's office and the secretary of defense, but they passed the buck down to the army. Now, how about that? Your only possible solution, as I see it, is to talk to General Kerwin into hiring outside lawyers to do it, and I can tell you right now, General Prugh would oppose that."

From that day to this, I don't know how I managed to say it, but I blurted out, "Then dammit, I will. But I need reassurance from you, Colonel Williamson, that the JAG will not oppose me. I need that before I can agree to a deal. You are asking a lot of me to keep silent about what I have already found out."

"I can promise you that and more. If you're lucky enough to find the proof that none of the soldiers shot up that town, you bring it to me first and I will take it from there. Don't worry about the other lawyers in JAG. You just satisfy me, and I'll do the rest. For starters, you will meet with me early Monday morning."

Then he did a surprising thing. He took the opposition memorandum and with affected pomposity proclaimed, "With this pen, I officially drop JAG's opposition to H.R. 6866." He drew a diagonal blue line through the original copy and handed it to me with these words, "This is yours to keep. By God, you earned it!"

"It's a deal," I said. And from that day forward, I kept that original memorandum.

Captain Murdoch officially drops JAG's opposition to H.R. 6866.

Lieutenant Colonel (Ret) William Baker

TWENTY-EIGHT

Jag Sets *the Legal Parameters*

The Meeting with JAG

It was very early Monday morning, June 5, 1972, when I met with Colonel Wade Williamson, Lieutenant Colonel Davis, and Captain Murdoch in Williamson's office around his conference table. Their faces were grim and distrustful.

Williamson opened the meeting by saying he understood that I was taking over the army's response to the proposed enactment of H.R. 6866 and that our office would be responsible for preparing a case for the secretary of the army to retract the action taken by President Roosevelt. He stated emphatically that JAG would not prepare the case but would have final review of any case we prepared. He got up, strode to a standing flip-top chart, turned over the first page—which was blank—and uncovered the next. On that page, he had written several premises on which, he said, any decision to reverse Special Order 266 had to be based.

1. The decision was erroneous as a matter of law.
2. The decision was erroneous as it was based on the concept of mass punishment rather than individual guilt.
3. The decision constituted an injustice as it was predicated upon racial discriminatory grounds.

After pausing briefly, Williamson turned from the chart and asked me if I understood what was going to be required of me from a legal point of view to support any one of the premises. From the tone of his voice and with his emphasis upon the words "law" and "legal," I suspected he intended to wrap me up in a tidy trap, where everything would appear neat and legitimate. But I never had much faith in the law for correcting injustices. I preferred relying upon what was "morally right" rather than what was legal. I knew there was a fundamental and profound difference. What is morally right is not always legal, and what is legal is not always morally right.

"No, sir, I don't know what you want in legal terms. Just tell me in simple terms what you want."

To get the concepts straight in my head and to keep them that way, I asked him if he would simplify the premises. I also wanted to know why we couldn't just call the premises "assumptions."

"You can call them whatever you want to call them," he said, "but I will try to simplify them as much as I can."

Shaking his head, he turned back to the chart, pointed to assumption No. 1, and simplified by flatly rejecting it. He said that Roosevelt's decision was, in fact, legal. It was based on ample precedents, and that at that time in history, both the president and the JAG found ample precedents for doing what they did. Then, closing the door to me to use that assumption, he said that over the years, JAG had reaffirmed the legality of the decision, and even today, they had no basis for reaching a contrary result. I interpreted his comments to mean that if I went out and tried to prove that the decision was illegal and brought it back to them, JAG would turn me down.

Maybe they had ample precedents, and maybe they didn't, but what if they didn't? Does an unjust precedent in the past doom one to suffer an injustice in the future? And if so, is that right? Moreover, it was characteristic of Roosevelt to assert something was right, simply because he, the president, said it. I jotted down on my notepad, "Check precedents."

Then he moved to No. 2. The action taken constituted an injustice, as it was based upon the concept of mass punishment rather than individual guilt. After a moment's hesitation, Williamson stated that JAG was not going to express a definitive opinion on the concept of mass punishment versus individual guilt. Or put another away (at least the way I perceived it), he was not going to repudiate the barbaric medieval logic procedure that if the authorities couldn't find the hand that stole the bread, they would chop off 100 hands, knowing the guilty hand would be among them. No, he was not going to renounce mass punishment!

I wondered how he could avoid discussing two of the most sacred pillars of our law—the presumption of innocence until proven guilty and the concept of due process. By not expressing an opinion, JAG refused to acknowledge that 1) the soldiers had not received a trial; 2) there had been a lack of due process; and 3) the soldiers were punished en masse.

Colonel Williamson must have realized the implication of what he had just said about JAG's refusal to issue a definitive opinion on mass punishment, for he quickly qualified that statement. "Of course, we all know that it is unlikely that a similar action of mass punishment would be taken today."

Whew! I was relieved to hear him disavow the concept of mass punishment in the present day, even though he was not going to say anything about the past. But he went on to warn me to be careful if I chose to use that assumption. "Great caution should be applied in giving retroactive effect to every change in the concept of due process."

I didn't have to read his mind to conclude what he meant, for he told me that President Roosevelt had cited a series of cases in which similar, if not identical, action was taken.

I made a mental note to determine if there had been a charge or evidence of a "conspiracy of silence" in the other cases Roosevelt cited.

Taking his pointer, Williamson jabbed the third assumption several times, almost punching a hole in the paper chart. Obviously, he was about to say something extraordinarily important about it. "If you choose to make a case that the action taken by President Roosevelt constituted an injustice as it was predicated upon racially discriminatory grounds, you better be prepared to support such a conclusion by specific findings of fact. And I warn you, the basic problem with racially discriminatory findings by you, by their very nature, impugns the integrity of President Roosevelt and his specific disclaimer of racial prejudice made in his message to Congress."

For a moment, I thought about Williamson's warning. I took it to heart, for I knew exactly what he meant. Racial discrimination was the last thing the U.S. Army ever wanted to be accused of, even in the past. Certainly, the army didn't want to be accused of continuing to support that past discrimination, and perhaps white America felt the same way.

After what seemed to me an endless silence, he looked hard at me as if to give his message time to sink into my head.

Four Courses of Action

Williamson furrowed his brow as he turned to the second page on his briefing chart. "As I see it, you have four courses of action, and all of them are difficult."

- A. Action by the adjutant general, independent of the secretary of the army
- B. Action by the Army Discharge Review Board
- C. Action by the Army Board for Correction of Military Records

D. Action of the secretary of the army, independent of the Army Board for Correction of Military Records

I scrambled to write the courses of action down on my yellow notepad. Of the four options, I was leaning toward action D—preparing a case strictly for the secretary of the army.

Our strategy would be:

1. Summarize the existing facts.
2. Search for hard evidence to prove that the soldiers didn't do it.
3. Rely heavily on the fact that no indictments were returned by the Cameron County Grand Jury, which was the only true forum of the judicial system faced by some of the soldiers.
4. Petition the secretary of the army to rectify the injustice, independent of the Army Board for Correction of Military Records, based upon manifest error of the past.

I wanted to hurry things along, as I didn't have much time. Before he could continue, I broke into his presentation. "Colonel Williamson, would you kindly simplify those alternatives that you are calling courses of action? Tell me which ones you consider feasible under your rules."

"I will not. It's important that you hear and understand the full implication of these courses of action. You should know what you're getting yourself into."

Then he picked up four notecards lying on the table in front of him, on which the four alternative and detailed explanations had been typed. He started to read and talk from the cards. "You might think it would be easy for the adjutant general, independent of any findings by the secretary of the army, to just issue an order rescinding Special Order 266. That's Course of Action A. It's not that simple and doesn't work that way, although JAG has previously expressed the opinion that the adjutant general has the authority to change records administratively to reflect the true facts."

He read the opinion numbers and the dates, "JAGA/1963/4143, 27 May 1963; JAGA 1960/3508, 12 Feb 1960."

"Sir, may I have copies of those opinions?"

"You may not," he said and continued to go through the advantages and the disadvantages of each course of action.

As he droned on and on, explaining everything in the minutest detail—disadvantage this, disadvantage that, you can't do this, you can't do that—I struggled to stay awake. The words on his chart began to blur. My head must have been bobbing because I heard him say, "Stay awake, Major!"

"I'm sorry, sir."

I sat up straight, wished I had a cup of coffee, and scrawled Xs over the first three options. They were completely out of the realm of possibility.

Williamson's voice lost the edge that characterized the beginning of his presentation. He eyed the fourth option on my pad and said, "Well, I see you didn't scratch that one out. I'm glad you didn't because that one may be your only hope. You probably thought that the other courses of action were out of reach—but the last one is perhaps the riskiest because it involves going directly to Secretary of the Army Froehlke without any intermediary. That places a political burden squarely upon his shoulders, without allowing him any wiggle room if anything goes politically wrong. I can tell you now that he may not like that, and he may wonder why you are coming directly to him. If he gives you a quick denial, the action is finished, dead. No appeal above him. He will simply write 'Denied,' and that'll be it."

There was another reason I wanted to go directly to Secretary Froehlke to present the soldiers' case. I wanted to stand before one person—and one person only—someone who had the power to make a decision and to whom I could passionately present an objective argument. A board of officers might be afraid to set a precedent. I believed that a complex case such as this one didn't stand much chance of success by being presented dispassionately in the present. Dry, dead facts about dead people—entombed in the bones of history—were not the stuff of inspiration.

"This ball is now in your court," he said. The meeting was over.

I went back to my office, facing a difficult task that required building a case upon facts so powerful, so clear, and so compelling that Secretary Froehlke would be convinced that justice demanded the reversal of Roosevelt's decision. I had to do it quickly, and I had to make sure it was politically acceptable to a conservative administration.

I have always followed the "Rule of Parsimony" or "Occam's Razor." To paraphrase the 14th-century philosopher William of Ockham (or Occam): "All things being equal, the simplest explanation tends to be the right one."

TWENTY-NINE

Disproving a *Negative*

Back to Square One

I left Williamson's office, went directly to the Law Library, and started my research all over again. Disproving a negative was going to be extremely difficult, if not impossible. I needed a new game plan and had to steel my resolve for the fight ahead. The first step was to establish a conceptual framework based upon logic, existing philosophy, or law. Hopes and dreams for success had no place here.

When I got to the library, it was virtually empty, except for the librarian. I sat at the reference table but didn't take a single book from the shelf. I needed to think.

I began weighing the elements of proof and the difficulty in disproving a negative. At the very heart of the theory is the claim of the existence or nonexistence of something and the fallacy of inferring general rules from limited, specific, empirical observations. This was shown to be unsound by David Hume, the 18th-century Scottish philosopher. It was misleading and inherently circular. I had learned in my philosophy classes at Howard University that this specious claim was a misuse of inductive reasoning.

Thus, knowing the inherent difficulty in disproving a negative, I could understand the problems faced by the Black soldiers, which I also would face unless I changed the philosophical paradigm associated with the historical presumption of innocence. JAG and Roosevelt had ignored the tenet that a person is to be presumed innocent until proven otherwise in a court of law. The courtroom is where the burden of proof lies, even the nonexistence of something.

First, I solidified in my mind my assumption that if I claim the existence of something, or if I make a claim about anything, then I must prove it. And the only logical way for me to prove it is to produce it, or produce evidence of it, and present it to the person to whom I am making the claim. Now the person to whom I am making the claim has no responsibility to prove that my claim is false. The burden of proof is on me. So, if the other person says, "I don't know, I have no knowledge of it, and you have not proven it to me," then there is no requirement for that person to disprove my claim.

Following that logic, I considered the fact that each soldier was put in a position of disproving that he participated in shooting up the town. Each one denied any knowledge of it, and, as Senator Foraker pointed out on the Senate floor, how else could he prove it except by denying it? Also, I considered the fact that each soldier was required to disprove that he knew who participated in the raid, even if he hadn't participated himself. The soldiers were punished for being unable to disprove that they didn't know, or put another way, they were punished for not knowing.

I imagined an argument between Hume and Major Blocksom. Blocksom claimed that all the catfish in the Rio Grande River were brown and that he knew it because so many of the townspeople in Brownsville had told him so. Thus, he knew it to be the truth. I envisioned further that Blocksom took Hume to the river, where he pointed out several brown catfish swimming in the Rio Grande. "See," says Blocksom, "I told you."

Hume would then blow apart this fallible generalization. He would probably say, "Not on your life can you infer that all the catfish are brown in the Rio Grande from those limited observations. You would have to drain the whole river to prove that and look for catfish everywhere in the river to prove it."

Then, I imagined that Major Blocksom demanded that the Black soldiers prove there were no black catfish in the Rio Grande River (that is, disprove a negative). To put it another way, he demanded that they prove they didn't shoot up Brownsville.

Suppose they tried to do just that by draining the river but returned and told Major Blocksom that they were unable to find any black catfish, and Blocksom said that is not good enough. He might further assert that because they didn't find any didn't mean none existed in the river. Perhaps they had not searched everywhere in the river. Some may have been embedded deep in the mud. He would accuse them of getting together and intending not to find any black catfish, engaging in a conspiracy, a situation not unlike the actual one they faced. I concluded that those charges would be impossible to refute by disproving the negatives.

One would have to conclude, as I did, that the burden of proof would be illogically and illegally shifted away from Major Blocksom. After all, in his argument, he made the claim of the existence of something, that all catfish in the river were brown. He should have to prove it—not the soldiers. The burden of proof was unfairly placed upon the backs of the soldiers—the persons not stating the claim. It seemed to me that the soldiers' burden of proof would be so great that no amount of evidence would be enough to prove anything and, in fact, would suggest that the outcome was rigged.

Under the adverse requirement of proving nonexistence (a negative), the reasonable thing to do was to assume nonexistence, and keep searching, which is the position of the great philosophers, the great jurists, and the law of civilized people. In this position, the burden shifts from requiring those accused of crimes to prove a negative over to requiring a presumption of innocence until proven guilty. The successful shifting of that burden must be my predominant strategy for success.

THIRTY

The Leckie and Wiegenstein *Experiments*

A Walk Back in Time

Days passed. I went in and out of the law library and back again to the Library of Congress. I sandwiched my research on Brownsville between my regular office work, other projects, and my project with the White House staff.

By the time I got to the Court of Inquiry investigation volumes, my brain was addled. These heavy red tomes featured more than 13,000 pages of testimony and exhibits. However, I wasn't so addled that I couldn't detect that the report was biased against the soldiers. That is when I determined that I had to go to the National Archives and study the primary documents, the old depositions, affidavits, telegrams, speeches, and court-martial records of the white officers.

As I walked up the steps of the National Archives, I had the strange feeling that I was walking back through time into history. If the truth were ever to be found, I would certainly find it in this neoclassical, Greco-Roman style temple with its colossal Corinthian columns, where the nation stores and maintains its most treasured historical records. Once in the building and at the reference desk, I requested the Brownsville file. After a two-hour wait, an attendant rolled in a cart carrying several small, dusty green file boxes.

Now I had the actual documents in my hands. These files were the ones that President Roosevelt and all the prior investigators had touched and worked with. These were the very texts upon which they made their decisions.

While skimming through the documents, I found a letterhead that said "The White House." It was addressed to the War Department and signed by the president. Roosevelt wanted the adjutant general to go over the testimony of Lieutenant Harry G. Leckie, claiming that Leckie had testified falsely before the Senate committee. First, Leckie was sent to Brownsville to investigate on behalf of the defense at the court-martial of Major Penrose. And second, Leckie gave several hundred rounds of government ammunition to an outsider. Roosevelt ended the letter, "Please report to me on all of his evidence."

Why did Roosevelt ask the personnel staff officer, the AG, rather than the JAG in our own legal department? Was Roosevelt's vindictive side beginning to show? His writings clearly reveal Roosevelt's animus toward Sanders, Leckie, and Penrose.

Roosevelt's letter to the War Department said the following:

> Sergeant Mingo Sanders, in spite of his reputation for personal courage, was as thoroly [sic] dangerous, unprincipled, and unworthy a soldier as ever wore the United States uniform and that, under no conceivable circumstances, should he ever be allowed in the army.

On the last day, when the three companies of the 25th Infantry were drummed out, Penrose watched in uncontrollable grief, saying, "There goes the best battalion in the army." Roosevelt read about the statement in the *Evening Star* newspaper and was livid. He demanded a full and immediate explanation for Penrose's reasons for making such a statement. Ultimately, Penrose ate his own words and denied both his laudatory comments about the Black troops and his interview with the newspaper.

The Brownsville Redemption

Roosevelt's letter led me to Lieutenant Leckie's testimony before the Senate Military Affairs Committee and the file on the court-martial of Major Penrose. I came to the part of the Senate hearings that I imagined must have made Roosevelt's blood boil. Leckie debunked Major Blocksom's theory that the bullets were fired from Company B barracks or from any other location within Fort Brown. In fact, Leckie showed that the bullets couldn't possibly have been fired from Company B's barracks.

The question Senator Foraker put to Leckie was, "Could the bullets that entered Yturria's house have been fired from Company B?"

Leckie was sure they couldn't:

> The reason that I say that they were not fired from B barracks is that they would have to turn an angle of 90 degrees in the air without having anything to deflect them in any way. And I do not know of any laws of motion for a bullet doing that.

Next, I turned to the court-martial record of Major Penrose. To my delight, there I found the rest of the story that caused Roosevelt angst and precipitated that War Department letter about Leckie. It, too, was based on Leckie's test results.

According to the record, General McCaskey sent Leckie to Brownsville to trace the shots that hit the various houses and to see what parts of the barracks could be seen from the Leahy Hotel second-story windows. Leckie was also to inspect the Ruby Saloon. What he found was revealing.

Leckie's investigation proved that, based on where the bullets struck the Cowen's house, all the shots had to have been fired from the rear. There were no bullet holes in the front of Cowen's house.

Lieutenant Colonel (Ret) William Baker

> **THE WHITE HOUSE**
> **WASHINGTON**
>
> Oyster Bay, N.Y.,
> June 20, 1907.
>
> To the War Department:
>
> I should like to have the Adjutant General go carefully over the testimony of Lieutenant Harry G. Leckie, of the United States Army, before the Senate Committee, in which it certainly looks as if Leckie had testified falsely. As, for instance, in stating that he went down to investigate simply as an impartial outsider, when it appears that he was sent there to investigate on behalf of the defense; and furthermore, it would appear from the testimony on page 3045 that this same Lieutenant Leckie was responsible for giving some hundreds of rounds of Government cartridges to an outsider. Please report to me on all his evidence,
>
> Theodore Roosevelt
>
> Enclosures

Letter from President Roosevelt to the War Department, 06/20/1907

The results of the tests at the Leahy Hotel highlighted several physical impossibilities. One could not observe Company C's barracks from the first window upstairs (the window toward the alley) in Herbert Elkins's room. Elkins told the Senate Committee that he saw flashes of gunfire from Company C's barracks. That view was obstructed by houses. Only about 10 feet (3 meters) of the upper end of Company B's barracks could be seen.

Katie Leahy swore to the Senate Committee that from her position in the upper window, she saw men shooting from both the lower and upper porches (galleries). Leckie found the view of the lower porch completely blocked by an orange tree. And only half of the upper porch could be seen from that window.

The Flash of a Rifle

Next, I turned to the Wiegenstein experiments. Lieutenant Henry Wiegenstein was admitted as an expert witness for the defense at Major Penrose's court-martial in March 1907.

On a bright, moonlit night on February 19, 1907, between nine and ten o'clock, Wiegenstein set up experiments to determine the accuracy of vision at night. One of his experiments simulated the conditions of an alley in a flat dry-bed gully, commonly known as an arroyo. He wanted to determine, according to his testimony, what could be seen by looking into the flash of a rifle from above, behind, or in front. He set up lanterns at two locations and posted military officers at the two locations to act as observers. As he moved a firing party, consisting of three civilians and eight soldiers, into positions, an observer shouted, "Lieutenant Wiegenstein, which way are the men facing?"

"I don't care to tell you; that's part of the test," Wiegenstein shouted back. Nor did Wiegenstein tell the observers their race or color. The men fired two volleys, then fired at will. Wiegenstein moved them up and down the simulated alley, firing at two different locations—point A and point B. The horizontal distance from the firing party to the nearest observer was about 9 feet (2.75 meters). The vertical distance was uniform at about 21 feet (6.4 meters). When the firing was completed, and the observers questioned, they said that they couldn't recognize any complexion by the light of the flash, that they couldn't see anything, not even the rifles.

Not satisfied, Wiegenstein took special pains to see if he himself could discern features or complexion. He stationed himself directly in the center of the firing party. He fixed his attention on the faces of the men immediately in front of him, not more than a one-step distance. He wanted to see if, at the instant of discharge, the flash of the guns would enable him to distinguish features or complexion. He couldn't, no matter how hard he fixed his attention on the faces as they stood before him, nor could he see the guns. The flash was instantaneous, and his eyes involuntarily followed the flash.

After the firing was completed, he marched the firing party along a path out of the gully to the road where the observers stationed themselves. Then he marched the firing party single file 9 feet (2.75 meters) from the observers. Wiegenstein said that the officers peered into the faces of the men separately as they went by. One of the observers remarked, "I would like to see white men marched by. I want to see if I can detect their features or complexion."

Wiegenstein testified he informed all of the observers that there were white men in the firing party as well as Black men and "also a Mexican."

After midnight, Wiegenstein conducted a second test. This time, unknown to the observers, he switched the firing party and used only Black soldiers. The main idea, as he testified, was to note if the effect of darkness, without moonlight, would cause the flash to be more pronounced and would enable the observers to distinguish the firing party complexion, which they had failed to do earlier on that same night while the moon was still shining. He repeated the same tests after the moon went down on a starlit night with no clouds. The results were the same. The observers couldn't tell whether members of the firing squad were Black, Mexican, or white.

On March 11, Wiegenstein conducted yet another test under starlit conditions. He selected seven soldiers. This time he included a sergeant and himself among the group. Again, he didn't tell the observers the color or race of the firing party, nor did he tell them that he himself would be a member of the group. He dressed himself identically to the men. But Wiegenstein put a white collar around the sergeant's neck, gave him his blouse and cap, switched the sergeant to his position, and had him give the commands for firing.

From that point, the firing party repeated the same tests as those done in February and got the same results. But before the firing was terminated and when the shotgun was fired, which created more light than before, Wiegenstein heard an observer say, "There's Wiegenstein, but you wouldn't know him if he didn't have on a cap." However, the man wearing the cap was the Black sergeant.

When the firing was finished, the sergeant marched the firing party out of the gully onto the road, where the observers posted themselves to determine if they could identify individuals by peering into their faces. They could not, as before.

But Wiegenstein added a new dimension to the test this time. Part of the experiment was conducted from a second-story window overlooking the street, and part was from the edge of a porch on the ground floor. He arranged for the observers to place themselves in the second story of a building and to look out a window into a side yard. Then he instructed one of the soldiers in the firing party to go into the side yard and act as if he were bent on making trouble. Then he was to run around to the front and join the firing party as they went into the street parallel to the front of the building and marched between the building and the streetlamp. At about the same time, the observers came to a front window and looked into the street as the firing party went by. Wiegenstein had previously measured the distance from the upper story to the street. It was about 45 feet (14 meters).

Turning around, the firing party marched back down the street between the same streetlamp and the building. This time the observers sat on the front porch while the soldiers marched onto the sidewalk within 10 to 12 feet (3 to 3.6 meters) from the observers. Again, the observers reported that they were unable to detect whether the firing party was Black, white, or Mexican, or the color of their clothing.

I now had something to take back to Wade Williamson that would contradict the testimony of the "eyewitnesses" and Major Blocksom's theory of where the shots were fired from.

THIRTY-ONE

The Eyewitnesses *to the Shooting*

What the Eyewitnesses Saw

Since Roosevelt cited what he termed "scores of eyewitnesses to the shooting," it was natural for me to reexamine the testimony of those witnesses. To get control of the testimony, I set up a credibility chart to help me move quickly through the numerous statements. I wanted to determine
1. if what the witnesses said made any sense
2. if they were under oath or not
3. if what they saw was actually possible based on their locations
4. what they said they saw
5. the darkness of the night, and so on…

I also wanted to know what evidence, if any, existed in the records to support, contradict, or refute their testimonies.

First of all, Roosevelt's count was incorrect. There weren't scores of eyewitnesses who were in any position to see what they claimed to have seen. By my count, there were only eight out of a total of 21 witnesses who, by their own statements, said they saw Black soldiers. My examination of their statements revealed that they weren't statements of facts at all. They were opinions, inferences, and guesses. They were not creditable—not worthy of belief by anybody—and certainly not able to meet the standard of probable cause in a legal case. But I couldn't just take my opinion back to Wade Williamson. I had to find something substantial to contradict the eyewitness accounts.

That it was a dark night was indisputable. All prior investigators agreed. Even witnesses who said they saw the soldiers shooting up the town admitted that it was a dark night. It had been raining, and it was heavily overcast.

First, applying the Wiegenstein test standards to the powers of observation of the 14 eyewitnesses cited by President Roosevelt in his second message to the Senate discredited all of their accounts. Their statements to the various investigators could be dismissed out of hand as unbelievable.

But, because Roosevelt believed them and insisted "…that there is no possibility they were mistaken," I went back and reread the key eyewitnesses' testimony given in a court of law—the court-martial of Major Penrose. Mr. George Rendall was a star witness cited by the president, so I started with his testimony.

While reading the transcript of his testimony, I imagined myself sitting in the courtroom, listening and making notes as a member of the jury, as I had done many times during my career as a military officer.

Rendall, a witness for the prosecution, was first to take the stand. Having already given his testimony to the Citizens' Committee and Major Blocksom, Mr. Purdy, the prosecutor, now considered Rendall one of his best witnesses. He was a mechanical engineer who lived with his wife on the second floor of the Western Union Telegraph building at the corner of Elizabeth and 15th Streets. The building was next door to Fort Brown and about 60 feet (18 meters) from the wall separating the town from the fort.

He testified that he was awakened by two pistol shots. He grabbed his glasses from the nightstand, went to the window, and looked out. He swore he saw "Colored soldiers" mount and jump over the wall into the street. He said he heard a voice saying, "Here we go." Furthermore, he claimed that he had heard that same voice before—it was the Black soldier who came to his house seeking a room to rent for his wife and son who were to join him in a week or so in Brownsville.

Under cross-examination, the defense counsel for Major Penrose asked, "How old are you, Mr. Rendall?"

"I'm 72 years of age."

"How long have you been wearing glasses?"

"I've been wearing glasses since 1866."

"You have lost vision in one eye, I believe, have you not? When did you lose that, Mr. Rendall?"

"I lost that in 1866."

The defense counsel asked Rendall a series of questions about whom he had discussed the case with and how many times. He said he had talked about it many times, over a hundred—but could not remember any specific person.

Defense continued with the cross-examination. "Could you see uniforms?"

"No, sir. I could not."

"Will you tell the court how you knew those were soldiers?"

"By their uniforms," Rendall said.

"And yet you say you couldn't see uniforms?"

"Those that I saw pass here." He pointed to the map. "I saw the uniforms and saw they were Negro soldiers."

"Did you see them jump over the wall at all?"

"I just saw the shapes and saw the men."

"Did you at any time during that night see any of those men that jumped over the wall close enough to see their uniforms or their guns?"

"No, sir, I didn't."

"Now, then, you got out of the bed and grabbed your glasses. Where did you go?"

"To the front window."

"And you saw some men. Which way did they go, and how many?"

"Up this way," Rendall said, pointing to the map. "Five or six."

"Did they have guns?"

"Yes, sir."

"Sure about that?" Defense asked.

Rendall hesitated, then said, "I wouldn't swear they had their guns."

"Do you know whether they were shooting a pistol or a gun?"

"No, sir. I wouldn't hesitate to say they were shooting pistols. I saw the flashes were near their faces, and the two I saw were Colored men."

"How could you tell that?"

"Because the flash of it showed their faces for a second. They might have been white men blacked, I don't know about that, but they were not white men."

"How far were those shots from you?"

"60 to 75 feet [18 to 23 meters]."

"Did you tell the Citizens Committee about that shot that went through your house?"

"I suppose so."

"Did you or did you not?"

"I don't know what I told them. I told them what I thought at the time. I was misled in the first place of the cause of it, and now I have doubts about the whole thing. As far as I am concerned, the troops offered nothing but friendship—and no one had any cause for anything."

"We want your best recollection, so this court can make up its own mind about the facts," said the defense counsel.

"Well, the facts, as far as I am individually concerned, is hardly facts. What I saw and what I heard I know pretty well, but a man with all his faculties, a young man in the prime of his life, might form a little different opinion."

Seeing, but Not Seeing

As I read or, better put, listened to the testimony and the grilling of the old man, I couldn't help but feel sorry for him. He said he had been misled in the first place about the whole thing, but by whom and for what reason? The cross-examination continued.

The defense counsel read back the part of Rendall's testimony where he stated he recognized the voice of the man who gave the command "Here we go" when the soldiers jumped over the wall. "Did you hear that evidence just read?"

"Yes, sir."

"Do you want this court to understand that the voice you heard giving commands that night was the same voice you'd heard the day before?"

"No, sir. I don't know positively if a man in that garrison ever went over the wall. What I saw at that distance was hard to tell."

"So, you don't swear that the man who gave a command that night was the same man you had been talking to the day before?"

"No, sir. I don't swear he was or he wasn't. It was my impression he was."

The defense then stood and pointed to three men standing in the back of the courtroom. "Stand up and look at the gentlemen in the back of the house. How many men do you see back there by the stove?"

"I see one man—two men."

"Is that all you can see back there?"

"Now I see five," Rendall said.

The defense counsel asked Rendall if he could see color. He said he could. But when asked to describe the men in the back, he could not discern much about the color of their clothing or shoes.

Defense then asked Rendall if the man on the left was a white man or a Black man.

"I judge he is a white man. He may have Colored blood in him. I don't know."

"What color is the man on the extreme right—your right?"

"He is a fair looking white man."

"You are sure about that."

"No, I'm not sure of that."

"How many men are there? Look carefully and tell us. Look carefully."

"I can see five. There may be one hiding behind the stove." Finally, Defense asked Rendall the condition of the weather that night.

"The condition was rather dark, starlight night," Rendall said.

The next person called to the stand was Mrs. Rendall, George Rendall's wife. I noted from her testimony that she had looked out the same window at the same time as her husband. She was some ten years younger than George, and both of her eyes were good. Yet she swore she couldn't tell the color or complexion of any of the men—in contrast to George, who claimed he had seen their color. However, he couldn't pick out colors in the courtroom even at a much shorter distance.

I dismissed the testimony of Teofilo Martinez, the caretaker in the Yturria house, because upon hearing the first shots, he quickly flattened himself face down on the floor and, by his own admission, stayed there all night. It was impossible for him to see anything.

Katie Leahy, the prized witness of the investigators, was the next witness to take the stand. No one could have been more anxious to see how Katie Leahy's testimony would stand up in a court of law than I was. Her testimony first came to my attention in Blocksom's report. Then an article in the *Washington Post* (June 7, 1907) I'd seen at the Library of Congress drew my attention to her again. The Post reported that she had testified before the Senate Committee on Military Affairs.

She said she recognized one of the soldiers as a "yellow nigger with spots," and she wished she had fought it out with them. That statement sounded preposterous. It sent me looking for her testimony before the Senate Committee on Military Affairs.

I found her testimony perfectly consistent throughout. She was positive about what she saw and very specific. She noted everything. She was in her nightgown when she heard the first shot, fired precisely at 11:55 p.m. because she looked at her clock. She could see the colors of the raiders' clothes and faces by the flashes of light from the gunfire. They wore khaki uniforms and some wore blue shirts. Their faces were black. They were Negroes. She could see the blue steel of the rifles and count the flashes of the guns.

How could the prior investigators believe she could recognize a freckle-faced person, the blue steel of the rifles, and all the rest that she claimed she saw from a distance on such a dark night? Especially, how she could see soldiers walking around and shooting from the lower porch of Company B, when the view was totally obstructed by an orange tree?

President Roosevelt had believed her testimony and relied on it. So had prior investigators, all except for Senator Foraker. He certainly didn't believe her, especially after she told him, "I saw through the leaves."

Once she was in a court of law, however, she was subject to cross examination. As I read the defense counsel's examination, I wished I could have been there to hear it. I didn't believe Katie Leahy's story.

Neither did the court or the defense counsel. Defense characterized Katie Leahy as an "overcharged bottle of seltzer." All you had to do was to push the right lever and let her gush. Her testimony thoroughly discredited her before the court.

The only testimony more absurd than Katie Leahy's was given by Herbert Elkins, Leahy's hotel clerk. Under direct examination, he testified that he was in his room on the second floor at about five minutes to 12 when he heard some shooting—about 15 shots just inside the wall or outside the wall. He went to the window and saw "two nigger soldiers" coming up the alley. He assumed they were the leaders. About 75 to 100 feet (23 to 30 meters) behind them, he saw eight to 15 other raiders.

When asked who these men were, he repeated, "They were nigger soldiers." How did he recognize them as such? He answered, "By the way they were dressed." He "knew they were niggers by looking at them. They had on khaki pants, leggings, belts, and some had on those light summer shirts. And some had on coats and some of them had on caps, and some hats." But Elkins said that he didn't notice what the two men in the lead were wearing.

Elkins claimed he saw the raiders turn up the alley. As they turned, they fired three or four shots into the front of Cowen's house. He saw the type of clothes they were wearing and the color but didn't know whether they wore hats. He was sure he saw the khaki belts. After that group of raiders ran uptown, somewhere toward the saloons, he supposed.

Elkins went on to testify that he saw soldiers shooting from Company C's barracks, some 80 feet (24 meters) away. Then he said he stepped into Judge Parks's room next door, and from the judge's window he saw shots fired from the upper balcony of Company B.

Making sure Elkins had plenty of opportunity to think about what he was saying, Defense repeated its question four or five times. Elkins said definitely that from his window he saw firing from Company C's barracks.

The defense counsel was just waiting to see if he would say that, and that is what he said. Now that was another impossibility. Elkins's view, or anybody's view, of Company C's barracks from the window of his bedroom on the second floor would be obstructed by the houses along the west side of the alley between 14th and 15th Streets, as the Leckie tests demonstrated.

The defense counsel moved closer to Elkins's face and pressed him. "Did you testify to Major Blocksom that you couldn't see the post from your window?"

"That I could not see the ground?" Elkins asked.

"You answer the question! Could you see the post from your window?"

Caught in the trap that the defense counsel had set for him, Elkins conceded. "No, sir."

"Could you see any portion of it?"

"I could see roofs and a little of the barracks."

Elkins surely had become rattled, for he gave even more preposterous answers to questions. He said he recognized the knob on the gun and the Springfield 03 rifle by the flash of gunfire.

Only part of Joe Dominguez's testimony for the prosecution required my special attention. The rest could be ignored. Dominguez stated on his own that he got confused. After testifying that he saw Black soldiers shooting into Cowen's house, he admitted that another policeman had told him that. He had seen nothing himself. He said he was mistaken and, "I would like to state to this court that I get so confused I don't know whether I am stating right or not."

So, was he stating right when he earlier testified that he heard shots fired toward the fort? He said it twice. In this instance, I don't think he was confused at all. Mayor Combe admitted that the citizens fired toward the fort, while the Black soldiers swore they heard bullets whizzing by over their heads.

I finished reading the testimony of all the eyewitnesses before the court. Not one claimed to have seen the raiders closer than 25 feet (8 meters), except Herbert Elkins, Katie Leahy, and the policeman Dominguez. But each had undermined their own words: What they claimed to have seen under the conditions of darkness and distance was nothing more than a string of impossibilities and contradictions.

Most troublesome to me, however, was the testimony of Paulino S. Preciado. He was the last person to see the bartender alive. He swore to Purdy, the prosecutor, that he saw the murder of the bartender in the courtyard of the Ruby Saloon. He said he saw the murderers under the light of the lamps and recognized them as Negro soldiers.

Again, I returned to Preciado's original sworn statement, given to the Grand Jury on September 10, 1906. Nowhere in his statement had he said anything about Black soldiers doing the shooting. To the contrary, he said, "I couldn't see anybody in the alley, as it was dark out there, and I was in the light. I heard no word spoken." *Maybe the bartender saw the murderers and recognized them. Maybe he saw local hired thugs. Maybe that's why the bartender was murdered, and why Preciado told the Grand Jury he didn't see anything—he was afraid.*

Next, I examined all of the original depositions and affidavits of the Black soldiers and their white officers. The soldiers' testimony was consistent, credible, and compelling with respect to their innocence.

I revisited the testimony of Tamayo, the post scavenger, who had been in the best position to see soldiers jumping over the wall—if, in fact, they had. But Tamayo swore on several occasions that the attack began on the town side of the garrison wall.

Another witness supported the soldiers' story. Wilbur Voshelle, a white man and the corral boss at the fort, swore he did not see a single soldier on the streets. He saw only two policeman and four armed citizens, and they were talking about soldiers.

THIRTY-TWO

Finding the *Proof*

An Abstract Notion

The eyewitnesses' testimony was flimsy and unreliable, but it did not prove the soldiers were innocent. It only proved that the eyewitnesses may not have seen what they reported they saw. Some of them lied deliberately. Others repeated the lies they had heard so often that they began to believe them.

If I couldn't find proof of innocence, "presumption of innocence" would have to be my fallback strategy. But I wanted more than the legal "presumption." Because, deep down, I feared that people would not really believe the soldiers were innocent—or at least some would not. I have heard people say, "Well, he did it. They just couldn't prove it. He had a smart lawyer." I didn't want this to be the case.

To find reliable facts, I dug deeper into Leckie's written testimony.

There I found an intriguing story

While in Brownsville, Leckie had found more disturbing evidence that annoyed Roosevelt. Leckie testified before the Senate that while he was in Brownsville having a drink at Crixell's saloon, Teofilo, one of the Crixell brothers, invited him to go out front with him. Once outside, Teofilo showed Leckie how close he came to getting killed. He pointed to a bullet hole in an upright post supporting the awning near the door of the saloon. "That's one of the shots fired that night."

The Brownsville Redemption

Leckie shook his head, "You're mistaken about that." Leckie rubbed his finger over the bullet hole. "That's about a .44 or .45."

"No," Crixell said.

A crowd of loafers, half-drunks, and drunks came out of the barn and gathered around the two men—the bet was on. Leckie bet a round of drinks that the hole had not been made by a steel-jacketed Springfield 03 rifle bullet. Leckie bored the bullet out with a brace and bit.

Leckie was correct. It was not a Springfield 03 rifle bullet, the kind the troops used. Instead, it was an all-lead bullet.

The bullet was later tested by a Dr. Hildebrand, who "found [it] to be of a different composition [lead, tin, and antimony] from any of the bullets used by the Black soldiers." In other words, the bullet could not have been fired from any of the soldiers' rifles.

Again, I searched for hard evidence in the record of the court-martial of Major Penrose. There I found yet another incongruity. The record showed that the seven empty cartridges and six clips Captain Macklin had found in the early morning after the shooting spree at the mouth of Cowen Alley were found in a little circle whose diameter was not more than 10 inches (25 centimeters). Macklin swore to this. However, if those bullets had been fired on the night of the raid, the mechanical action of the Springfield rifle ejector would have scattered the empty shells randomly over a 10-foot (3-meter) area. I knew this from my military experience with the Springfield 03 rifle, which I had fired many times.

The defense counsel pointed out this discrepancy to the court. "Those shell casings had been put there for a purpose."

After reading that, it became apparent to me that there had indeed been a conspiracy at Brownsville, but not the one of silence so often mentioned. It was a conspiracy by other parties yet undiscovered. Who put those empty shell casings there, and for what purpose? Why would the Black soldiers place those shell casings in that little circle?

What soldier would be so dumb as to leave that kind of incriminating evidence behind in the path of his shooting spree? That would be irrational.

At Last, a Literal Smoking Gun

In his summation argument in the court-martial of Major Penrose, the defense counsel alluded to a "microscopic test" carried out by experts on the 33 empty shell casings found on the streets of Brownsville. But he had been unable to get the results from the Senate. That excited me. Maybe that test would provide the critical piece of evidence I needed. I dug farther into the little green boxes in the National Archives and pulled out several documents that were rolled in a neat little bundle and tied with a faded red cord. To my delight, among those papers was the Microscopic Investigation Report from the ordnance experts at the Springfield, Massachusetts, Armory, containing the results of the relevant ballistic tests.

Those experts had subjected the 33 exploded shells picked up in the streets of Brownsville to microscopic examinations. When analyzed together with other evidence, I was able to state conclusively that the 33 shells had not been fired in Brownsville at all. They had been fired on the rifle range at Fort Niobrara, Nebraska.

I went back to the Senate hearing report, which I had quickly skimmed over earlier in my research. Now I studied and focused on the testimony of several Black soldiers, white officers, and Major Penrose, in particular.

In March 1907, after Major Penrose had been acquitted of the charge of "neglect of duty to the prejudice of good order and military discipline" for his men's alleged culpability in the Brownsville raid, he was called before a Senate committee to testify about his troops' participation. By this time, Penrose had changed his mind. He no longer believed his men were guilty.

The testimony I found in Penrose's folder turned out to be of critical interest. Penrose's own recollections validated the ballistic tests report. "Those shells," he said, "were brought down from Fort Niobrara to Brownsville," he asserted. "They were in open [boxes] on the back porch of Company B. They were open there several days; I don't remember how long."

The details of the ballistic test were fascinating. I understood the Microscopic Investigation Report because of my experience at the Ballistic Research Laboratories. I hoped that I would be able to explain it to Williamson without undue complexity and tedium.

The Critical Proof

To perform the ballistics tests, all 167 of the Black soldiers' rifles were shipped to the Springfield Armory. Each rifle was fired twice, and then its exploded shell casings were examined under a microscope. Those shell casings were then compared to the examinations of the 33 shell casings that were found on the streets of Brownsville.

The results were stunning—there were four guns that provided an identical match between the microscopic indentations found on the heads of all 33 exploded Brownsville shell casings and those found on the heads of shell casings belonging to Company B. The experts said it was beyond a reasonable doubt. My heart sank.

How did the experts identify these four guns out of the 167 they tested? That was easy. Three of them were identified by serial numbers, which in turn identified the soldiers assigned to those rifles. But wait!

Lieutenant Lawarson had testified that those men had been present and accounted for, and their rifles were clean and locked in the racks. Had the guns been fired at some other time and place? Had the spent shells been planted? My hopes suddenly revived.

The fourth gun provided the inconvertible, absolute, and conclusive proof I had been looking for. That rifle, the fourth gun with serial number 45683, was originally assigned to Sergeant William Blaney at Fort Niobrara. On that fateful night in Brownsville, August 13, 1906, Blaney was not at Fort Brown at all but on a four-month furlough. Before he left his post in Nebraska for vacation, he turned in his rifle to Quartermaster-Sergeant Walker McCurdy, who placed Blaney's name on a small piece of paper, placed that paper in the bore of the gun, and locked it in the arms chest before it was transported to Fort Brown. In fact, Sergeant Blaney had never been in Brownsville.

On the night of the attack, company commander Lieutenant Lawarson verified the count of all the rifles. He and McCurdy had carried an oil lantern over to the locked storeroom, unlocked it, unscrewed the top of the arms chest, and found Blaney's rifle—still locked in the chest with the piece of paper still in the bore of the gun. Both men swore to this at the Senate hearings.

Thus, *it was impossible for that fourth gun to have been fired in Brownsville.* An actual "smoking gun" had been found! And as the saying goes, "eliminate the impossibilities, and what remains must be the truth." But, it was truly a miracle that of all the possible guns, the shells matched the only rifle that could be proven not to have been used that night in Brownsville.

The experts had conclusively demonstrated that Blaney's rifle had to have been fired on the rifle range at Fort Niobrara, Nebraska (or any place other than Brownsville), and the empty shell casings found on the streets of Brownsville were planted.

The Brownsville Redemption

Two other test findings—double indentations and double insertions—confirmed the impossibility that those empty shell casings picked up in Brownsville were fired from the four guns on the night of the attack.

Double indentations meant that the experts found two dents on the head of some of the empty shell casings, which indicated that the firing pin had struck the head of the bullet twice before it finally fired.

Each time the rifle failed to fire, the ejector would have thrown the bullet 10 feet (3 meters) away on the ground, requiring the shooter to retrieve it and insert it again. It was highly improbable that a raider would be so foolish as to take the time to scramble around in the dark searching for an ejected cartridge, and highly unlikely he would ever find it in the dark. But it could easily be done on a rifle range in daylight during target practice. (I have seen it happen many times.) Several of the soldiers and officers testified that it happened on the rifle range at Fort Niobrara.

The same thing would be true for double insertions. If a soldier tried to insert a cartridge into a rifle two or more times, he would have to pull the bolt backward, and the ejector would throw the cartridge out of the chamber 3-10 feet (1-3 meters) away. The testers found that nine of the empty shell casings had been put in the gun two or more times before the rifle finally fired. Again, what kind of night raider would fiddle with a cartridge? Moreover, the officers and men swore that the need for double insertions had happened several times at Fort Niobrara during target practice.

Finally! After running into many dead ends, I had found in the National Archives the pieces of technical evidence that I believed would prove conclusively that the soldiers were not involved in the shooting. They were, in fact, unmistakably innocent.

THIRTY-THREE

Pardon or *Exoneration?*

"You got it half right."

It was late, almost nine o'clock at night, near closing time at the National Archives. There were only two or three of us left, and the attendants were turning off the lights at the desks. After stuffing my briefcase with copies of my research, I left the Archives by the back door.

The next morning, I met Wade Williamson at his office. I was decidedly upbeat. Putting aside all sense of protocol, I spread my documents out on the colonel's desk, not waiting for him to go to his conference table. When I started to explain the key elements in the documents that I had underlined, Williamson said, "Wait, Baker, I can read."

Williamson went through the documents, nodded his head from time to time, jotted down notes on a yellow pad as he turned page after page, and asked me pointed questions. Then after about three hours, several cups of coffee, and as many trips to the bathroom, he put the papers down.

I was anxious.

He pushed his chair back from his desk, folded his arms, and said, "Boy, I think you got something here."

Then he looked embarrassed and quickly added, "Baker, you know I didn't mean anything by calling you 'boy,' it was just a figure of speech."

The Brownsville Redemption

Even though I had been dealing with Wade Williamson for only a short time, one thing I knew for sure—he wasn't a racist, and he wasn't calling me "boy" in a pejorative sense.

"Now don't you be over-sensitive," I told him, "because I see your neck is getting red."

He laughed. Then he commended me for finding what he called all "this stuff" in the Archives. But then he added a "but."

"How're you going to explain it to the army staff in a one-page summary sheet?"

"I'll brief them first."

"You'll never get enough time. Look, we've been here almost three hours. Half of it I understand, half of it I don't. This stuff's technical."

"I know I can explain it," I said.

"Yes, but that's not good enough. You got it half right. Facts alone never win anything, Baker. You've got to have a compelling legal argument! What you got here doesn't do anything to satisfy the legal argument raised by President Roosevelt that, as commander-in-chief, he had the legal power backed by precedents to discharge those soldiers 'without honor' by executive summary action."

What is he doing, moving the goalposts, changing the rules in the middle of the game? I needed more? I remembered him telling me to get the facts. Well, I had better get moving.

Beat down almost below the bricks, my head bowed, once again I trudged off to the National Archives to search for evidence to discredit the legal precedents—the central core in Roosevelt's argument. After crossing the street on the Pennsylvania Avenue side, I noticed for the first time the Shakespeare quote on the statue near the back door entrance. I was struck by its message: "What is past is prologue."

What I found indoors was also quite revealing. A letter from the White House dated December 7, 1906, stated that the president wished Taft to "give him some instances, of which he knows there must be many," where commanders have discharged men without honor and without a court-martial. Taft replied on December 10, 1906, that *no precedents* in the regular army had been found prior to the discharge of the Black soldiers of the 25th Infantry. Rather, Taft sent him some examples of cases that were clearly not analogous to Brownsville.

I went back to Williamson's office and showed him what I had found. There *were* no precedents. He agreed—the foundation on which JAG based its opposition had collapsed.

The Legal Argument

After all the research, consultation with JAG and other staff directorates, hits, and misses, it was now time to sit down and write the legal argument. Hiding out in one of the conference rooms with all my files and reference books stacked on the tables, desks, and on the floor, I wrote the first draft. When I finished, I had written 40 pages.

I showed it to Wade Williamson, and he promptly rejected it. "This will never fly. You need help. Cut this thing back. The lawyers in the secretary of defense's office will never let this out."

I distilled the information into a two-page summary sheet and a five-page legal argument with ten appendices.

There were five key elements:

1. The soldiers satisfied the criteria for honorable discharges. I proved this declaration by referencing their records that stated their service was honest and faithful.
2. The action taken by President Roosevelt constituted an injustice as it was based upon the concept of mass punishment rather than individual guilt.

3. The action taken constituted an injustice, enacting an extreme form of disgrace and punishment. It took away valuable property rights, retirement income, and other benefits.
4. The action taken constituted an injustice as it was partly predicated upon racial discrimination.
5. The action taken was erroneous as a matter of law. There were no precedents for the action in the regular army.

I wrapped the whole argument into a case of manifest error. A gross injustice had been done because the presumption of innocence had been abandoned.

Vindication

On August 7, 1973, based upon the case I developed, the secretary of the army decided to exonerate the soldiers. I was ecstatic. Then I learned that there was a hitch. The exoneration was put on hold. Some of the top lawyers in the Defense Department advocated a pardon by President Nixon as more appropriate than exoneration. I objected to the idea of a pardon because that would indicate that the soldiers were guilty after all.

Back at Williamson's office, he cautioned me. "Baker, you got to be careful. There's a document floating around among the top people that purports to be a confession by one of the Black soldiers."

I burst out laughing.

Williamson got up and closed his office door. "Baker, what in the hell's wrong with you?"

I tried to answer him, but I couldn't. Putting my hand over my mouth, I tried to stop laughing. I felt tears streaming down my cheeks. It felt good and a relief. Words wouldn't come. I kept laughing.

"What's so damn funny?"

Finally, I managed to get control of myself and got a few words out. "It's nothing. Forgive me."

This time I didn't have to go back to the Archives. I knew that the so-called "Boyd Conyers confession" was a fraud, and I explained it to Wade Williamson.

"Do you have something to prove this?" Williamson asked. "Yes, sir, in my files."

"Get it and give it to me."

I retrieved Sheriff Arnold's sworn statement from my files. Sheriff Arnold swore that the "confession" was false. Williamson read it and said, "This is good enough. Leave it to me."

But I promised myself that I was going to track down the source of that document containing that old false confession. I would find its sleeping place, drive a stake through its heart, and "kill it thoroughly dead." I found it in an information folder that had been prepared by the public relations staff for the top-level people.

Once the Conyers story had been revisited and explained, the Defense Department lawyers dropped the pardon idea.

On Monday morning, September 25, 1972, Richard Belnap, the legal advisor to the adjutant general, whom I'd already met at Williamson's office, brought the draft order to my office and asked me to review it for the last time. I had reviewed a draft list before, but I still went over it again, making sure, name by name, that no soldier was left off the order.

Exoneration at Last

The order amended War Department Special Order 266 of 1906, recharacterized the discharges of the Brownsville soldiers and changed their status from "discharged without honor" to "honorably discharged," thereby exonerating all of them. Then I noticed that an old clause I had objected to before had been reinserted in the final draft. That clause stated, "No back pay, allowances, benefits or privileges shall accrue by reason of the issuance of this order to any heirs or descendants."

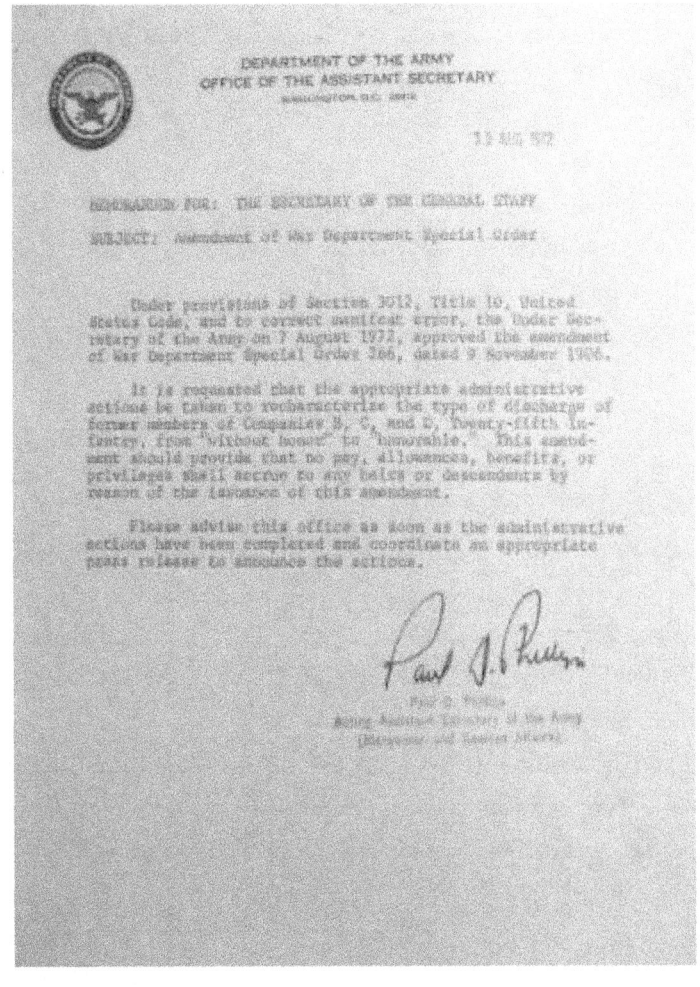

Letter from the Department of the Army agreeing to change the soldiers' discharge orders from "without honor" to "honorable."

Lieutenant Colonel (Ret) William Baker

I was irritated and greatly disappointed that that old clause had crept back into the order. I had fought it twice—lost and won and now lost again.

So, I took what I had. The amended order was completed on Tuesday, September 26, 1972, and delivered to me by Belnap. It was packaged with the legal case upon which the secretary of the army acted to reverse President Roosevelt. I rushed into General Brooks's office and gave it to him. After Brooks reviewed it, he gave it back to me and told me to lock it in our safe until the chief of public information could put out a news release. After it appeared in the newspapers, I was to take the order to the National Archives.

About mid-afternoon, General Brooks's secretary stuck her head in my office door and told me that Brooks wanted to see me right away in the secure conference room. I got up and walked to the room wondering, *What's this all about?*

After I entered the conference room, General Brooks made sure the door was locked. Then he introduced me to Mr. Don Miller, the deputy secretary of defense for equal opportunity. Brooks came straight to the point. "Bill, Don plans to announce the decision that the army has exonerated the Brownsville soldiers at the reunion of his old regiment. What do you think about it?"

General Brooks was putting me on the spot, and I knew it. Perhaps he thought I would speak truth to power.

I hesitated. Both men looked at me intently while I struggled for a politically correct answer. When I waited too long to say anything, Miller spoke up. "I'd announce it at the 369th Infantry Regiment celebration in New York City."

"When?" I asked.

"That would be…" Miller pulled out his calendar and glanced through it. "Sunday, October 8."

The Brownsville Redemption

Miller's proposal would delay the exoneration because the order had to be posted to the records in the National Archives to legally correct the records. He gave me the perfect opening to oppose it. "That'll take too long, don't you think? It might leak out."

"No, it won't. Lock it in a safe!" Miller said. "It's already locked up," Brooks said.

I pointed out that we would be taking a big risk. JAG and several staff officers knew about it. Suppose somebody leaked it to, say, John Connolly, the former Democratic governor of Texas, now turned Republican, or any other politician. He could go to President Nixon and kill it on the spot.

Miller discounted my concerns as unlikely and said he thought it should be announced to a Black audience. His old regiment would make the perfect venue.

When I heard him say that, I was convinced he had already made up his mind. Nothing I could say would matter, so I politely excused myself and left.

Togo West was a brilliant young Black officer working as the civil rights staff attorney for the secretary of the army. After I left the secure conference room, I went over to his office and told him about Don Miller's plan for the public announcement of the exoneration.

"Why, he's trying to upstage the secretary of the army. I won't let him do that," West said. He put on his suit jacket and went directly over to the secretary of the army's office.

When a day went by without hearing anything, I feared something had gone wrong. What if the exoneration had hit a political snag? Suppose there was a last-ditch effort to stop it? After all, the November election was coming up. What could I do?

Lieutenant Colonel (Ret) William Baker

DEPARTMENT OF THE ARMY
OFFICE OF THE ADJUTANT GENERAL
WASHINGTON, D. C. 20315

LCC/hcw

DAAG-ASO-O (7 Aug 72)   22 September 1972

SUBJECT: AMENDMENT OF ORDERS

Action: Amendment

So much of: Paragraph 1, Special Orders 266, War Department, 9 November 1906

As reads: "discharged without honor from the Army by their respective commanding officers and forever debarred from reenlisting in the Army or Navy of the United States, as well as from employment in any civil capacity under the Government."

How changed: Is amended to read: "honorably discharged from the Army by their respective commanding officers."

Is amended to add: No back pay, allowances, benefits or privileges shall accrue by reason of the issuance of this order to any heirs or descendants.

Is amended to delete: The discharge certificate in each case will show that the discharge without honor is in consequence of paragraph 1, Special Orders, No. 266, War Department, November 9, 1906.

Pertaining to member(s) of: Company B, 25th Infantry
First Sergeant Mingo Sanders
Quartermaster Sergeant Walker McCurdy
Sergeant James R. Reid
Sergeant George Jackson
Sergeant Luther T. Thornton
Corporal Jones A. Coltrane
Corporal Edward L. Daniels
Corporal Ray Burdett
Corporal Wade H. Watlington
Corporal Anthony Franklin
Cook Leroy Horn
Cook Solomon Johnson
Musician Henry Odom
Private James Allen
Private John B. Anderson
Private William Anderson
Private Battier Bailey
Private James Bailey

The Brownsville Redemption

```
DAAG-ASO-O  (7 Aug 72)                    22 September 1972
SUBJECT: Amendment of Orders

Private Elmer Brown
Private John Brown
Private William Brown
Private William J. Carlton
Private Harry Carmichael
Private George Conn
Private John Cook
Private Charles E. Cooper
Private Boyd Conyers
Private Lawrence Daniel
Private Carolina DeSaussure
Private Ernest English
Private Shepherd Glenn
Private Isaac Goolsby
Private William Harden
Private Charley Hairston
Private John Holomon
Private James Johnson
Private Frank Jones
Private Henry Jones
Private William J. Kernan
Private George Lawson
Private Willie Lemons
Private Samuel McGhee
Private George W. Mitchell
Private Isaiah Raynor
Private Stansberry Roberts
Private William Smith
Private Thomas Taylor
Private William Thomas
Private Alexander Walker
Private Edward Warfield
Private Julius Wilkins
Private Alfred N. Williams
Private Brister Williams
Private Joseph L. Wilson

                              Company C, 25th Infantry
Quartermaster Sergeant George W. McMurray
Sergeant Samuel W. Harley
Sergeant Newton Carlisle
Sergeant Darby W. O. Brawner
Sergeant George Thomas
Corporal Charles H. Madison
Corporal Solomon P. O'Neil
Corporal Preston Washington
```

Lieutenant Colonel (Ret) William Baker

DAAG-ASO-O (7 Aug 72) 22 September 1972
SUBJECT: Amendment of Orders

Corporal Willie H. Miller
Corporal John H. Hill
Cook George Grier
Cook Lewis J. Baker
Musician James B. Armstrong
Musician Walter Banks
Artificer Charles E. Rudy
Private Clifford I. Adair
Private Henry W. Arvin
Private Charles W. Askew
Private Frank Bounsler
Private Robert L. Collier
Private Erasmus T. Dabbs
Private Mark Garmon
Private George W. Gray
Private Joseph H. Gray
Private James T. Harden
Private George W. Harris
Private John T. Hawkins
Private Alphonso Holland
Private Thomas Jefferson
Private Edward Johnson
Private George Johnson
Private John Kirkpatrick
Private Edward Lee
Private Frank J. Lipscomb
Private West Logan
Private William Mapp
Private William McGuire, Jr
Private Thomas L. Mosley
Private Andrew Mitchell
Private James W. Newton
Private George W. Perkins
Private James Perry
Private Oscar W. Reid
Private Joseph Rogers
Private James Sinkler
Private Calvin Smith
Private George Smith
Private John Smith
Private John Streater
Private Robert Turner
Private Leartis Webb
Private Lewis Williams
Private James Woodson

3

The Brownsville Redemption

DAAG-ASO-O (7 Aug 72)
SUBJECT: Amendment of Orders   22 September 1972

                         Company D, 25th Infantry
First Sergeant Israel Harris
Quartermaster Sergeant Thomas J. Green
Sergeant Jerry E. Reeves
Sergeant Jacob Frazier
Corporal Temple Thornton
Corporal David Powell
Corporal Winter Washington
Corporal Albert Roland
Corporal James H. Ballard
Musician Hoytt Robinson
Musician Joseph Jones
Cook Charles Dade
Cook Robert Williams
Artificer George W. Newton
Private Samuel Wheeler
Private Charles Hawkins
Private Henry Barclay
Private Sam M. Battle
Private Henry T. W. Brown
Private John Butler
Private Richard Crooks
Private Strowder Darnell
Private Elias Gant
Private James C. Gill
Private John Green
Private Alonzo Haley
Private George W. Hall
Private Barney Harris
Private Joseph H. Howard
Private John A. Jackson
Private Benjamin F. Johnson
Private Walter Johnson
Private Charles Jones
Private John R. Jones
Private William E. Jones
Private William R. Jones
Private Edward Jordan
Private Wesley Mapp
Private William A. Matthews
Private James Newton
Private Elmer Peters
Private Len Reeves
Private Edward Robinson
Private Henry Robinson

Lieutenant Colonel (Ret) William Baker

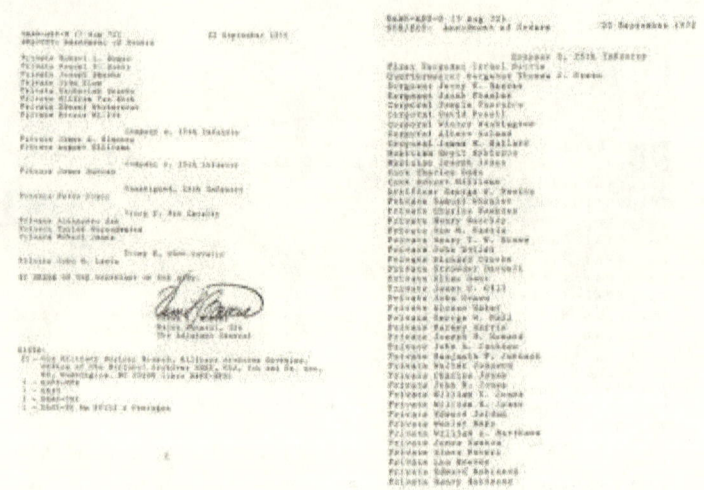

Department of the Army Amendment of Orders and the names of the 167 soldiers, 09/22/1972

I devised a simple strategy but a risky one. I would take the order to the National Archives early in the morning on Friday, September 22, 1972, and deposit it there. That would, in effect, complete the exoneration. I wouldn't wait on any press release from the Pentagon or Don Miller. Publicity was not my business anyway.

Then I was summoned to the office of the assistant secretary of defense for public affairs and was told that Melvin Laird might make the public announcement on Sunday, September 24, 1972, on the nation-wide TV news program "Meet the Press." The public relations experts had prepared notes for him, and they wanted me to check the accuracy of those notes.

A Beautiful Day in My Heart

That Thursday night, the eve of the day I was to deliver the order to the Archives, was a bad night. I didn't sleep well. I had dreams one gets on the night before exams in a difficult course, say, nuclear physics. Dreams of bizarre impossibilities occurred all during the night. I woke up in a cold sweat each time.

One dream was unusually strange and frightening. With the documents secured in my briefcase, I dreamed I went to the Archives. The inscription at the back entrance had changed from Shakespeare's "What's past is prologue" to Dante's inscription over the gates of hell: "Abandon all hope, ye who enter here."

A man met me at the door and said, "Welcome, Colonel Roosevelt, we've been expecting you for a long time. I see you have something for us."

"You're mistaken. My name is Baker," I said.

Turning his head slightly to the side while smiling, the man said, "No, it's not. Come in, Colonel Roosevelt."

When I stepped through the door, to my amazement, the Archives had turned into a beautiful green forest.

I tried to ask a question, but the man cut me off. "Give me the papers!"

When I tried to unlock my briefcase, my key wouldn't fit. The man handed me a key and said, "Try this one. It fits."

I took the papers from my briefcase and handed them to him. He read the papers and handed them back to me. "We can't accept them."

"Why?"

"They are ashes of the past." Frightened, I turned to leave.

"Wait, Colonel Roosevelt, you can't get out that way. You must go this way." He pointed toward the green forest.

When I started to walk toward the forest, it turned to ashes before my eyes.

"Where's the door?" I asked.

"Colonel Roosevelt, you must walk on the ashes of the forest." The next morning, I got out of bed feeling pretty groggy, as if I had spent the entire night drinking. I made my way to the bathroom. After taking a cold shower, I put on my finest military uniform, my dress blues. I didn't own a set of whites, but if I had, I would have worn them. It was a day of celebration.

Friday morning, September 22, 1972, was a day when autumn had barely arrived. No leaves had started to turn color. Summer was still hanging on. It was gray, heavily overcast, warm, and humid—but it was a beautiful day in my heart.

I walked out of the front door of the Pentagon. There was no army sedan waiting for me, only my old black un-air-conditioned Pontiac. I got into it and drove across the 14th Street Bridge, turned right onto Constitution Avenue, and on to the front entrance of the National Archives. I went through the front entrance—not the back door this time—and delivered the order.

The World Is Told the Truth

My family, a group of friends, and I sat in front of the television on Sunday, September 24, 1972, waiting for Secretary Laird to announce the good news about Brownsville. Members of the press grilled him seemingly about everything, the war in Vietnam, the volunteer army, and so on. He never said anything about Brownsville, even though there were opportunities to squeeze it in.

Would the public release be made on Monday? Surely it would be. Monday went by—nothing on the evening news. Tuesday came and went—nothing in the newspapers, TV, or radio. By Wednesday, when there still was no announcement, I began to think that maybe Melvin Laird killed the public release for political reasons and might soon ask if the order had been delivered to the Archives. Finding out that it had been, he would no doubt conclude he had been handed fait accompli, which is abhorrent to the military chain-of-command. Might he still try to stop the whole thing? I began to worry. Now I'm in trouble. The order is in the Archives. Suppose some researcher stumbled upon it in the records and notified the press?

I was about to go out of my mind. Then it occurred to me, call the Archives. What a relief when I found out that the order had not been filed in the records. I asked Dr. Elaine Everly, the archivist in the Old Military Branch, to wait for the official announcement by the Department of Defense before giving any publicity to the order. She agreed. Why didn't I think of that before?

On Thursday morning, September 28, 1972, the Department of Defense made the announcement. And on Friday, September 29, 1972, it seemed that newspapers all over the country carried the story. The New York Times carried it in a front-page article, "Army Clears 167 Black Soldiers Disciplined in a Shooting in 1906."

The Washington Post had a different title on page A3, "Army Clears Black Soldiers in 1906 Brownsville Incident."

It was official. The whole world knew the truth—the Brownsville soldiers were innocent.

Lieutenant Colonel (Ret) William Baker

THIRTY-FOUR

The Old Man's *Claim*

Dorsie Willis is Still Alive

The main reason propounded by the adjutant general for the no back pay, no benefits clause in the order was to avoid setting a precedent by making payments to surviving soldiers. Besides, no one I dealt with in the Pentagon believed any of the soldiers were still alive. Even the Justice Department had said that in writing. So, it follows that the real reason for the no back pay, no benefits clause was to prevent making payments to living descendants. Living descendants were a more likely probability.

Even I doubted that any of the soldiers were still alive, but I hadn't given up hope. Anxious to find some of the soldiers, I requested authority and funds to search for survivors. My superiors were against it. They told me there were no funds in the budget for such a project, and moreover, they said I needed to get back to work developing the army's Affirmative Action Plan and developing plans to improve race relations in the army.

One day Bob Dews came to my desk to give me a message. His face was sad, and he had an air of formality about him. "General Brooks is leaving. He's being replaced by Colonel Ernie Frazier."

I was puzzled. Then Dews added quickly, "Don't worry about Harry. It's a step up the career ladder for him. It'll probably guarantee a second star for him."

The Brownsville Redemption

Then he got down to the real reason he came to see me. "Bill, I have been asked to tell you that there are people in this building who don't want Brownsville embellished anymore. You've done your job. You're being pulled off the case. Turn your files over to the adjutant general's staff."

I felt numb and, for some strange reason, unworthy. Only once before had I felt that way—when I returned from the war in Vietnam. I looked up at Bob. "Vietnam, all over again, no appreciation, huh?"

"I'm just the messenger. Don't shoot me," Bob said and left. Fortunately, that was not the end of it.

One morning in early October, the secretary told me that a General Mark W. Clark was on the phone and wanted to speak to me. I picked up the phone. A gruff, commanding man's voice came through loud and clear. "Mark Clark here. Are you the lad who knows something about back pay for the Brownsville boys?"

Sure enough, it was Mark W. Clark, the famous World War II four-star general. He told me that he knew a remarkable old Negro who had shined his shoes for the last 30 years—and wanted to know what the army was doing to grant him back pay.

I almost leaped through the telephone. Could it be? Could it be? Words rushed out of my mouth, "General Clark. General Clark. Who's alive? Who are you talking about?"

"Don't you know?" the old general said.

"No, sir. I don't."

"You don't know? Nixon's aides told me to talk to you."

I was embarrassed for myself and the army. I mumbled something like, "Let me get back to you."

"Well, you answered my question. You don't know anything. You're not doing anything for Dorsie Willis."

Sensing that he was about to hang up on me, I said, "General Clark, how can I reach you? I'll get back to you."

"All right. You can reach me at the Francis Marion Hotel in Charleston. Don't call me back till you have the answer to my question."

That call from Mark Clark filled me with hopeful anticipation that the army would change its position on back pay and benefits and provide funds for me to organize a search for survivors. I rushed into General Brooks's office and told him that we might have a survivor. Brooks wanted to know his name and how I had found out about him. In my excitement, I had neglected to first tell him about my conversation with Mark Clark. When I told Brooks that I had spoken to a living World War II legend in his own right, I got Brooks's full attention.

Newspapers around the country had also discovered Dorsie Willis, and his picture appeared in stories across the country. On October 5, 1972, the *Minneapolis Star,* in a front-page banner headline, heralded the story of Dorsie Willis: "Army justice was 66 years late to a man in Brownsville Affray."

A huge public outcry ensued almost simultaneously with the publicity surrounding Dorsie Willis, charging the army with discrimination in the no back pay, no benefits clause. Letters flowed into the secretary of the army's office praising him for exoneration of the soldiers but asking what the army was going to do about helping Dorsie Willis. Copies of those letters were forwarded quickly down through the chain of command to me by intermediate staff officers. Obviously, no one had told them I was no longer on the case. Dorsie Willis became a political hot potato.

Weeks passed, but the Dorsie Willis problem wouldn't go away. On Friday, October 27, 1972, Mr. Plant, special assistant to the undersecretary of the army, passed the chain of command and called me directly. "Colonel Baker, I understand that you're handling the actions pertaining to survivors of the Brownsville Incident. What's the status of benefits for Dorsie Willis?"

After hesitating for a moment and not knowing how to respond, I said, "Mr. Plant, our office isn't handling survivors' benefits. You should talk to the adjutant general."

On November 3, 1972, Secretary Froehlke received a letter from Congressman Augustus F. Hawkins criticizing the no back pay, no benefits clause. Among other things, Hawkins stated, "Frankly, I consider this language discriminatory [language in the order], and I wonder if you could give me the reasoning behind it."

A day or so later, our secretary told me that I was wanted immediately upstairs at a meeting in the assistant secretary of the army's office. I quickly grabbed some of my Brownsville files and hurried upstairs. I walked into a spacious office. There I found several high-level staff officers sitting at a long mahogany table. Some I knew, some I didn't. All of them had quizzical looks on their faces.

A well-dressed man sat at the head of the conference table. I didn't remember having ever seen him before. He seemed to be in charge and acted as if he knew me. "Colonel Baker, what was your rationale for including that dumb no back pay, no benefits clause in your case?"

"I didn't have a rationale then, and I don't have one now. I put it in the case because General Bowers insisted on it. That's the only way I could get it by him."

"Got any proof of that?" the man said. "Yes, sir."

"Where is it?

I fumbled through the file I had brought along. Luck was with me. I found the memorandum prepared by Mr. Fraker and signed by Colonel J.C. Pennington for the adjutant general on June 30, 1972, a long time prior to the development of my case. I got up from the table, walked over to where the man was sitting, laid the memorandum down in front of him, and put my finger on the paragraph of the memo that was the origin of the no back pay, no benefits provision.

"That's all, Colonel Baker," the man said.

Even though I had been taken off the project, the staff at the higher levels kept forwarding me letters about Dorsie Willis. On November 17, 1972, the secretary of the army received a poignant letter from Mr. J.C. Cornelius, a wealthy banker from Minneapolis, Minnesota. He wrote that "my greatly admired friend, General Mark W. Clark," at his request, was doing all he could to find out whether or not his good friend Dorsie Willis was entitled to any benefits.

After reading that letter, not only did I feel helpless, I also felt guilty that I hadn't gotten back to General Clark about benefits for Dorsie Willis. Why did I feel that way? I simply had nothing to tell him. Moreover, I had been taken off the project.

The Search for Dorsie Willis

Congressman Donald M. Fraser, in a letter on November 22, 1972, asked the army to issue Mr. Willis an Honorable Discharge certificate. That letter increased the pressure against the army for doing nothing and saying nothing about the plight of Dorsie Willis. The secretary of the army was being put on the spot personally for the army's inaction. He was feeling the heat, and he wanted some answers.

Having many projects to work on, I kept busy. But my main interest was still on Brownsville. Time went by fast after the long Thanksgiving weekend, and it was now mid-December. I kept my ear to the ground, listening for any information about Dorsie Willis.

Colonel Frazier, the soon-to-be director of our department, and General Brooks were summoned into a hastily called meeting with

The Brownsville Redemption

General Bernie Rogers, our new boss. Rogers had just replaced General Kerwin. I wasn't asked to attend.

But about 15 minutes later, I was called into the meeting. Colonel Frazier was talking when I entered the room. "General Rogers, we don't have the staff to search for survivors. Back pay and benefits are not our responsibilities. Bill Baker is overloaded."

General Rogers turned to me. "Colonel Baker, what do you have to say about this? What can we do to help Dorsie Willis?"

Before I could think clearly, words came pouring out. "We could do a lot more than nothing." Then I realized that I had been too blunt. "Sir, I mean the army...not anybody personally."

I knew that I had better show General Rogers that I wasn't just a bag of emotions, so I said, "Let me put it this way, sir. The first thing we must do is identify this man who calls himself Dorsie Willis. Yes, there was a Dorsie Willis at Fort Brown. I know that. But is this the same man? Is he a legitimate survivor? We don't know that yet. If he is, we must issue him an Honorable Discharge certificate. The discharge certificate would enable him to apply for veterans' benefits. Also, we should determine if he is due any back pay or some sort of reparations.

"We should not allow the case of this man to be made into a cause célèbre by the news media or any other outside organizations. That's what's happening now. We must move rapidly to seize the initiative."

"That's a mouthful. Now, you tell me who's going to do the work?"

Ernie Frazier glared at me. "I'll do it," I said.

"You don't have enough time. You have too much on your plate now," Frazier said.

"I can do both like I've been doing. I'll work at night. I'll give up my Christmas vacation and work during the holidays."

General Rogers spoke up. "Let's give Bill a shot at it."

I went back to my office thinking that I had settled it: I was back on Brownsville. Later that day, I prepared a position paper for General Rogers recommending identification of Mr. Willis and issuance of an Honorable Discharge certificate, if appropriate.

When I made that recommendation, I knew that one of the most powerful generals in the army with respect to military personnel policy, Major General Verne Bowers, the adjutant general, had opposed the issuance of the Honorable Discharge certificate to any possible survivor just a few weeks ago, even though he knew that the issuance of such a certificate would have "no legal effect on statutory entitlements to which these individuals [Brownsville survivors] would otherwise be entitled." That is what JAG told him back on November 9, 1972.

When my position paper was staffed recommending the issuance of an Honorable Discharge certificate to Mr. Willis, if his identity could be established, the adjutant general opposed it. It took outside pressure from letters to the secretary of the army to get him to change his position.

The Criminal Investigation Department Steps In

On the day before General Brooks's departure, I was called into Colonel Frazier's office for a special meeting on Brownsville. For all practical purposes, Colonel Frazier was now the new director of our office, and he had moved into General Brooks's office. He had a pleased look on his face when he introduced me to three men wearing cheap-looking, bell-bottom polyester civilian suits. As if on cue, all three of them immediately took out their badges and showed them to me. They were military policemen (MPs) from the Criminal Investigation Department (CID).

The Brownsville Redemption

Colonel Frazier said, "Bill, I have asked the CID to identify Dorsie Willis. Take them to the conference room and brief them on Brownsville. They'll go to Minnesota and get this over quickly."

"Gentlemen, would you excuse us?" I said. "I want to speak to Colonel Frazier privately."

"What do you want to talk with me about? I just got you some help," Frazier said.

Colonel Frazier and I had a long and sometimes heated debate about the wisdom of sending criminal investigators out to Mr. Willis's home in Minneapolis. I was against it and told him so. I also told him my belief that the CID was the most distasteful department of the military police. Some of their methods were questionable and secretive. To seriously consider sending them out to investigate an old, arthritic man who had committed no crime was a despicable thing to do. And I told him so.

My words hit a nerve. Maybe I should've been more tactful. He stood up. His face was red, and the veins in his neck bulged. As he talked and pounded his fist on his desk, he got louder and louder. He was becoming a wild man. I knew he hadn't been drinking; he was a teetotaler. Every time I tried to say something, he drowned me out, saying, "Shut up! Shut up! Shut up!"

Finally, desperate to stop him, I yelled, "Colonel Frazier, you're making a colossal mistake!"

"I told you to shut up! Don't interrupt me when I am talking. Now go do what I told you."

The three CID agents were waiting for me in the conference room. *How can I get rid of these guys?* was the first thought that crossed my mind. Ernie Frazier had told me that they didn't know anything about Brownsville. I was betting on their ignorance. To be sure, I had better confirm it. So I began, "I know you fellows are smarter than Brown &

Baldwin detectives, the Secret Service, the Grand Jury, and five prior military investigators. But you should know that they failed."

"Failed at what?" one of the agents asked.

"I'll get to that in a minute. First, I need to know who is in charge and what authority you have to investigate an American civilian."

One of the agents spoke up. "I'm in charge. Did I understand you to say that Dorsie Willis is a civilian?"

"That's right, Colonel," I said. "How does that square with the Posse Comitatus Act?"

"It doesn't. Ernie didn't tell us that Dorsie Willis was a civilian. He must be slipping. He must have forgotten everything he ever learned as a CID agent. I know him from way back. I'll talk him out of this."

The Real Dorsie W. Willis

It was the 26th of December. The corridors of the Pentagon were quiet, and people were still out on Christmas vacation. But I wasn't. I was working. By now, Colonel Frazier and I had patched things up. With the telephone not ringing as much and hardly any meetings to attend, I was able to catch up on my projects and put in some serious time searching for evidence that would confirm that the real Dorsie W. Willis, who was a young soldier in 1906, was still alive.

I viewed his records in the National Archives, read interviews he gave to various newspapers, and reviewed the testimony and affidavits he made to prior investigators. I knew a lot about him. I was confident that I would be able to say whether or not he was the Dorsie W. Willis within a week or so. Thus, I felt it was time to answer some of the mail about Willis, buy some time, and work to neutralize the negative publicity the army had recently endured. I so advised Ernie Frazier.

The Brownsville Redemption

On December 26, 1972, on behalf of the secretary of the army, Ernie Frazier notified Congressman Donald Frazier that the army would assist Dorsie Willis in establishing his identity as a legitimate survivor. The effort would require research in the National Archives to find documentation and a personal interview of Willis by a "knowledgeable person." Based on the findings, the army would be in a position to determine his identity as the lone survivor of the Brownsville night of terror. Upon proper identification, Willis would be issued an Honorable Discharge certificate.

The next day, December 27, at his home in Minneapolis, Minnesota, Dorsie Willis gave an extensive interview to Andrew H. Malcolm. His report, "How Brownsville Raid Changed Life of Black G.I.," was filed as "Special to the *New York Times*" and appeared on New Year's Eve. Willis told Malcolm his sad story while providing me with valuable information that would have to be verified by direct contact with him.

Now that the army had officially gone on record offering Dorsie Willis assistance, and he was talking freely to reporters, I felt that it was the right time for me to make contact with him. I called him on the telephone and introduced myself. I tried to reassure him that my job was to assist him in convincing the army that he really was Dorsie W. Willis. I was going to help him, not interrogate him.

The first thing he said to me was, "It's a trick! You're playing a trick on me." Then he hung up the phone.

Well, that was a mistake. It was a mistake making a cold call to an old man who had no good reason to trust me or anybody else in the army. I needed an introduction. So, I turned to Mr. J. C. Cornelius, the president of the Northwestern Bank in Minneapolis, who readily agreed to call Dorsie Willis and persuade him to talk with me. The next time I called him, he was most gracious. I didn't have to ask him a single question. He talked on and on about Brownsville and his life after being discharged. His story was essentially the same things he had told several reporters.

More Detective Work

On Monday, January 8, 1973, I developed a detailed, four-step procedure for a board of officers to follow that would assist Willis in establishing his identity.

One of the first things I did was develop a systematic approach to solving the identification problem. From the outset, I ran into problems. Fingerprint technology was not available until 1918, so that was out. I was about to fly off to Jackson, Mississippi, to get a copy of Willis's birth certificate when I learned that Mississippi did not record births or deaths until 1912. I couldn't find any record of his dental work. What surprised me most, however, was not only could I not find any historical photos of Dorsie Willis, but in addition, he had no photos of himself as a young man. All of the witnesses who had known him and could identify him as a member of the 25th Infantry were probably dead. He had outlived all of them. Recordings of his voice in a historical context were not available. So voice prints were out. I was getting nowhere fast.

When everything seemed to have failed, I found historical signatures of Dorsie W. Willis in the National Archives. I also saw more recent signatures (1954) in JAG's records where Willis had appealed to the army for an honorable discharge. I hired a graphologist, or handwriting expert, to confirm their authenticity. I arranged for Mr. John H. Orr, an examiner of questionable documents, to meet me at the National Archives on January 5, 1973. With the approval of the archivist, I had the expert examine original historic signatures signed by Willis on January 5, 1905, and three original signatures he had executed on affidavits in 1954. On the basis of his examination, the graphologist concluded that the same person had executed those signatures.

The experts' determination on the signatures heartened me, but I knew that evidence alone wouldn't be enough. What I needed were his medical records. I kept digging farther into the box of records, examining paper after paper. Finally, on Friday, January 12, 1973, I found them. As I began reading the descriptive data on the physical induction card, my hands began to shake with excitement. Like a miner who had been digging for years to find that perfect golden nugget, I had found my undeniable proof. My hands shook so rapidly, I had to grasp my right wrist with my left hand and hold it tightly so I could read the document.

Right here was what I needed—a full description of Dorsie W. Willis: Color of eyes, color of hair, complexion, height, and weight. And scars—a quarter inch (.6 cm) on his left cheek, a 1-inch (2.5-cm) scar on his left wrist, one 1.25 inches (3 cm) on his left forearm, and another one-eighth of an inch (.3 cm) on his right forearm. Three other scars were described in the induction physical—one each on his back, right thigh, and left foot.

From that information, public statements Willis had made, depositions, and affidavits, I was able to develop a complete profile of a young man who was 18 years old and a private in the U.S. Army stationed at Fort Brown, Texas. I knew what he looked like then, but I didn't know what he would look like today, as an old man in his eighties. Now armed with these distinguishing characteristics, we could positively identify him and confirm the existence of the last living legacy of the Brownsville Affair.

Lieutenant Colonel (Ret) William Baker

Meet Dorsie Willis (1886–1977)

On Thursday, January 11, 1973, I flew on Northwest Orient Airlines to Minneapolis, Minnesota, with Colonel Robert J. Kirk, a personnel expert, and Doctor L. Thomas Wolff, a medical doctor. There we interviewed Reverend Curtis Herron, pastor of Zion Baptist Church. We learned that he knew Dorsie Willis and that the old man was a faithful member of the church.

The next morning at nine o'clock, we went to the seat of financial and economic power in Minneapolis, Northwestern Bank. Jack Cornelius, the bank president, ushered us into his spacious and elaborate mahogany-paneled office. Cornelius told us he had known Dorsie Willis for 40 years, and during those years, as far back as the 1930s, Willis had told him of the unjust treatment he had received as a result of the Brownsville Incident. He had come to know Willis as a friend and described him as a hard worker who had shined shoes in his bank building for many years. Cornelius said he admired Willis's intelligence, integrity, and civic responsibility. Then he shared a story of how Willis saved enough quarters from his shoeshine business to send an inner-city child to summer camp every year. "In spite of how the army had treated him," Cornelius said, "Dorsie loves our country."

We were scheduled to interview Willis at his home at two o'clock that afternoon. I was so anxious, I called Mr. Willis to ask him if we could come a little earlier. He said, "Yes." I could hardly wait to get there.

It was a cold but sunny afternoon. We arrived at Willis's home around 1:30. The house, a little white stucco bungalow on Minnehaha Street, was covered with snow, and his yard glistened with ice melt.

A well-dressed distinguished-looking old man, with a face as if cast in bronze, stood at the open door, leaning on a walking cane. His

The Brownsville Redemption

cheeks were fully fleshed, and he had a square chin, stocky build, and gray silver hair. He greeted us warmly and welcomed us into his home.

Dorsie W. Willis, 1972, One of the two last survivors of the Brownsville, Texas Incident, 1906, Courtesy of U.S. Army Signal Corps

Sitting down in his old-fashioned leather chair seemed difficult for him. He eased slowly and carefully into it. It must have been painful. The chair and the man seemed too big for the tiny living room.

When I looked into his eyes, sadness looked back at me. Now knowing his history, I knew it was a sadness of many years—and mourning for all his friends and fellow soldiers who had passed on before him, leaving him the last man standing. His approaching mortality was reflected deep in the hollows of his eyes. He would be celebrating his 87th birthday the following month, and we both knew there would not be many more. His expression told us that he had been waiting for us, the U.S. Army, for a long, long time. His eyes seemed to ask us the question, "Why did you have to wait until now?" Nothing had adequately prepared me to meet this man. I didn't know where to start, even though I had written out several questions on a yellow pad that was still in my briefcase. I was supposed to lead the interview. I fidgeted awkwardly with the latch on my briefcase. Failing to get it open, I gave up trying.

Willis's attention was drawn to my briefcase. He looked at it, then at Colonel Kirk's briefcase sitting on the floor, then at Dr. Wolff's black medical bag. After the four of us had sat in silence for what seemed like a long time, the old man finally spoke up softly. "You gentlemen look educated, but are you civilized?"

Then he smiled, and we all smiled. Even under these circumstances, I realized Dorsie Willis had a sense of humor. When he smiled, I noticed a scar on his left cheek. After I saw that scar, I dropped my plan for direct questioning and conducted an open-ended interview.

The story the old man told us was at once extraordinary, revealing, and compelling. His narrative coincided remarkably with my research. When he appeared to tire, I thought it time to end the interview. I wanted to get back to Washington, report our results—and get this man his Honorable Discharge certificate. I had seen and heard enough.

But we needed to do a physical examination. I asked him if he was willing to submit to a medical exam. He agreed. Dr. Wolff took Willis into a back room for privacy, where the doctor conducted the exam. The doctor identified the scars that were described on Willis's medical record at the age of 18.

We took a vote. It was unanimous—this man was, in fact, the Dorsie W. Willis we were looking for. He was a legitimate and confirmed survivor of the Brownsville Incident, and he should be recognized as such by the Department of the Army.

The Brownsville Redemption

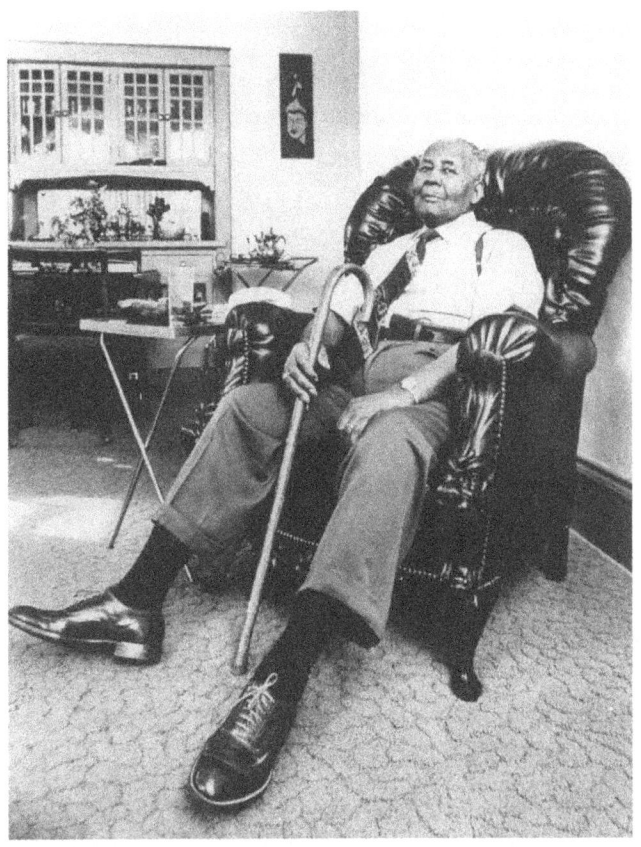

Dorsie Willis at his home in Minneapolis, January 12, 1973

After 69 Years of Injustice, Justice

On Friday, February 2, 1973, Secretary of the Army Robert F. Froehlke approved the report. Almost immediately, controversy arose over who would present Dorsie Willis with his Honorable Discharge certificate. There were a number of wild suggestions. My new immediate superior, Ernie Frazier, made it known that he would clear his calendar and make the presentation himself. Of course, I wasn't consulted. I didn't care much about it, except that I was concerned that the army would select the wrong official. I didn't want someone who was ignorant of the historical significance of the affair and what the awarding of the Honorable Discharge would mean to the 87-year-old man humbly standing before him.

Secretary Froehlke eventually selected Major General Dewitt C. Smith, Jr., the second-ranking public affairs official and press expert in the Pentagon, to represent him and make the presentation. Froehlke selected me to assist General Smith. The staff attorney Togo West explained the rationale. "Major General Smith should be accompanied by the staff officer (Lt. Col. Baker) most familiar with the case. Since Lt. Col. Baker happens to be Black, the team would be racially balanced."

At that time, I didn't know anything about General Smith. I checked around the Pentagon and found out that DeWitt Smith, in addition to his outstanding public relations reputation, was a soldier's soldier, a fair man, and a big supporter of equal opportunity. I went to his office to see him and asked if I could write his presentation speech, which was customary for staff officers to do for generals and high-level civilian officials. He thanked me but declined. He said he preferred to write it himself but promised to let me read it before he delivered it.

I made all the arrangements for the presentation. I got approval from Reverend Herron and Dorsie Willis to conduct the ceremony on Sunday, February 11, 1973, at the Zion Baptist Church in Minneapolis. I sent notifications to interested members of Congress, requested press coverage, and so on. Then I went back to the Pentagon and asked General Smith's secretary if the general had finished writing his speech. She said, "No, Colonel Baker. He's really tense about this speech. I've never seen him like this before. I'll let you know when he completes it."

On Friday evening, the day before we were to leave for Minneapolis, General Smith still hadn't prepared his speech. I was worried.

The Brownsville Redemption

The next morning, February 10, 1973, General Smith and I caught a plane for Minneapolis. On that flight, I noted he was writing furiously. He sat in a seat in front of me, and at about 20 minutes into the flight, he turned around and handed me a pencil-written speech. "Bill, read this and tell me what you think."

I read the speech in awe. How could this man write such beautiful, powerful words that conveyed so much in such a short period of time? I gave it back to him and simply said, "Marvelous!"

On Sunday afternoon, February 11, 1973, following the regular church service, the ceremony was held in a packed church with standing room only. People filled the back and both sides of the aisles. Willis and his family sat in the first rows. General Smith and I stood at the pulpit, wearing our Dress Blue uniforms.

General Smith, addressing the congregation in general, and Dorsie Willis in particular, said, "We are trying to substitute justice for injustice, to make amends, to say how much we of this generation—white men as well as Black—regret the errors and injustices of an earlier generation. Colonel Baker and I signify the army's disapproval of mass punishment. Mr. Willis, you honor us by the quality of the life you have led, by your outstanding citizenship, and by the faithful service you rendered the United States Army..." (*New York Times* quote of the day [in part], 2/12/73).

When General Smith had finished his speech, Dorsie Willis knew the moment he had waited for so long had come. He stood up and hobbled alone to the edge of the pulpit, stood as erect as he could, and leaned on his cane. He was followed by his wife, Olive Willis, and family members. Photographers, TV camera technicians, and men and women scrambled on their knees and hands along the floor in front of the pulpit, jockeying for a good view of the scene. With TV cameras rolling and flashbulbs popping, General Smith presented Dorsie Willis his Honorable Discharge certificate.

Dorsie Willis took the certificate, looked down at it momentarily, raised his head, and looked up past us. I could only imagine that he was looking back into time, to the days of his youth—to a time of broken promises and crushed dreams that could never be repaired or restored. The certificate reclaimed his honor, but not the life he had imagined.

General DeWitt Smith and Lt. Col William Baker shake hands with Dorsie Willis as they present his compensation check for $25,000.

It was not until the congregation gave him a standing ovation that he smiled.

The choir began singing the "Battle Hymn of the Republic." The words flowed into the hearts of many people with yet a deeper meaning, for I saw them crying while singing, "Mine eyes have seen the glory of the coming of the Lord…"

Later at the cake and coffee reception in the basement of the church, I presented Dorsie Willis with an American flag. He said to me, "I'm going to use this flag to put on my coffin."

The *Washington Afro-American*, February 17, 1973. The American flag was presented to 87-year-old Dorsie Willis (right) during ceremonies at the Zion Baptist Church in Minneapolis, Sunday, while his wife, Olive, and son, Reginald, watched proudly as Willis was exonerated after being reduced to shining shoes for 40 years. Making the presentation is Lt. Col. William Baker (UPI Telephoto)

After the ceremony and after General Smith flew back to Washington, I was inundated with requests for interviews by reporters. They assumed that I was a public relations spokesman for the army, which I wasn't, but nevertheless, I was uncomfortably pressed into that role.

The army's plan was that I would remain in Minneapolis to assist Willis in filling out forms for his veteran benefits and not to talk to reporters. However, I was grilled about back pay, reparations, and benefits for Dorsie Willis. What was the army going to do? I ducked, dodged, and danced away from the questions as best I could.

One of the interviews I gave was to Andrew H. Malcolm. His report, "Army Returns Honor to Discharged Black," was filed as "Special to the *New York Times*" and appeared on Monday, February 12, 1973.

Sometime later, another Brownsville survivor surfaced—Edwin Warfield. He was also confirmed as legitimate and presented with an Honorable Discharge certificate. That made it two out of the 167 disgraced and dishonored soldiers, who would go to their graves knowing full well that they had been innocent of any crime.

"I'm going to use this flag to put on my coffin." Dorsie Willis, February 11, 1973. Courtesy, U.S. Army Signal Corps

BOOK III

Aftermath

THIRTY-FIVE

Compensation or *Reparations?*

A Bid to Compensate

Negative publicity continued to build against the army for its failure to rescind the no benefits clause in the order. Congressman Hawkins fired off a follow-up letter to Secretary Froehlke, which was blunt in every detail. "I do not consider [army] replies responsive to my inquiries..." He pressed Froehlke for answers to his previous questions. He wanted the answers in detail and in simple terms. Why didn't Froehlke consider the language in the order discriminatory? Why did Dorsie Willis and the other survivor have difficulties receiving benefits? Hawkins threatened congressional hearings and legislation if the army failed to act soon.

When the army didn't heed his warning, Congressman Hawkins introduced on February 20, 1973, H.R. 4382, a bill to "confersionable status on veterans involved in the Brownsville Texas Incident..." His bill would require the administrator of the Veterans Administration to make compensatory payments of $40,000 to veterans involved in the Brownsville Incident and $20,000 to their heirs.

The Chairman of the House Veterans Affairs Committee requested Melvin Laird, secretary of Defense, and Donald Johnson, head of the Veterans Administration (VA), to submit their views on the pro-posed legislation. As customary, the Nixon administration required such reports to be submitted through its Office of Management and Budget so that a consistent policy position could be presented to the Congress.

Lieutenant Colonel (Ret) William Baker

Donald Johnson of the VA opposed the bill in his written reply on May 16, 1973. On June 10, 1973, Major General Verne Bowers, in his proposed reply for the secretary of the army, simply deferred comments to the Veterans Administration on the merits of the bill. Richard Belnap, a legal adviser to General Bowers, brought copies of Johnson's reply and General Bowers's proposed reply to my office for my review and agreement.

I disagreed with both Johnson and General Bowers on their replies and wrote a memorandum analyzing their positions and stating my objections. My analysis of the VA's position was easy. I concluded that all of the VA's opposition points said essentially the same thing, and all of them were wrong. They contended that retroactive benefits for the Brownsville soldiers would be discriminatory to other veterans who had not been granted benefits for commission of similar offenses.

But there *were* no other similar cases of mass punishments or precedents in the regular army. All legal authorities agreed on that.

In deferring to the VA, General Bowers, in effect, recommended that the army submit a negative report to Congress. Such a report would, like Pontius Pilate, attempt to wipe the army's hands clean of the whole sorry Brownsville affair. This effort would be a complete dodge of the unjust consequences of that affair, which was solely perpetrated by the War Department (now Defense Department), and not the modern Veterans Administration. Moreover, for the army to defer any comments to the VA, based upon the contention that Hawkins's bill fell outside its purview, was to accept a narrow interpretation of its responsibility.

My view was that the army should make restitution for the damage it had done in the form of direct reparations to the survivors or their heirs. I recommended that the army support Hawkins's bill with respect to the monetary aspects, that payments should be made by the army in individual lump sums to survivors or their heirs, and that the funds should come from the army, not the VA.

In my opinion, though, Hawkins's bill was flawed in a major way. Unlike the notorious Willie Sutton, who reportedly once said, when asked why he robbed banks, "That's where the money is," the Hawkins bill was trying to get funding where there was little or no money. Everyone knew that the VA was almost always broke. The Defense Department was where the money was—and that's where I wanted to get it from.

General Bowers flatly and roundly denounced my plan. His opposition didn't totally surprise me. He had been unsympathetic towards the soldiers all along. But now that his office was responsible for carrying out the remaining tasks on Brownsville, he was in a strategic position to block benefits—and that is exactly what he was trying to do.

Why did he choose to step out from behind the curtain of simply deferring to the VA to outright opposition now? It occurred to me that I used the wrong word in my argument for benefits. It was my fault. By using the word "reparations," I plunged the benefits argument into controversy. Bowers thought he could gain allies now, for it was common knowledge that the mere notion of paying reparations was anathema.

When the adjutant general still wouldn't agree to support the Hawkins bill, I recommended that our office nonconcur. Since we were at loggerheads, Colonel Loma Allen, the new deputy director of our office, took the matter up the chain of command to General Bobby Gard for resolution, but General Gard was not in his office.

He was in California, testifying against Daniel Ellsberg for leaking the Pentagon Papers to the *New York Times* and the *Washington Post*. A conference telephone call was made to him.

After the conference call, Colonel Allen came to my office and stood over my desk. I looked up at him, waiting for the decision. He told me that General Gard had asked three questions: 1) who agreed with the adjutant general; 2) who disagreed; and 3) what was the VA's position?

"We told him that everyone agreed except you, Bill."

"You mean everybody?" I asked.

"That's right," Allen said.

Then he told me that General Gard said we would go along with the VA and oppose the legislation and that I should write a paragraph ending the controversy and support the adjutant general's position.

At that point, it mattered little to me what Bobby Gard said. I knew what I had to do. With Colonel Allen still standing over my desk, I turned to my typewriter and typed out a paragraph taking the opposite position of the VA:

> "Whereas this office does not support that part of the bill which would award benefits to second-generation children, the concept of benefits to actual veteran survivors or their widows is a fair objective through congressional legislation."

Eliminating benefits to second-generation children, as much as I hated to do it, was my way of ending the controversy over reparations. From then on, I substituted the word "compensation" for "reparations" when referring to back pay and benefits. I had to compromise if I were to get benefits for Dorsie Willis and the widows of the soldiers, all of whom were old and not far removed from institutional care. They were poor people, and medical bills were already falling heavily upon them. They needed the money now.

The Brownsville Redemption

Colonel Allen was still looking over my shoulder, and he didn't like what he saw. "Bill," he said, "this isn't what General Gard said. You have defied him."

It was true; I had defied General Gard's instructions, but certainly not lightly. A charge of insubordination could be serious. But moral cowardice was worse.

I took the paper out of the typewriter. My hand shook so badly that it was difficult to sign my name. I handed it to the colonel. "Colonel Allen, please take this to General DeWitt Smith."

Smith was the next general in our chain of command. He had recently been moved from public relations to the position of assistant chief of staff for Personnel, reporting directly to Lieutenant General Bernie Rogers. In that position, Smith slightly outranked the adjutant general, who also worked for Bernie Rogers. Fortunately for me, Smith overruled Bobby Gard and the adjutant general. General Smith persuaded General Bowers to include in the army's reply to Congress part of my paragraph:

> "...some compensation to surviving members of the Brownsville incident or their widows is a fair objective through legislation..."

I barely managed to keep the army on the side of supporting "compensation," for, without the army's support, any bill was doomed. But I hadn't in any way won a victory.

On June 5, 1973, I read a story hot off the wires of UPI:

> THE NIXON ADMINISTRATION IS OPPOSING A BILL TO GRANT COMPENSATION TO Families Of 167 Black Soldiers Dismissed From The Army In 1906...Rep Hawkins...Said. The Measure Is Being Opposed By Both The Veterans Administration And The

Lieutenant Colonel (Ret) William Baker

> Office Of Management And Budget. Administrator Donald Johnson Said Hawkins's Bill Would Set An Undesirable Precedent And Discriminate Against Other Veterans. UPI 0605 02:42.

Now that Hawkins had gone public against the Nixon administration, I feared positions would harden. Something extraordinary needed to be done. Not knowing exactly what to do, almost by reflex, I picked up the telephone and called Donald Johnson at VA headquarters. I was surprised when he took my call—and mildly shocked when he listened to my views on the phone and agreed to meet with me. It was risky business for me to step outside of the Pentagon's realm of control and meet with another government official. But the risk was worth taking. I took a cab to his office, but when I got there, he was gone. Instead, he left word for me to brief his staff.

In an emotional yet fact-filled presentation, I told them the story of Brownsville, and I ended by warning them that the tide was running against them and that Hawkins's bill would pass. My friends in the White House could turn this thing around, convince President Nixon to sign the legislation, and as a consequence, the budgetary cost and burdensome staff work would be unhappily forced upon them.

Then I struck a deal with them. If the VA would drop its opposition to the bill, I would guarantee that the funds would come out of the Defense Department budget for retirees. I also assured them that the army would assume the administrative responsibility for payments. The staff made no commitments to me but agreed to pass the information along to Johnson.

After leaving the VA, I hailed a cab and went to the White House (Old Executive Office Building), and met with the staff of Roy Ash, the new director of OMB. I told them essentially the same story about Brownsville, the main element being that the army was historically responsible for the injustice. Therefore, the army should pay restitution in a lump sum and should accept the administrative burden associated with payments.

Compensation Is Due. But…

On or about June 6, 1973, the new secretary of the army, Howard H. ("Bo") Callaway, who had succeeded Secretary Froehkle, received a letter from the executive office of the president, OMB, which essentially rejected General Bowers's reply letter with one exception, the paragraph that said *some compensation is a fair objective through legislation*. The Nixon administration wanted to know specifically what form that compensation should take and would the army be willing to absorb the cost. Gone was the VA's opposition to any compensation.

The administration agreed with the VA that claims should be submitted to the Department of the Army, not the VA, since claims would not be related to regular veterans' benefits. On June 8, 1973, in response to the Nixon administration OMB letter, Belnap prepared another letter for the adjutant general and brought it to me for concurrence. I couldn't agree with it, and I told him why. After first praising him, telling him what a good and honest man I believed he was, I then told him he hadn't taxed his imagination or ingenuity. He simply copied the same old letter using different words to say the same thing, and more to the point, he hadn't addressed the new offer by the Nixon administration. My major objection was that Belnap had not included in his draft letter an unambiguous, unqualified commitment by the army to pay for the compensation out of the army's or Defense Department's funds.

"Well, what do you want me to do?" Belnap said.

"I want you to introduce me to General Bowers and see if he will talk to me directly."

"I don't know about that. He's a busy man. What changes do you want us to make?"

"They want us to pay for this out of our budget. The VA wants us to do the work! Mr. Belnap, can't you see that!"

I typed the changes that I wanted to include:

> The Department believes some compensation to surviving members of the Brownsville Incident or their widows is a fair objective through legislation. A lump-sum payment should be considered through legislative enactment to those men...or to their unremarried widows. Such legislation should provide for payment currently available to the Department of Defense for military retired pay.

In other words, I wanted the Defense Department to cough up the money because the VA was probably broke.

Handing him the proposed changes, I said, "Take me to General Bowers. I want to explain it to him directly. We can work it out." Belnap said I should come with him to Colonel J.C. Pennington's office. He was the executive officer to General Bowers, the gatekeeper, and the defacto second man in charge. We went around to his office on the E-ring corridor. Belnap told me to wait outside in the lobby while he consulted with Pennington.

This was the first time I had been in the suite of the adjutant general's office. The sumptuous lobby was richly appointed with thick oriental carpets, and red and brown leather chairs. A great big overstuffed brown leather couch sat in front of and against a long rectangular mahogany table with beautiful colorful lamps on top. Lining the

The Brownsville Redemption

mahogany-paneled walls were portraits of serious, sternlooking men, all previous adjutant generals.

Standing outside the open door to Pennington's office, I could hear they were arguing.

Belnap's voice was low but distinctive. "We must convince General Bowers to accept Baker's changes."

Pennington's voice was loud and argumentative. "General Bowers will not take orders from a junior officer. Baker is not our boss."

"But he's right on this issue. Let's go see General Bowers."

When I heard them getting up, I moved away from the door over toward one of the portraits.

The two men went into General Bowers's office and closed the door. They weren't in there very long. Pennington came out first and walked right past me without saying a word. A few seconds later, Belnap came out, walked up to me, shook his head, and said, "Colonel Baker, for your own sake, please back off." Having said that, he gave me a little written green memo slip, which I still have today. Then he turned on his heels and went to his office. I read the note.

The adjutant general had refused to speak to me. It was evident to me that he wouldn't be persuaded by words, and certainly not from me. He had taken a hard line. In writing, he had said that he would not change his position unless directed to do so by his immediate superior officer, Bernie Rogers, a three-star general. When any soldier says he will not act unless given an order—that is pretty strong stuff.

Bypassing Colonel Frazier and Colonel Allen, I went to see General Smith and told Joyce, his secretary, that I needed to speak to the general. I showed him the note, and Smith told me to try to find out what JAG's position was on the changed language. At about five o'clock that evening, I learned informally that General Prugh, the judge advocate general, said he would also oppose our changes. With that, Smith said for me to let him handle it.

Since Bernie Rogers was not available to resolve the dispute, I later learned that Smith took the issue to General Creighton W. Abrams, the chief of staff of the army, for resolution. Abrams, a former tank commander during World War II in General George Patton's Third Army, was known for making quick decisions. He overruled the adjutant general and the judge advocate general, putting the army squarely in support for compensation and, just as important, willing to foot the bill.

On June 13, 1973, Secretary of the Army Callaway signed the letter to the chairman of the House Committee on Veterans Affairs, ending the controversy in the army, and the Nixon administration raised no more objections to Hawkins's bill.

During the whole time I struggled to put the army on record to support Hawkins's bill, I openly worked with Senator Hubert H. Humphrey's staff. I had been assisting them, at their request since February 13, 1973, to formulate a bill to make compensatory payments to veterans involved in the Brownsville Incident. Senator Humphrey's administrative assistant had enough political clout to get authorization from the secretary of the army's Office of Congressional Legislative Liaison for me to work with them without going through the time-consuming bureaucratic chain-of-command process.

Working with Senator Humphrey's staff was reassuring. The people I worked with were advocates for the Brownsville soldiers, and I felt confident that Senator Humphrey would succeed in getting some sort of bill through the Senate. On June 14, 1973, he introduced bill number S. 1999, one similar to Hawkins's bill, for himself and Senator Walter Mondale. For processing, the bill went to Senator Vance Hartke, chairman of the Senate Committee on Veterans Affairs.

The Brownsville Redemption

About three weeks after Senator Humphrey introduced his bill, Belnap rushed into my office and showed me a letter dated July 10, 1973, from Senator Vance Hartke. It was addressed to Secretary of the Army Bo Callaway. The senator requested the army's position on Humphrey's bill.

I assumed that the army's response to Humphrey's bill would be identical to the response on Hawkins's bill, thus avoiding any more controversy. Or so I thought.

But Senator Hartke asked Callaway to provide additional information: To develop in the next two weeks a compensatory schedule (mathematical model) to calculate the amounts of payments for the Brownsville survivors. He also requested a "comprehensive historical outline of past compensation awards, especially as to amounts, dates, and factors considered, including items of legitimate damages." Finally, Hartke suggested Callaway consider, among other alternatives, paying $25,000 to surviving Brownsville veterans, $10,000 to widows—and $5,000 to children, if no widow.

To satisfy Hartke's request, the adjutant general made inquiries to the comptroller of the army, the Board for Correction of Military Records, and JAG, seeking information about past compensatory awards in situations analogous to the Brownsville Incident. Since those agencies didn't find any records, Belnap asked me if I would develop a reasonable formula for determining a fair lump-sum payment schedule for each soldier-survivor involved in the Brownsville Incident and each surviving unremarried widow.

Belnap said the payment schedule must be done in a day or two because of the tight Senate deadline and the requirement to get concurrence by the army general staff. Also, the Nixon administration had to approve any payment schedule.

> **OFFICE OF THE ADJUTANT GENERAL**
> **MEMO**
>
> 8 June 73
>
> ~~Col Baker~~ /RB
>
> Your proposed rewording was presented to TAG. He advised that he does not concur in the proposed rewording and will not change the report unless directed to do so by Gen Rogers.
>
> RBB

Office of the Adjutant General Memo, June 8, 1973. "Col. Baker, Your proposed rewording was presented to TAG [The Adjutant General]. He advised that he does not concur with the proposed rewording and will not change the report unless directed to do so by Gen. Rogers." Source: RBB (Richard B. Belnap)

"Look," I told him. "That's not my job. It's the adjutant general's responsibility. Go back and tell General Bowers to have his staff make the calculations." Belnap started for the door.

"Wait!" I called to him. "Richard, you know I'm just joking." I had never called him by his first name before, and he had never called me

"Bill." I couldn't hide my enthusiasm. I was so happy that he had asked me to make the calculations.

He handed me the letter from Senator Hartke and said, "Thanks, Bill."

I went to work. I developed a payment schedule. My calculations showed that Dorsie Willis would receive $126,598. When I finished, I trotted over to Belnap's office and gave him the compensatory pay schedule. Later, when Belnap told me that Colonel Pennington, chief of staff for the adjutant general, and JAG agreed with the compensatory pay schedule, I felt good. I was riding high.

Two weeks went by. The deadline came and went. It was the end of July, and I hadn't heard anything about a reply to Senator Vance Hartke. I was about to call Richard Belnap when my telephone rang.

Belnap was on the other end of the line. "Bill, could you come over to my office right away?" His voice sounded tentative.

The "Japanese Problem"

What disaster has happened now? I hurried over to Belnap's office. He told me that the civilian politicians had rejected the compensatory pay schedule of $126,598. They were supporting the $25,000 for Dorsie Willis and $10,000 for unremarried widows—and nothing for heirs.

What could I do now? I needed time, but time I didn't have. So, I called my contact on John Ehrlichman's domestic staff in the White House. I was told that the Nixon administration would support no more than the $25,000 and $10,000 payments. When I asked why, I was told it is the "Japanese problem."

Questioning my contact further, he explained that the current thinking of the administration and some other politicians was that America soon would have to free its conscience and absolve its guilt for the Japanese internments during World War II. From 1942 until 1946, the federal government imprisoned 120,000 Japanese American citizens and aliens—men, women, and children—for the sole reason of having Japanese ancestry. Compensation for thousands of them was expected to be costly. Because of that likelihood, they could not allow Brownsville to set a costly precedent.

On or about August 3, 1973, the new secretary of the army reported to Senator Vance Hartke that research provided no record of past compensatory awards analogous to the Brownsville Incident. Therefore, no basis for compensation was available. However, the army would have no objections to $25,000 for soldier survivors and $10,000 for unremarried widows. However, it still objected to any payments to heirs or descendants. (The compensatory payment schedule that I had devised—and was agreed to by the army staff—was not mentioned.)

General Smith was unhappy about this proposal. He wrote me a note:

> Why did the assistant secretary of the army take this position? Originally, when Togo West was there, I thought they were sympathetic to Mr. Willis et al. Did Mr. Bennett think this was right and the wise thing to do? Ask informally and quietly.

I knew the answer already. The decision came from on high, from the Nixon administration—and not from my old friends in the assistant secretary of the army's office. It pained me that I couldn't divulge my source to General Smith.

The chief of legislative liaison, Major General Thomas H. Tackaberry, who worked for the secretary of the army, was carrying out political orders when he rejected my compensatory payment schedule.

He wrote that my formula was based on highly speculative assumptions and that such a formula could establish "an undesirable precedent."

Where could I go, and what could I do to reverse this defeat? Nowhere to go above the political structure of the army, I was sure. There was nowhere to go in the Nixon administration. I had been told the reason. Nowhere to go in the Congress, except to Senator Humphrey's staff. I could give them the compensatory payment formula, but that would be disloyal to the army, and I couldn't do that. We had our internal fights, but in the end, the uniform army on the general staff supported me.

Even if Congress endorsed my payment formula and passed Humphrey's bill, Nixon would probably veto it. I must do nothing to hurt the chances of the "some compensation position" I had managed to get the Pentagon to support. Those old people needed money now—not a political fight that would surely last beyond their lifetimes.

Humphrey Makes a Move

In order to be successful, I have always believed that everyone has to struggle up to the top of his mountain. However, one must not misjudge it by continuing the climb and falling off the other side where disaster may await. With only lukewarm support from the Reagan I knew both Congressman Hawkins's bill, H.R. 4382, and Senator Humphrey's bill, S.1999, were doomed to fail in their present forms. The only thing I could do now was to wait and hope that the "some compensation clause" would stick and at least the $25,000 and $10,000 amounts would survive.

It was now the middle of November. I could not wait any longer for some news—good or bad. I called Senator Humphrey's staff and learned that Humphrey, the "Happy Warrior," had attached his bill as an amendment to H.R. 9474, the Veterans' Pension bill, and on November 16, both houses had agreed on the one bill. The $25,000 and $10,000 survived the conference process! All it needed to become law was the signature of President Nixon.

Thanksgiving passed with no word from the White House. I knew there were problems over there with the Watergate break-in scandal, and rumors started surfacing that Nixon would resign. It might seem ironic, but I hoped he would hold on at least until he could sign that legislation.

66 Years Later, Compensation

On December 5 at three o'clock in the afternoon, I received a call from Roger Currier, special assistant to Secretary of the Army Callaway. He told me that Callaway received a call from the White House staff. President Nixon invited me to the White House to witness the signing of H.R. 9474. I asked Currier if anyone else from the Pentagon was invited. He said, "Nobody else, just you."

On December 6, 1973, at twelve noon, wearing my Dress Blue uniform, I stood in the White House Oval Office and watched President Richard M. Nixon fumble with a fountain pen, struggling to hold it between his fingers. The pen kept slipping out of his hand as he nervously signed the Veterans' Pension Act, granting $25,000 compensation to the one (then known) soldier-survivor of the Brownsville Incident and $10,000 to each surviving unremarried widow. Public Law 93-177, 93rd Congress was enacted to take effect on January 1, 1974. After receiving one of Nixon's souvenir fountain pens, I left the White House, feeling that my job was done.

Well, I was wrong about that. Even before the act took effect, the day after Nixon signed H.R. 9474 into law, I began receiving telephone calls saying President Nixon had "an interest" in presenting the $25,000 check to Dorsie Willis at the White House. One of the calls was from Donald Johnson, Veterans Affairs Administrator—a man I had belatedly come to respect. He told me that President Nixon "desires Mr. Willis to be brought to the White House for an appropriate ceremony." He asked me to check on the availability of military aircraft to transport Mr. Willis.

Other queries came from the General Counsel of the Veterans Affairs Committee, Senator Humphrey's office, and other congressional leaders. One suggestion was to have the army bring Willis to Washington, D.C., and have Bo Callaway present him with the check in the Pentagon. Congressional leadership responsible for the legislation would be invited to the presentation ceremony as well. Others wanted the Willis family brought into the Capitol Building for the event.

President Richard M. Nixon signs Public Law # 93-177, the Veterans' Pension Act December 6, 1973, granting $25,000 to any surviving Brownsville Incident veteran and $10,000 to any unremarried widow. Lt. Col. William Baker, congressional leaders, American Legion president and past presidents, and White House staff look on. Courtesy, White House Communications Agency

Before trying to satisfy all those competing interests, I called the aging Willis on December 7 to determine his wishes in the matter. He said it didn't matter to him. "I will do anything you want me to do." But two days later, Willis told me Congressman Hawkins had asked him to have the ceremony in his office in California.

Before I went any further, I called Willis's doctor, Donald Brown, in Minneapolis and asked him what he thought about it. He said, "Colonel Baker, we're barely keeping Mr. Willis alive. I don't recommend he take a trip to Washington or California."

Now how was I going to convince these politicians that it was too risky to bring Dorsie Willis to either Washington or California? I had to scare them off. In telephone calls to the various staff people, I simply relayed what Dr. Brown told me, planting seeds of what would be a public relations disaster in their minds. "What if the old man fell dead in the White House Oval Office, on the Pentagon steps or steps at the Capitol Building?" That did it. My telephone stopped ringing.

Secretary of the Army Callaway settled the presentation question. He decided that since almost all of the work, historical and current, which resulted in the exoneration of the Brownsville soldiers, as well as the legislation granting compensation, was largely the result of army initiatives and persistence, it followed that the army should present the payment check to Mr. Willis. Accordingly, he decided that the ceremony would be conducted at an appropriate place in Willis's hometown. General Smith would represent him—assisted by Major Vincent Gomez and me. Interested congressional leaders would be invited.

The army published orders making me a Class A agent responsible for drawing the checks on the U.S. Treasury and paying $25,000 to Dorsie Willis and $10,000 to eleven unremarried Brownsville widows.

Restitution, At Last

On January 10, 1974, General Smith, Vince Gomez, and I traveled to Minneapolis and hosted a presentation ceremony in honor of Dorsie Willis at the Marquette Inn. Near the end of the luncheon ceremony, and after remarks by General Smith and several testimonial speeches by Dorsie Willis's friends, I presented Mr. Willis with a $25,000 check, and thanks to a ruling from the IRS, it was tax-free.

Lt. Col Baker leans down to shake the hand of Dorsie Willis.

"I'm very grateful for [the check]," Dorsie said. "It's a great birthday present. But it comes too many years too late. I'd hoped for $70,000, figuring $1,000 for each year of the sixty-six years I waited, plus $4,000 for medical costs I've had over the years. But this is all right."

Lieutenant Colonel (Ret) William Baker

General DeWitt Smith and Lt. Col. William Baker with the presentation check for $25,000 made out to Dorsie Willis.

Three years later, on August 24, 1977, at the age of 91, Dorsie Willis passed away. Five days later, on a bright sunny day, the now exonerated former soldier was buried with full military honors in the National Cemetery at Fort Snelling, Minnesota. I was there. The Military Honor Guard folded the flag and handed it to me. It was the same flag I had given him at the presentation of his Honorable Discharge certificate. I said a few words at the request of his widow, Olive Willis, and then I presented her with the flag. A lone bugler sounded taps. The honor guard fired the gun salute and Dorsie Willis, honorably discharged U.S. army veteran, formerly Company D, Brownsville station, was finally at rest.

The Brownsville Redemption

Dorsie W. Willis, 1973 with Lt. Col. William Baker and armed escort to deposit compensation check in the bank. Courtesy U.S. Army Signal Corps

Lieutenant Colonel (Ret) William Baker

DEPARTMENT OF THE ARMY
OFFICE OF THE DEPUTY CHIEF OF STAFF FOR PERSONNEL
WASHINGTON, D.C. 20310

10 January 1976

I, the undersigned, certify that I received U. S. Treasury check number **82,680**, for Twenty-Five Thousand Dollars ($25,000.00) from Class A agent, LTC William Baker, 252-46-7464.

DORSIE W. WILLIE

The Brownsville Redemption

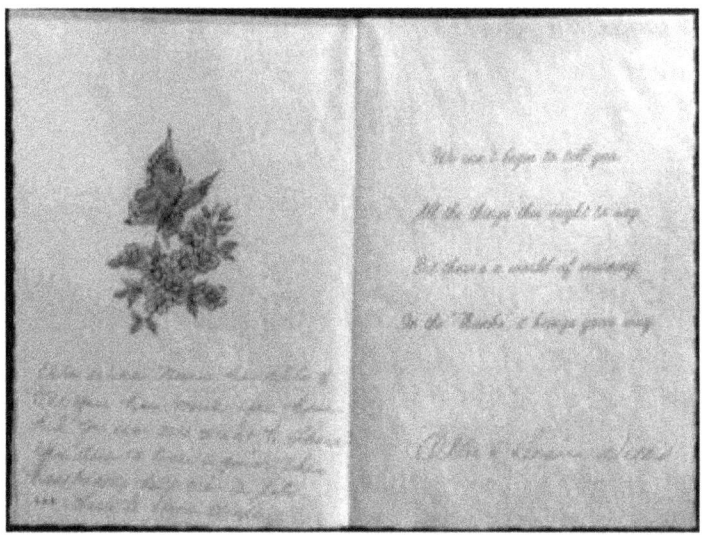

The thank-you note sent to Lt. Col. William Baker from Ollie and Dorsie Willis

Lieutenant Colonel (Ret) William Baker

THIRTY-SIX

Who Actually *Did the Shooting?*

Unanswered Questions

My quest for answers to unanswered questions about Brownsville did not end with the exoneration of the soldiers or with the death of Dorsie Willis. It led me to seek out the white descendants in Brownsville and to go to the old Fort Brown, now partly commercially developed as a resort. The University of Texas at Brownsville and Texas Southmost College occupy part of the old fort, coexisting with some of the old buildings that were standing on the night of the raid.

I located many of the white descendants, but only two of them would talk to me. The others refused. Perhaps they wouldn't want to say anything that might lead to the discovery that one of their grandfathers might have been a murderer.

Ralph Cowen, a prominent citizen and businessman, talked with me freely, saying that his mother and some of his older relatives believed the Black soldiers were dealt a dirty deal by Roosevelt. Cowen said he spent some time in Louis Cowen's old house and saw the bullet holes in it. He drew me a sketch showing where the old house once stood. I talked to Cowen several times over the years and asked him many questions, but he did not remember hearing anything from his older kinfolks that would give me a clue as to the identity of the raiders.

At the Brownsville Historical Society, I was introduced to Henry Krause, a dignified, well-spoken man who retired as a former State Department diplomat. I was told that he knew a lot about the history

The Brownsville Redemption

of the incident, and he did. Starting from old Fort Brown, Krause took me on a walking tour of Brownsville, and we retraced the route of the raiders. He pointed out some of the extant buildings and explained where some of the old buildings once stood. We turned the corner from what used to be Cowen Alley, came down 13th Street, turned that corner onto Elizabeth, then walked down a short distance. He paused and pointed to a shabby brick structure. "Over there in that building is where my great-grandfather ran a saloon."

"Who was he?" I asked.

"Joe Crixell."

I did not tell him that I remembered Joe Crixell all too well from my research. While playing cards in his saloon, he yelled, "Nigger!" when the first shots rang out. "Close up boys, here come the niggers." He said it, without any evidence as to the identity of the raiders. Crixell was gunned down in the middle of Elizabeth Street just a few years after he swore to many lies about the soldiers. Like Ralph Cowen, Henry Krause did not remember hearing anything from his relatives connected to the identity of the raiders.

The Brownsville trail led me further across the Rio Grande River into Matamoros, Mexico, where I followed up on what turned out to be blind leads. Some of the Brownsville residents told me that the answer to who raided the town could be found across the river. I found nothing there.

Who murdered Judge Parks, the creditable witness who saw the raiders but did not recognize them as Black soldiers? That question troubled me. To my disappointment, I could not find anything that connected Parks's death to the identity of the raiders.

I did find out who killed Judge Welch. He was murdered by Alberto Cabrera from Starr County, Texas, but I was unable to connect Cabrera in any way to the Brownsville Incident.

While unanswered questions and imponderables still dogged me, there were answers to questions about the soldiers that became absolutely clear to me. Did Dorsie Willis and the other 166 men carry secrets to the grave, concealing the identity of the raiders? Hardly. Did the soldiers have a motive for raiding the town? Not likely, and certainly not to protest segregated bars and trivial incidents. This position became especially clear when placed in a larger context of the gravity of the crime.

None of the preceding investigations found one scintilla of evidence that would lead to the conviction of any of the soldiers in a court of law. But somebody shot up that town and terrorized its citizens. Who was it? This mystery led me to reexamine the motives of some of the citizens and the key evidence implicating them, which had not been done by any of the prior investigators.

The Evidence Reexamined

The evidence was clear that the citizens did not want Black soldiers stationed in their town. Some of them threatened to drive them out in a week or so. The white saloon owners lost money when the white soldiers were replaced by Black soldiers. The alleged rape of a white woman whipped up hysteria among the citizens, some of whom openly threatened to attack the fort. All of these facts suggested that some of the town's citizens had a motive to frame the soldiers to provide a pretext to force them from Brownsville.

Given my suspicion that the plot was hatched in Tillman's Ruby Saloon, I found the behavior of John Tillman and his friend, Paulino S. Preciado, the publisher of a local Mexican newspaper, strange.

When the raiders came up Cowen Alley, shooting wildly at every light they saw, Preciado said he had heard several shots near the back

The Brownsville Redemption

gate of the Ruby Saloon. He followed the young bartender out the back door of the Ruby Saloon. He claimed he saw the killers come through the open gate from the alleyway, "advance two or three paces" into the courtyard, and shoot down Frank Natus. Light shining from the saloon's open back door allowed Preciado to recognize the raiders as Black soldiers. This is what he told Assistant Attorney General Milton Purdy under oath in December 1907.

But earlier in September, Preciado told a different story to the Grand Jury. He swore he had not seen anything. Moreover, on the night of the shooting, he swore to the justice of the peace, who conducted the inquest over the dead body, that unknown parties fired about seven shots inside the courtyard of the Ruby Saloon and killed Frank Natus. He said as much in his sworn statement, which he wrote out in longhand.

One can pick his or her choice of the contradictory statements to believe. For me, I believe Preciado did see the murderers in the light flowing into the alley from the open back door of the saloon—and he knew who they were.

I believe Frank Natus, the bartender, also saw the killers and recognized them. And that is the key. The raiders realized Natus knew who they were—and killed him for it. And that is also why Preciado swore he did not recognize the killers in his testimony at the inquest, and he told the Grand Jury the same thing.

Months later, in December, when Preciado thought it was safe, he added to the growing body of lies blaming the soldiers. He also thought he could shake down the U.S. government for $10,000 in a lawsuit for an alleged wound where he claimed a bullet grazed his arm.

Not satisfied with Preciado's veracity, I went back to the National Archives and reexamined Frank Natus's original death certificate. It stated:

There were two bullet holes inflicted by the same projectile. The orifice of the entrance was the right side between the 8th and 9th ribs, and the bullet went directly through the body. The orifice of exit was in the left side, about two inches lower than the orifice of entrance.

According to Dr. Fred Combe, who examined the body, the wound was caused by a [single] high-power bullet.

I found it remarkable that, if Preciado is to be believed, seven shots were fired at what had to be short-range. Only one bullet hit Natus, and that lone bullet was never found (or, perhaps never turned in to the authorities). Maybe somebody found the bullet, disposed of it, or put it in the coffin and buried it with him.

After reexamining the bartender's death certificate in the National Archives, I traveled to Brownsville and searched for his grave in the old Brownsville City Cemetery, tombstone by tombstone. I found nothing. Finally, and by happenstance, I saw a large, upright, aboveground crypt almost hidden by weeds and overgrown brush. There I found the name Frank Natus inscribed among other names of people buried in a marble crypt. A poor man, an orphan, buried in that crypt. Why?

After that, I turned to Bruce Aiken, historian, author, and member of the Texas Historical Commission. Like many historians, Bruce firmly believed that the soldiers were the raiders, but when I pressed upon him my distrust of Preciado's story and his possible involvement in the plot, he said, "We ought to open the crypt." The crypt was never opened.

John Tillman's behavior in the face of danger that fatal night was extraordinary. His bartender had been shot dead. He knew danger was nearby for anyone foolish or brave enough to go out into the street. Yet Tillman did. Why did he feel safe walking down the middle of Elizabeth Street during the height of the shooting? If the raiders were Black soldiers, why did they not shoot him? I suspect that Tillman knew the raiders, and the raiders knew him.

Frank Natus's Crypt, Old Brownsville City Cemetery. Lt. Col. William Baker's Private Papers. Photo: Joe Hermosa, Brownsville, Texas

The jammed rifle story was an oddity, too. Much of what Katie Leahy said she saw was an impossibility, including her tale about seeing a raider's rifle jam. But where did she get that story? Herbert Elkins said he saw the same thing. If they did not see it, someone must have told them about a raider having trouble with his gun. No Black soldier would have known or told her that.

However, there was, in fact, a jammed rifle that night. Jose Garza carried it. He was one of Mayor Combe's part-time policemen who was not on duty that night. When Mayor Combe saw him with the rifle, he took it away from him but noticed that the rifle was jammed. There was an exploded cartridge shell casing in the bore of the gun, and the ejector failed to eject it when the gun was fired. Mayor Combe swore to this. Another oddity was Joe Crixell's explanation. The saloon keeper offered a quick, incredulous explanation for the jammed gun. "It doesn't work. It's probably been like that for a long time." Mayor Combe accepted the explanation, but should he have?

That the raiders knew Police Lieutenant Joe Dominguez is beyond doubt. Four witnesses remembered hearing the raiders call out different versions of the same words but saying essentially the same thing. "There goes the son of a bitch! Get him! Give it to him. There he goes, shoot him!"

There was no evidence that any of the soldiers even knew Joe Dominguez—and more to the point of motive, Dominguez spoke well of the soldiers and had not had any negative contact with them. As far as I could determine, the soldiers did not have any accounts to settle with the policeman. But the raiders surely did, and they tried to kill him.

Except for the shooting of Joe Dominguez, which appeared to be the settling of a score, and the killing of Frank Natus, I concluded that the raiders weren't trying to kill anyone, let alone women and children. With the firing of an estimated 300 to 500 rounds of ammunition, it would be a near-miracle that more people weren't killed or wounded or that more bullet holes weren't found in buildings. Unless the raiders were simply poor marksmen, maybe they weren't really trying to shoot anybody. This latter explanation appeared to me to be more plausible when placed in context with the other facts that I unearthed.

Experience taught me to look for patterns—or the lack of them—in about everything I observe, study, or do. To me, it was evident, and it should have been obvious to prior investigators, that because the raiders fired consistently at houses and buildings wherever they saw lights, they created a pattern of their behavior. This was compelling evidence that they were trying to conceal their identity by shooting out the lights. It also suggested to me that the raiders were civilians rather than soldiers.

The Brownsville Redemption

I say that because I walked and ran the historic route, some 350 yards that the raiders took, to better visualize what happened in 1906. I concluded that the route of the raid into town and back to the fort was not favorable to the soldiers. But it was favorable to civilians who could seamlessly melt back into the rush of people running about the town.

No soldiers in their right minds would plan an attack like the Brownsville Affray and seriously believe that it would work. It started with firing from the porches of their barracks (as alleged by the citizens), which would alarm the whole town and wake up the white officers at the fort. Some of their compatriots were then expected to jump the wall, while other soldiers continued to cover the attack by randomly shooting into town, endangering the lives of their fellow soldiers from friendly fire.

To carry out such a plan, they would first have to break into the gun racks or steal the keys from the pockets of the charge of quarters. Then they would have to steal 300 to 500 rounds of ammunition, shoot up the town, sneak back to camp undetected, fall in line, and answer their names at roll call. Later that night, they would have to clean their rifles in the dark in order to pass rigid inspections by the white officers and complete all of this activity without being discovered. Yet this fanciful scenario is precisely what some of the citizens claimed happened. It is also what six investigations said occurred, forming the basis for the drastic action taken by President Roosevelt.

The chance that this occurred in the manner alleged was an impossibility that I eliminated. What remained must be the truth. It did not happen.

Now just for the sake of argument, and maybe a little enlightenment, if some of the soldiers shot up the town, would it be impossible, under the circumstances alleged by the citizens, for dozens of the other soldiers not to know their identities? This line was Roosevelt's argument. If that supposition were true, then the men who knew had kept that secret for years while enduring several investigations, the rigors of cross-examinations, and relentless pursuit by detectives and Secret Service agents. They resisted bribes of money, whiskey, and employment and suffered threats of imprisonment and death by hanging in Texas. Was it possible that they could have withstood such an ordeal for years without being discovered or without at least one of them cracking and pointing the finger at the raiders if he knew? It was not possible.

The Heart of a Conspiracy

I found creditable evidence that a Black citizen of Brownsville named Mack Hamilton knew who the raiders were. Hamilton worked for John Tillman at the Ruby Saloon, primarily serving the few Black soldiers who came into his segregated back room. According to Napoleon B. Marshal, a Black lawyer, and Brigadier General Aaron S. Daggett—the soldiers' defense counsels during the military court of inquiry hearings—Hamilton said he overheard white civilians in Tillman's Ruby Saloon conspiring to attack the fort. They even asked Hamilton, a former soldier who most likely knew Fort Brown, to be their guide.

On the night of the raid, Sheriff Garza locked up Hamilton and kept him in jail for a week. The detention was for his own protection since there was a rumor circulating in the Mexican community that Hamilton knew as many as 16 people who made up the shooting party and that the ringleader was a photographer.

After I examined the sworn testimony of ex-corporal Willie H. Miller, I was convinced that Hamilton had crucial evidence to tell the Senate Committee, the Military Court of Inquiry, and the jury at the court-martial of Major Penrose, but they wouldn't let him testify.

Corporal Miller was Hamilton's cousin. On the night of the raid, Miller was trapped in an uptown Mexican saloon, drinking beer during the shooting. He had been on a 24-hour pass in Mexico and did not know about the curfew. Miller went to Hamilton's house, presumably after the shooting stopped, but before the sheriff threw Hamilton in jail. Miller swore before the court of inquiry that Hamilton told him that the citizens wanted him to join them and to go to the post that night and take somebody out. But he refused. Miller testified that his cousin wouldn't give him the names of the conspirators because he was afraid they might find out that he talked and "people might do something to him down there."

The Senate Committee did, in fact, bring Hamilton to Washington but found a flimsy excuse for not calling him to testify. "He seemed to be in a terror-stricken frame of mind," Marshal said, further explaining that Hamilton was afraid of retribution against his family and wanted transportation for them to be moved out of Brownsville. It appeared that even the U.S. Senate was afraid to put him on the stand for what was termed a case of "extreme humanity...." Or were the senators afraid that his testimony would break the case wide open and embarrass a sitting president?

Later that year, Captain Howland, the recorder "prosecutor" for the Court of Inquiry, also wouldn't allow Hamilton to testify. Howland opposed the subpoena for Hamilton, offering a thin excuse. "There is no money to bring Hamilton here."

Even at Penrose's court-martial, the defense counsel for Penrose was unable to get Hamilton to testify before the court. He was too frightened to take the stand.

The absence of any bullet holes in any of the buildings at Fort Brown gave rise to the question, "If the Brownsville people did the shooting, isn't it remarkable that not a single building at Fort Brown was struck?" In my opinion, that kind of reasoning ignores testimony that the soldiers heard bullets whistling high over the garrison and Mayor Combe's testimony that some of the citizens fired at the Fort. The easy conclusion is that the raiders did not hit anything simply because they aimed high.

But Hamilton had a better answer:

> It was their purpose to shoot over the buildings and not to shoot into them...the object being to draw the men out and draw their fire, so it would appear that the men did the shooting there in the city of Brownsville.

I believe that baiting the soldiers to shoot back into the town was at the heart of the plot of the Brownsville, Texas, conspiracy.

At the end of my search for evidence, I reflected on the incident, its aftermath, relevancy, and ramifications. What was it all about? I knew it was not just about a 10-minute shooting spree in Brownsville, Texas. It was about much more, and to me, it was not simply about racism, although there was plenty of that. Numerous threads came to my mind—honor versus dishonor, mass punishment versus individual guilt, manifest error, an error so egregious that it was deemed bad on its face, injustice versus justice, due process of law, the presumption of innocence, and other constitutional guarantees vs. the summary action of President Roosevelt to punish by executive order. It was about all of those themes intertwined with the principle that might makes right—a throwback beyond the Enlightenment to medieval times and the ancient Greeks. Of course, President Roosevelt was a modern man. But with the Brownsville Incident, he still believed that might made right. Therefore, he, the president, the stronger, the most powerful, decided what was right and imposed his will on the weaker.

The Brownsville Redemption

Knowing that might makes right won in Brownsville and Washington for 66 years caused me to distrust certain judicial expressions that often give the illusion of justice—the sort of stereotyped bromides that politicians and judges are given to, such as, "All men are equal before the law," and the inscription over the U.S. Supreme Court building, "Equal justice under law." President Roosevelt made similar statements as he rationalized his action against the Brownsville soldiers. His statements were barren then, and such lofty pronouncements are barren now and will always be barren, for they assume the law is just.

I am convinced that justice is not always inspired or achieved by the law, and certainly not by well-meaning platitudes, and not even by just having constitutional rights. Those rights must be activated. It was goodness, the God within, and struggle that achieved a measure of justice for the soldiers. What they got was delayed, imperfect, but redemptive. Truth prevailed. And in this case, "truth, crush'd to earth" did rise again.

Too many innocent people live out their lives in prison, waiting for justice.

Noted historian and winner of the Pulitzer Prize, Doris Kearns Goodwin, in her book *The Bully Pulpit*, wrote, "Roosevelt's handling of the Brownsville affair is a permanent scar on his legacy." In his book *Theodore Rex*, Roosevelt biographer Edmund Morris left no doubt that the evidence showed that the "Black soldiers were innocent, and Roosevelt knew it."

It is my position as well—that the Black soldiers were innocent, and President Roosevelt knew it. All of the facts and evidence that I uncovered so many years after the incident pointed to the truth. But what more could the Black soldiers have done to prove their innocence? Nothing.

Lieutenant Colonel (Ret) William Baker

THIRTY-SEVEN

The Officers' Fates and *Seeds of Doubt*

A Change of Mind?

President Roosevelt wrote a letter to Secretary of War William Howard Taft, requesting whether the white officers "are or not blamable." He ordered a "thorough investigation."

Major Penrose was acquitted of the charge of "neglect of duty, to the prejudice of good order and military discipline" for his men's alleged culpability in the Brownsville raid. Penrose recanted his earlier report that the Black soldiers under his command raided the town.

Captain Edgar A. Macklin was tried by court-martial in April 1907 for neglect of duty on one count, having been the officer of the day on August 13, 1906. He was acquitted.

Captain Samuel P. Lyon was tried by court-martial and acquitted. These white officers were acquitted based on evidence that Roosevelt had denied to the Black soldiers.

Sometime later, after the president drummed out the Black soldiers, he was walking along the Potomac River with his old friend Owen Wister. Apparently, he had reconsidered the disparity in his treatment of the Black soldiers and their white officers' commanders. "When you turned those niggers out of the army at Brownsville," Wister asked Roosevelt, "Why didn't you order a court of inquiry for the commissioned officers?"

The Brownsville Redemption

"Because I listened to the War Department, and I shouldn't [have]," Roosevelt replied. He paused. "Of course, I can't know all about everything."

Defensively, he launched into a long disquisition on the fickleness of financial advisors. Wister heard him out. Roosevelt continued, "And so, the best you can do is to stop, look and listen—and then jump…Yes. And then jump. And hope I've jumped right."

Extraordinary, I thought. Roosevelt *had* entertained the thought he could have made a mistake in dishonorably discharging all 167 Black soldiers. He was not sure if he had done the right thing. He just didn't know. He hoped he had. But it was too late, too late.

The defense counsel for Major Penrose in his court-martial said:

> …but we become a world power, and while I recognize and appreciate that certainly during this generation, and whether there is going to be prejudice against the Negro…I certainly hope for the good of this country—and that the time is not very far distant—when the uniform of the United States will protect the Black man or the brown man, just as it does the white man. That prejudice is of that general nature that we all recognize against the Negro race…but particularly against the African; but I certainly hope that we, and each of us, will make it our effort to cultivate sentiment in this country that will protect these Colored men.

Unfortunately for the Black troops of the 25th Infantry stationed in Brownsville on August 13, Texas, 1906, Roosevelt's later doubts notwithstanding, that sentiment did not arrive in time to save them.

Appendix A

Text of the letter AMENDMENT OF ORDERS by Secretary of the Army Verne L. Bowers, revising the text "discharged without honor" to read "honorably discharged." Included here are the names of the 167 soldiers (edited to appear in alphabetical order by rank).

22 September 1972
DEPARTMENT OF THE ARMY
Office Of The Adjutant General Washington, D.C. 20315

SUBJECT: AMENDMENT OF ORDERS Action: Amendment

So much of: Paragraph 1, Special Orders 266, War Department, 9 November 1906.

As reads: "discharged without honor from the Army by their respective commanding officers and forever debarred from re enlisting in the Army or Navy of the United states, as well as from employment in any civil capacity under the Government."

How changed: Is amended to read: "honorably discharged from the Army by their respective commanding officers."

Is amended to add: no back pay, allowances, benefits or privileges shall accrue by reason of the issuance of this order to any heirs or descendants.

Is amended to delete: The discharge certificate in each case will show that the discharge without honor is in consequence of Paragraph 1, Special Orders, No. 266, War Department, November 9, 1906.

Pertaining to member(s) of: Company B, 25th infantry

First Sergeant Mingo Sanders
Quartermaster Sergeant Walker McCurdy
Sergeant George Jackson
Sergeant James R. Reid
Sergeant Luther T. Thornton
Corporal Ray Burdett
Corporal Jones A. Coltrane
Corporal Edward L. Daniels
Corporal Anthony Franklin
Corporal Wade H. Watlington
Cook Leroy Horn
Cook Solomon Johnson
Musician Henry Odom
Private James Allen
Private John B. Anderson
Private William Anderson
Private Battier Bailey
Private James Bailey
Private Elmer Brown
Private John Brown
Private William Brown
Private William J. Carlton
Private Harry Carmichael
Private George Conn
Private John Cook
Private Charles E. Cooper
Private Boyd Conyers
Private Lawrence Daniel

Lieutenant Colonel (Ret) William Baker

Private Carolina DeSaussure
Private Ernest English
Private Shepherd Glenn
Private Isaac Goolsby
Private Charley Hairston
Private William Harden
Private John Holoman
Private James Johnson
Private Frank Jones
Private Henry Jones
Private William J. Kernan
Private George Lawson
Private Willie Lemons
Private Samuel McGhee
Private George W. Mitchell
Private Isaiah Raynor
Private Stansberry Roberts
Private William Smith
Private Thomas Taylor
Private William Thomas
Private Alexander Walker
Private Edward Warfield
Private Julius Wilkins
Private Alfred N. Williams
Private Brister Williams
Private Joseph L. Wilson

Company C, 25th Infantry

Quartermaster Sergeant George W. McMurray

The Brownsville Redemption

Sergeant Darby W. O. Brawner
Sergeant Newton Carlisle
Sergeant Samuel W. Harley
Sergeant George Thomas
Corporal John H. Hill
Corporal Charles H. Madison
Corporal Willie H. Miller
Corporal Solomon P. O'Neil
Corporal Preston Washington
Cook Lewis J. Baker
Cook George Grier
Musician James E. Armstrong
Musician Walter Banks
Artificer Charles E. Rudy
Private Clifford I. Adair
Private Henry W. Arvin
Private Charles W. Askew
Private Frank Bounsler
Private Robert L. Collier
Private Erasmus T. Dabbs
Private Mark Garmon
Private George W. Gray
Private Joseph H. Gray
Private James T. Harden
Private George W. Harris
Private John T. Hawkins
Private Alphonso Holland
Private Thomas Jefferson
Private Edward Johnson
Private George Johnson

Private John Kirkpatrick
Private Edward Lee
Private Frank J. Lipscomb
Private West Logan
Private William Mapp
Private William McGuire, Jr.
Private Andrew Mitchell
Private Thomas L. Mosley
Private James W. Newton
Private George W. Perkins
Private James Perry
Private Oscar W. Reid
Private Joseph Rogers
Private James Sinkler
Private Calvin Smith
Private George Smith
Private John Smith
Private John Streater
Private Robert Turner
Private Leartis Webb
Private Lewis Williams
Private James Woodson

Company D, 25th Infantry

First Sergeant Israel Harris
Quartermaster Sergeant Thomas J. Green
Sergeant Jacob Frazier
Sergeant Jerry E. Reeves
Corporal James H. Ballard

The Brownsville Redemption

Corporal David Powell
Corporal Albert Roland
Corporal Temple Thornton
Corporal Winter Washington
Musician Joseph Jones
Musician Hoytt Robinson
Cook Charles Dade
Cook Robert Williams
Artificer George W. Newton
Private Charles Hawkins
Private Henry Barclay
Private Sam M. Battle
Private Henry T. W. Brown
Private John Butler
Private Richard Crooks
Private Strowder Darnell
Private Elias Gant
Private James C. Gill
Private John Green
Private Alonzo Haley
Private George W. Hall
Private Barney Harris
Private Joseph H. Howard
Private John A. Jackson
Private Benjamin F. Johnson
Private Walter Johnson
Private Charles Jones
Private John R. Jones
Private William E. Jones
Private William R. Jones

Private Edward Jordan
Private Wesley Mapp
Private William A. Matthews
Private James Newton
Private Elmer Peters
Private Len Reeves
Private Edward Robinson
Private Henry Robinson
Private Robert L. Rogan
Private Samuel E. Scott
Private Joseph Shanks
Private John Slow
Private Zachariah Sparks
Private William Van Hook
Private Samuel Wheeler
Private Edward Wickersham
Private Dorsie Willis

Company A, 25th Infantry

Private James A. Simmons
Private August Williams

Company G, 25th Infantry

Private James Duncan

Unassigned, 25th Infantry

Private Perry Cisco

Troop C, 9th Cavalry

Private Alexander Ash
Private Taylor Stroudemire
Private Robert James

Troop H, 10th Cavalry

Private John W. Lewis

By order of the secretary of the army: Verne L. Bowers

Major General, USA
The Adjutant General

Lieutenant Colonel (Ret) William Baker

AUTHOR'S BIOGRAPHY

Lieutenant Colonel William Baker (Ret) was born in Amsterdam, Georgia, on November 26, 1931, and grew up in nearby Attapulgas. His mother, Julianne Lee Baker, died when he was just 11 months old. After his father, Roosevelt Baker, remarried, he was adopted by Ned Keaton, a freed slave, and his wife, Angeline. The Keatons raised William as their own grandson.

The Brownsville Redemption

In 1949, Baker graduated valedictorian of his class from the college preparatory program at Attapulgus Vocational High School. He won Georgia State Quiz contest, which earned him a full scholarship to Howard University, where he was a member of Alpha Phi Alpha Fraternity and a charter member of the Delta Epsilon Boule, Sigma Pi Phi Fraternity. As the top-ranked cadet in the university's ROTC program, he received the Distinguished Military Graduate Award. He graduated cum laude.

Baker received his MBA in Controllership from Syracuse University, then distinguished himself at the Ballistic Research Laboratories, Aberdeen Proving Ground, in Maryland. In 1969, while at Aberdeen, he published *The Role of Cost Discounting in Weapons Systems Evaluations*, co-authored with his assistant, Robert Williams. It was published by the U.S. Department of Commerce in 1969 and sold around the world for more than 40 years. This work is now archived by the National Science Foundation.

In 1972, Baker was assigned to the Office of Equal Opportunity at the Pentagon, where, in addition to other duties, he developed Operation Aware in conjunction with the White House staff. This program permitted Black soldiers to air their concerns directly to influential Black businessmen as well as the Department of the Army.

Bill Baker's crowning life's achievement was the reinvestigation of the Brownsville Texas Incident of 1906. After extensive research, he prepared a case for the secretary of the army that resulted in the reversal of President Theodore Roosevelt's decision to dishonorably discharge the soldiers of the First Battalion, 25th Infantry. Based on Baker's research, the secretary of the army made the decision to correct the injustice and change the soldiers' discharge to "Honorable."

The resolution was signed by President Richard M. Nixon, bringing national acclaim to Baker and the United States Army. Baker received the coveted Pace Award from the Secretary of the Army and the Legion of Merit in 1973 as a result of his painstaking work.

Baker was awarded two Bronze Stars, two commendation medals with oak leaf clusters, and various other medals for service in Korea, NATO, and Vietnam. In his post-military retirement, he was employed as a financial manager for Rohm and Haas Chemical Company (now Dow Chemical) in Philadelphia, PA. He retired in 1993.

Secretary of the Army Robert F. Froehlke described Baker's contributions best when he said, "Baker's achievement has brought favorable acclaim to the Army in the field of Civil Rights and has had a positive commitment to elimination of racial injustice."

Lieutenant Colonel Baker died on September 24, 2018, just weeks after the ink on the final page of his manuscript had dried. With devoted dedication and perseverance, his wife, Dr. Bettye Foster Baker, then took up the banner of his legacy. Her tireless effort has succeeded in bringing the incredible story of Baker's proudest achievement to light.

DEPARTMENT OF THE ARMY
THE PACE AWARD: 1973
FOR EXCEPTIONAL SERVICE
AWARDED TO

Lieutenant Colonel William Baker

Lieutenant Colonel William Baker, Office of Equal Opportunity Programs, Office of the Deputy Chief of Staff for Personnel, distinguished himself by exceptional performance of duty during a reinvestigation of the Brownsville Incident of 1906. This event resulted in every soldier assigned to the all black unit of the 1st Battalion, 25th Infantry being discharged without honor and barred forever from re-enlisting in the Army or Navy and from civilian employment with the Government. After extensive research, Lieutenant Colonel Baker prepared a case upon which the Secretary of the Army made the decision to correct the injustice by changing the discharges of these soldiers to honorable. In addition, he developed the process for identification of survivors; assisted in the location of a bona fide survivor; and formulated the Army position favoring Legislative approval of a bill which was signed by the President and provided compensation to survivors and unmarried widows of soldiers involved in the Brownsville Incident. Lieutenant Colonel Baker's accomplishments reflect great credit upon himself and have brought national acclaim to the United States Army.

WASHINGTON, D. C.

_____
Secretary of the Army

Lieutenant Colonel (Ret) William Baker

SOURCE NOTES

This reconstruction is based primarily on official government reports and on original source documents in the U.S. National Archives. The original source documents are located in boxes 4499 through 4504, the adjutant general document file number 1135832. I have referenced many of these materials in the narrative of the book. By far the most important materials I relied on were—the sworn affidavits, depositions, testimony of the soldiers, townspeople, and officials; courts martial records; and technical reports by ballistic experts and others.

The government reports constituted the official records of the Brownsville Affray as the incident was called at that time in history. These records included three presidential messages, War Department reports, the hearings of the Senate Military Affairs Committee, the courts-martial reports of Major Charles W. Penrose and Captain Edward Macklin, and the military court of inquiry proceedings, all published by the U.S. Government Printing Office in Washington. D.C. These published reports included many volumes, some of which constituted thousands of pages. They purported to tell the story of what really happened at Brownsville.

Although these published government documents offered valuable information, as I reviewed and analyzed them, I grew to distrust much of their information and I rejected many of their conclusions.

Other sources included telegrams, cablegrams, memoirs, contemporary newspaper accounts, letters, and autobiographical materials of some of the major characters.

The Brownsville Redemption

The second part of the book, "My Quest to Exonerate the Innocent," is based largely upon the evidence culled from the same government records and the same original source documents in the National Archives I relied upon for the reconstruction, plus official government letters and memoranda from 1971 to 1974; my interviews with one of the last surviving soldiers, Dorsie Willis; my private papers; and my memory.

Lieutenant Colonel (Ret) William Baker

SELECTED MEDIA RESOURCES AND ABBREVIATIONS

Institutions

National Archives, 700 Pennsylvania Avenue, NW, Washington, DC 20408

Library of Congress, 101 Independence Avenue, SE, Washington, DC 20540

The Law Library in the Pentagon, 1400 Defense Pentagon Arlington, VA 22202

U.S. Army War College, Army Heritage and Education Center, 950 Soldiers Dr. Carlisle Barracks, PA 17013-5021

The Brownsville Historical Association (Society), 641 E Washington St. Brownsville, TX 78520

The University of Texas at Brownsville, 1 W University Blvd. Brownsville, TX 78520

Books

Dostoyevsky, Fyodor, 2001. *Crime and Punishment.* Translated by Constance Garnett. Dover Publication, Mineola, New York. "His profound understanding of the tragic side of life and the workings of the psyche make him one of the greats of Russian literature. His fascination with the theme of crime and the problem of conscience arose from his own firsthand experience." Dostoyevsky's protagonist...experiences a profound sense of alienation from humanity after his crime, and his isolation from society accentuates his moral dilemma. Embodied in this inward struggle is the notion of good and evil vying for supremacy of the soul, and a recurring of Dostoyevsky."

Voltaire, 1884. *Candide*. Edited by Francois-Marie Arouet, 112 pages. (0-486-6689-3). Doctor Pangloss in Voltaire's satire Candide proclaimed that "This is the best of all possible worlds," notwithstanding all kinds of disasters he encountered.

Goodwin, Doris Kearns, 2013. *The Bully Pulpit*. Simon and Schuster, p. 515. "Roosevelt's handling of the Brownsville affair is a permanent scar on his legacy."

Morris, Edmund, 2002. *Theodore Rex* (Modern Library Paperback Edition). Morris said that Roosevelt had a failure when he agreed with the white citizens of Brownsville and had succumbed to white racist pressure.

Alighieri, Dante, **1935**. *The Divine Comedy*. A long poem in book style. Sources of the select passages are: The Divine Comedy of Dante Alighieri 1265-1321. Inferno, Purgatory, Paradise. New York: The Union Library Association, Print. Inscription over the gates of hell: "Abandon hope all ye who enter here."

CI Senate Document, 701, 61st Congress, 3rd Session, 1910. Report of the Proceedings of the Court of Inquiry Relative to the Shooting at Brownsville, TX. Twelve Volumes. (US Government Printing Office 1911).

CMA Committee on Military Affairs, U.S. Senate. Senate Document, 402, 60th Congress, 1st Session (1907).

Lieutenant Colonel (Ret) William Baker

Affray At Brownsville, Tex. Hearing Before the Committee on Military Affairs, US Senate. (US Government Printing Office 1907).

DAMlDepartment of the Army Memoranda, Letters and Notes, 1971-1974. These documents are listed by their subjects and file symbols. They should be available at Department of the Army or its record storage facilities.

NAUS National Archives—boxes 4499 through 4504, the adjutant general document file number 1135832.

PG-CM-M-P *Affray at Brownsville*, Texas, August 13 and 14, 1906 Proceeding of a General Court Martial...in the Case of Edgar A. Macklin, (Government Printing Office 1907).

SD-155 (Part 1) Senate Document, 155, 59th Congress, 2nd Session, 1906Summary Discharge or Mustering Out of Regiments or Companies Message From The President of the United States (US Government Printing Office 1906).

SD-155 (Part 2) Senate Document, 155, 59th Congress, 2d Session, 1907. Summary Discharge or Mustering Out of Regiments or Companies Message From The President of the United States (US Government Printing Office 1907).

SD-389 Senate Document, 389, 60th Congress, 1st Session (1908). The Brownsville Affray.

SD-430 Senate Document, 430, 60th Congress, 1st Session (1908). Names of Enlisted Men Discharged on Account of Brownsville Affray with Applications for Reenlistment.

SD-587 Senate Document, 587, 60th Congress, 2nd

Session (1908). Special Message of the President of the United States. Contains the Report of Investigation of Mr. Herbert J. Brown. (US Government Printing Office 1908).

SR-355 Senate Report No. 355, Parts 1 and 2, 60th Congress, 1st Session (1908). The Brownsville Affray. (US Government Printing Office 1908).

WBPP William Baker Private Papers

Newspapers

BDH *Brownsville Daily Herald*

NYT *The New York Times*

SPPE *St. Paul Pioneer Press*, St. Paul., MN, Monday, February 12, 1973

TBHC *The Brownsville Heritage Complex*

WP *The Washington Post*

Periodicals

JBB Bishop, Joseph Bucklin. *Theodore Roosevelt and His Time.* (Scribner's, 1920.)

JMC Carroll, John M. *Twenty Fifth Infantry.* (The Old Army Press, 1972).

CC Clark, Champ. *My Quarter Century of American Politics.* (Harper's, 1920).

DB Du Bois, W.E.B. *The Souls of Black Folks.*

JBF   Foraker, Joseph Benson, 1916, *Notes of a Busy Life* (2 vols.). (Stewart and Kidd Co., Cincinnati, 1916.)

JBF   Foraker, Joseph Benson, April, 1908, "A Review of the Testimony in the Brownsville Investigation." (North American Review, April 1908.)

JF   Foraker, Julia Bundy. "I Would Live It Again." (Harper's, 1932).

JHF   Franklin, John Hope. From Slavery to Freedom. (Knopf, 1967).

CF   Fuller, Charles. *The Brownsville Raid*. (A Play by Charles Fuller produced by the Negro Ensemble Company, 133 Second Avenue, New York City, 1975)

EM   Morris, Edmund. *Theodore Rex* (Modern Library Paperback Edition 2002).

ABP   Paine, Albert Bigelow. *Captain Bill McDonald: Texas Ranger*. (J.J. Little & Ives Co., New York, 1909).

HFP   Pringle, Henry F. *Theodore Roosevelt*. (Harcourt, Brace, 1931).

MCT   Terrell, March Church. *A Colored Woman in a White World*. (Ransdell, Inc. Publishers, Washington, D.C., Arno Press, New York, 1980).

JAT   Tinsley, James A. *The Brownsville Affray*. (Master of Arts Thesis, University of North Carolina, Chapel Hill, 1948).

—"Roosevelt, Foraker, and the Brownsville Affray." (Journal of Negro History, January 1956).

JEW   Watson, James E. *As I Knew Them*. (Bobbs-Merrill, 1935).

JDW-1 Weaver, John D. *The Brownsville Raid.* Paperback. (W.W. Norton & Co., Inc, New York, 1973).

JDW-2 *The Senator and the Sharecropper's Son: Exoneration of the Brownsville Solders.* (College Station, 1997).

Lieutenant Colonel (Ret) William Baker

BACKSTORIES

Foreword

The Dreyfus Affair, a political crisis in France beginning in 1894 and continuing through 1906. The controversy centered on the question of the guilt or innocence of army captain Alfred Dreyfus, a Jew from Alsace. Dreyfus was accused of selling military secrets to the Germans. In December 1894, he was convicted of treason.

At first the public supported the conviction and was willing to believe Dreyfus, who was Jewish, was guilty. Much of the early publicity surrounding the case came from anti-Semitic groups (especially the newspaperLa Libre Parole, edited by Édouard Drumont), to which Dreyfus symbolized the supposed disloyalty of French Jews. Source: https://www.britannica.com›event›Dreyfus-affair.

Alan Riding, July 7, 2006

https://www.ny-times.com/2006/07/07/world/europe/07dreyfus.html

Chapter 2. Thirty-five Years Later: The Pentagon, June 1, 1972

The second letter was written by Army lawyers (JAG): DA Letter to Congressman F. Edward Hebert, Chairman, Committee on Armed Forces, House of Representatives. To direct the to rectify certain official action as a result of the Brownsville Raid, 1906 (April 23, 1971). This letter states the views of DA in opposition to H.R. 6866. File Symbol DAJA-AL 1972/4295. See DAML.

The third letter: DA Letter to George P. Shultz, Director of Management and Budget. This letter reiterates the Army's opposition to H.R. 6866. Ibid.

Another amazing result of the incident: The principal sources used for this account of the split in the African American community and its response to the summary dismissal of the Black soldiers are JAT, pp. 45-49, 53 56, 60; 93-94 and 96; and AJL, pp. 59-128.

Chapter 3. Brownsville, Texas, 1906 Anger and Fear Take Over

Weeks have passed since last May: War Department General Order 98, May 26, 1906, ordered Companies B, C, and D 25th Infantry to Texas. SD-701, p. 1625.

At the outset, trouble was predicted. Ibid. **citizens were making violent threats:** CMA, pp. 2941-2942, 2949. SD-701, pp. 2116-2119, 2121-2124.

Was that letter complaining about the soldiers that Wreford wrote: NA, box 4501.

Chapter 4. Brownsville Awaits the Final Decision

The fact that a certain amount of race prejudice: SD-155 Part 1, p. 301.

"He's been fornicating with a Mexican woman!" 3rd Indorsement. Fort Reno, Okla, Jan.16, 1906 [1907] to letter from Sam P. Wreford to President Theodore Roosevelt 01-03-1907. NA.

The record also revealed that Sam Wreford has paid no taxes in Brownsville for several years and that he is, in fact, a resident of *Mexico!"* Ibid.

These are the brave soldiers who captured El Caney: BDJ/31/06, pp. 1, 3.

"Talks About a Fight." he began to read from the paper: Ibid, p.1.

Practices nepotism with his sister: I first heard about this type of demagoguery used in the old South by George Smathers against the late Senator Claude Pepper in a race for the U.S. Senate in Florida during the 1950s.

Chapter 5. Buffalo Soldiers Are Coming to Brownsville

"The people in Texas are gonna give you hell! Don't go down there!" This account was drawn from the deposition of John Amos Holoman, January 8, 1908, p.24. NA.

"...their five white officers dreaded taking the troops to Texas." SD-701, p. 1625.

He had been schooled at West Point: SR-355, Part 2, p. 2. Officials at West Point deny that Penrose was a graduate. Letter to Lt. Col Baker, 12/13/2002 from U.S. Military Academy. WBPP.

From the standpoint of health and physique: The description of Major Penrose was based on his medical records as recorded by doctors at Walter Reed Army General Hospital. NA.

"...these damn niggers trading down here." CI, p. 724.

Chapter 6. The Troops *Go To Town*

"It seems kinda funny I can't buy salve in a drugstore.": PGCM-P, p. 1090.

"**Why, you Black son of a bitch**, *don't you know this is a white man's town?:* Deposition, Private McGuire taken by Lt. Col. L. A. Lovering. NA. Also see SD 155-Part 1, p. 160.

It was rumored that back in 1904 Bugs headed a secret society of thugs: This account of Bugs' character was drawn from a sworn statement dated January 1907 by Samuel P. Holman. It was attached to a letter from Holman to Roosevelt, December 30, 1908. Holman was a deserter from the Army when he made the statement to Detective Browne.

"Private John Amos Holoman...had a talent for making money." The description of Holoman's money making ventures was taken from his deposition.

"Then he began pistol-whipping him about the head and shoulders." There are several versions of Tate's pistol-whipping of Private Newton. Newton's version is in his affidavit, Penrose reporting, SD 155-Part 1, p. 69. Tate's version, SD 155-Part 2, pp. 454-455. Deposition, Private Frank J. Lipscomb, taken by Lt. Col. L. A. Lovering: NA. Also see SD 155-Part 1, p. 133. Ibid, pp. 209-210.

"**You damned niggers are too smart around here, anyway.**" SD 155-Part 2, p. 479.

Chapter 7. "The Yellow Rose of Texas"

"**That's a colored soldier's song.**" The best historical evidence I could find shows that the song "The Yellow Rose of Texas" was probably

Lieutenant Colonel (Ret) William Baker

written by a Black person. Private Reid was correct. The song had been sung by Black soldiers for years, long before Texas became a state. There was a fair skin African-American woman named Emily West Morgan who was "the Yellow Rose of Texas." See "In Search of the 'Yellow Rose of Texas'" by Mark Whitelaw. http://www.markw.com/yelrose.htm.

Mrs. Evans, a white woman, alleged that she had been accosted by a big Black soldier: PGCM-P, pp. 1146-1148.

"...report this outrage on my wife." CMA, p. 2381.

"...with the number of Mexican prostitutes in this town, I hardly think rape would be necessary." PGCM-P, p. 1147.

"...as prostitutes are too common in town." SD 155-Part 1, p. 69.

Chapter 8. Midnight Attack on Brownsville, August 13, 1906

...a big black dog had cornered several children who were huddled in a group: PGCM-M, p. 181. **then Trooper began racing up and down along the wall, barking loudly.** PGCM-M, p. 61. **sixteen to twenty men emerged from the darkness near the garrison wall:** The location of the beginning of the attack was reconstructed from the testimony of the two most credible witnesses in a position to know. Testimony of Private Joseph H. Howard, Sentinel on Post No. 2.: PGCM-M, p .60. Also see: PGCM-P, pp. 1057-1058. See deposition of Matias G. Tamayo, post scavenger [garbage collector] 12/29/06, p. 2. NA.

...a single frame house...stood alone, its lights still burning: The description of Cowen's House, how it was shot up, and how the family was terrorized was drawn from the testimony of Anna A. Cowen. CMA, p. 2790-2803.

"A student lamp...was shot out. The lantern in the kitchen...shattered with a single shot, as was a large Rochester lamp." Ibid., pp. 2794, 2795. The raiders were bent on shooting out the lights for obvious reasons.

"Madame, Madame! 'Tis the day of judgment!" Ibid., p. 2794.

"The soldiers are going to kill us!" Ibid.

Louis Cowen's house was being shot up: Anna Cowen and her husband Louis Cowen testified that the soldiers did not have a "grudge" against their family. Ibid., pp. 2796, 2809-2810.

"...they fired sporadically at the Western Union Telegraph building, Yturria's house, and Martinez's Cottage from their position in Cowen's Alley." I reconstructed the route of the attack from the trail of damages and by sorting out the conflicting testimony of many witnesses. *Also see map of Brownsville: JAT,* p. xvi.

"**Git the light.**" The single shot missed the oil lamp in Hale Odin's room in the Miller Hotel. Deposition of Hale Odin before Assistant Attorney General Purdy, 1/4/07, pp. 7-9. NA.

"**Close up your doors. Here come the niggers.**" Joe Crixell's testimony, CMA, pp. 2483-2518.

Mr. S. C. More testified he heard a raider say, "**There goes the son of a bitch. Let's git 'im.**": Deposition of S.C. Moore, January 1, 1907, p. 1. NA.

"**The colored soldiers are firing into houses and killing the people!**": PGCM-P, p. 118. Policeman Dominguez testified he heard the raiders say, "**Give him hell!**" Ibid., p. 118.

"...fired a volley in the direction of the policeman, shooting him in the arm and shooting his horse." Ibid.

"...one of the men was having trouble with his gun." CMA, pp. 2893-2923. "Don't go out! I heard noises in the alley." See Nicholas S. Alanis' testimony. PGCM-P, pp. 422-427. Also see his testimony before Assistant Attorney General Purdy, pp. 100-102.

"A group of five or six armed men appeared in the alley and fired." Preciado's testimony before Assistant Attorney General Purdy. NA.

"Frank exclaimed, 'Ay Dios' and fell down." See contradiction in Paulino Preciado's testimony before the grand jury, p. 1. NA.

"A lantern was burning in Fred Starck's house. A hail of bullets hit the two-story house, knocking out the lantern." CMA, p. 154.

"Fred, hug the wall. They are shooting down the street." CMA, p. 2383.

"Don't go any farther, mayor. You will be shot." Ibid., p. 2384.

"What are you doing with that rifle, Garza?" Ibid.

...there was an empty cartridge inside the magazine, which the ejector had failed to eject: *See Joe Crixill's testimony. Ibid., p. 2515.*

Chapter 9. Did the Soldiers Shoot Up The Town?

"...the soldiers have shot up the town." That was the "universal expression." CMA, p. 2385.

"I don't know what the word fear means." PGCM-P, p. 86.

Yellow nigger with spots. WP, (June 7, 1907). Also see PGCM-P, p. 86.

"I served with those troops,...know them to be...efficient. Splendidly armed...valuable lives will be lost." CMA, p. 2386.

"Your men have gone into town...killed one man..." Ibid., p. 2387.

"...I can hardly believe that..." Ibid.

"...no evidence that any weapons had been fired." Ibid., pp. 1933-1934.

"Well, Macklin, it looks as if our men...." Ibid., pp. 1933.

"...what do you think of this evidence? Your men did this." Ibid., p. 2392.

"...this is almost conclusive evidence...." Ibid.

Chapter 11. A Citizens' Committee Investigates

"...your men did this shooting." CMA, pp. 2394-2395.

"No one else has those arms or ammunition." Ibid., p. 2395.

"I would give my right arm..." Ibid.

"Regret to report serious shooting..." SD 155-Part 2, pp. 430-431.

"We know that this outrage...." SD 155-Part 2, p. 449.

"God damn him!" Ibid.

"I don't know if they were Negroes...." Ibid.

"...we ask you to have the troops...removed...and replaced by white soldiers." Telegram to Roosevelt from Citizens Committee, 8/15/06. SD 155-Part 1, pp. 20-21.

"Come out, you Black sons of bitches." Affidavit of Private Map, 9/25/06. SD 155-Part 2, p. 516.

"...we will kill all of you." Affidavit of Private Rudy, 9/12/06. SD 155-Part 2, pp. 512-513.

"I saw some civilians running...." Affidavit of Corporal John H. Hill, 9/24/06, p. 69. NA.

"After further investigation...." Telegram, Penrose to Military Secretary, Dept. of Texas, 8/14/06. NA.

Chapter 12. The Blocksom Investigation

"SAVE US FROM NIGGER HUSBANDS." JDW-1, p.115.

"The cause of the disturbance..." SD 155-Part 1, p. 38.

"...recommended the removable...." Ibid.

"Our position is misunderstood." SD 155-Part 1, p. 26.

Roosevelt approved...recommendation...ordered the removal: SD 155-Part 1, pp. 34-35.

Chapter 13. A Texas Ranger *Comes to Town*

...don't have the authority to enter the fort: I based this account on, ABP, p. 324. "that Brownsville business." Ibid.

"Why, them hellions." Ibid. McDonald faced down: I based this account on Paine's book. Ibid., p. 198.

"...you'd like to take it up." Ibid.

"...done took it up." Ibid.

"I'm Captain McDonald...here to investigate...show you niggers something. Put up them guns!" Ibid., p. 328. Quotations are from McDonald's autobiography as told to Paine.

"You, as their officers,..." Ibid., p. 337.

"Judge, nobody gonna move..." Based in part from Paine. Ibid., p. 345.

"Military authorities are trying to take our prisoners..." Ibid., p. 346.

Chapter 15. Fort Reno Days of Forced March

Author's note. I named the hills the troops ran up and down after two hills at Fort Knox, Kentucky, that I used to drill my troops on during basic training.

Chapter 17. A "Conspiracy of Silence"

He imbibed too much and fell out the window. Senator Foraker questioned whether Judge Parks was pushed or fell out of the window. CMA, p. 2423.

He didn't see a single soldier on the streets. Deposition of Wilbert Voshelle, 10/24/06, p.1. NA.

"That the raiders were soldiers...cannot be doubted." SD 155 Part 2, p. 427.

"All enlisted men of the three companies present...discharged...without [honor]..."Ibid., p. 429.

"It must be confessed that the colored soldier is much more aggressive...." Ibid., p. 430.

Chapter 18. The Grand Jury Investigates

"...[the] unprovoked, murderous midnight assault..." CMA, pp. 3297-3298.

The soldiers now being held in jail were entitled to go free. SD 155-Part 1, pp. 107-108.

"...evidence did not point with sufficient certainty to any individual..." CMA, p. 3242.

"The reasons for the selecting of these men..." SD 155-Part 1, p. 66.

Chapter 19. The Ultimatum

"...to secure information that will lead to the apprehension and punishment..." SD 155-Part 2, p. 527.

"...every Black soldier stationed at Fort Brown would be discharged 'without honor...'" Ibid.

"I lived with them..." CMA, p. 2733.

"You have until nine o'clock..." SD 155-Part 2, p. 530.

"Unless you men with guilty knowledge come forward..." Ibid., p. 527.

"All of you have entered into a general understanding..." Ibid., p. 529.

They must all be punished: Ibid., p. 531.

"Theodore Roosevelt came to me...shared our supply of hardtack with his command." Affidavit of Sergeant Mingo Sanders, 9/24/06. Sergeant Mingo Sanders knew Colonel Roosevelt in Cuba and thought he would not let him down. p. 1. NA.

Chapter 20. President Roosevelt Makes His Decision

"…blacker than black….": SD-389, p. 14.

…calling them murderers, midnight assassins, criminals: See Roosevelt messages to the Senate. Ibid., pp. 14-20.

…accused all of them of engaging in a "conspiracy of silence": Ibid., p. 14.

Roosevelt made his decision. Ibid., p. 8

War Department issued Special Order 266: NA. Also see SD-389, pp. 8-10.

Chapter 21. A Public Outcry

"…I've come on behalf of the colored soldiers." The major source I have used on Taft's suspension of Roosevelt's order is the account given by Mary Church Terrell in her memoir. MCT, pp.268-271.

"…suspend the order dismissing the soldiers…" Ibid. "Is that all you want me to do, Mary?" Ibid.

"…suspend an order issued by the president of the United States…" Ibid.

He suspended the order of the president. SD 155-Part 1, p.187. Also see NYT, 9/20/1906, p. 1.

"Discharge is not to be suspended…" JAT, pp. 51-52. Taft revokes suspension. SD 155-Part 1, p. 189.

Chapter 22. Without Honor *The Drumming Out*

"There go the best men, the best soldiers..." The source of this quote is an interview with Major Penrose in the Washington, D.C. *Evening Star*, 9/27/06. Roosevelt complained about the article. See letter from the White House to Taft, 9/27/06. NA

Chapter 23. The Gridiron Club Dinner Debate

Roosevelt and Foraker were destined to collide: The major sources I used for reconstruction of the debate are cited here in their short form abbreviations. CC, pp. 443-449; JEW, pp. 70-73; AWD, pp. 178-189; JBB, pp. 31-32; JBF, pp. 249-257; WP, 1/28/07.

"I wants to see de President. I'se an old nigger..." JDW-2, p. 125.

"All coons look alike to me." AWD, p. 180. Also see JEW, p. 71.

The Mob! The Mob! The Mob! JBF, p. 255.

"The government ought not to conduct the business." Quote is from a speech TR gave in Harrisburg, Pennsylvania, on 10/4/06. JBB, p. 32.

He shook his fist: CC, p. 445.

"No man in this country is so high." JBF, p. 251.

"...When legal and human rights are involved." Ibid.

"...academic discussion." Ibid., p. 255.

"Mr. President, there was a time." Ibid., p. 252.

"Some of those men were bloody butchers...ought to be hung." CC, p. 447.

Chapter 24. The Last Investigation

"Louis Cowen was the head devil...Cowen was really..." AJL, p.64.

Brown & Baldwin detectives spread out. See letter from Browne to Taft,5/9/1908NA.

"Browne reported...that Boyd Conyers...had confessed." Letter from H. J. Browne to G.B. Davis, JAG, 6/15/08. NA.

"I have...sufficient evidence...to convict, and hang..." Letter from H. J. Browne to G.B. Davis, JAG, 7/30/08. NA.

"This report enables us..." SD-587, p. 3.

"It's the most absolutely false..." JBF, p. 306.

It was signed into law...creating a military court of inquiry. JAT, p. 124.

It concluded that the soldiers shot up the town. CI, p. 1635.

"...allowed fourteen men to re-enlist." Ibid.

Chapter 25. The Pentagon *June 1972*

"....supplemented it in the shape of a successful conspiracy of silence...": SD 389, p. 14.

Chapter 26. The Search for Evidence of a "Conspiracy of Silence"

"Almost no evidence against men arrested...,": SD 155-Part 2, p.437.

Testimony as to the expression heard...Black sons of bitches... Ibid., p. 458.

"The following men...prove an alibi." Ibid., p. 457.

"The president directs that you proceed..." Ibid., p. 527.

"The uniform denial indicated a possible general understanding...but I could find no evidence of such understanding." Ibid., p. 529.

"I could get no information...assumed a wooden, stolid look..." Ibid., p. 528.

"The secretive nature of the race...," Ibid.

"...plenty of precedents for the action taken." SD 389, p. 15.

"[I] lay before the Senate the following facts..." Ibid., p. 11.

"...the evidence proves conclusively that a number of soldiers..." Ibid., p. 14.

"Their contents proved surprising." NYT, 11/22/1906.

"Extraordinary...Not a particle of evidence..." Ibid.

Chapter 28. JAG Sets the *Legal Parameters*

...he had written several premises: DAML, file symbol: DAJA-AL 1972/4430 (20 Jun 72). Memo Col. Williamson to Maj. Baker, 30 Jun 1972. Affirmative Action by DA to recharacterize discharges as a result of the Brownsville incident.

Chapter 30. The Leckie And Wiegenstein *Experiments*

"Roosevelt ended the letter..., 'Please report to me on all of his evidence.'" NA.

"The reason that I say that they were not fired from B barracks..." CMA, p. 3222.

"...they had to be fired from the rear." PGCM-P, pp. 1126-1127.

"Wiegenstein set up experiments." Ibid., pp. 989-1028.

"which way are the men facing?" Ibid., p.1012.

"I don't care to tell you..." Ibid. "I would like to see white men...want to see if I can detect...." Ibid, p. 991.

"I informed all of observers. "Ibid.

"There's Wiegenstein..." Ibid., p.997.

But the man who had on the cap was the Black sergeant: Ibid.

Chapter 31. The Eyewitnesses to the Shooting

Roosevelt cited what he termed "scores of eyewitnesses" SD 389, p. 11.

"...that there is no possibility of their having been mistaken." SD 389, p. 20.

"Rendall,...was the first witness to take the stand." See Rendall's testimony. PGCM-P, pp. 6-25, 43-45.

"Mrs. Rendall, George Rendall's wife, followed him to the stand." PGCM-P, pp. 25-43.

Katie Leahy, the prized witness of the investigators. Ibid., pp. 73-93.

"The defense counsel characterized Katie Leahy..." Ibid., p. 1230.

"I saw through the leaves." CMA, p. 2902.

Only Herbert Elkins's testimony was more absurd: PGCM-P, pp. 442-479.

...he said they were nigger soldiers: Ibid., p. 443.

"By the way they were dressed, he knew 'they were niggers by looking at them.'" Ibid.

"They had on khaki pants..." Ibid.

"You answer the question!" Ibid., p. 473.

"...in Dominguez's own words he stated that he got confused." Ibid., p. 131

"He admitted that another policeman...he knew nothing of his own knowledge." Ibid., pp. 130-131.

"I would like to state to this court that I get so confused..." Ibid, p. 131. See Dominguez's testimony. Ibid., pp. 116-153.

Most troublesome to me was the testimony of Paulino S. Preciado. See his testimony to Assistant Attorney General Purdy. NA.

"...the last person to see the bartender alive." Ibid. I returned to the original sworn statement, given to the Grand Jury.

"I couldn't see anybody in the alley, as it was dark out there and I was in the light. I heard no word spoken." Ibid.

Chapter 32. Finding the Proof

"That's one of the shots fired that night." CMA, pp. 1892-1894.

"That's about a .44 or .45." Ibid. It was an all-lead bullet: Ibid.

"...tested by Doctor Hildebrand, 'Found to be a bullet of a different composition...from any of the bullets used by the Black soldiers..., a bullet such as the soldiers could not have fired from their rifles.'" SR 355 Part 2, pp. 42-43.

"...seven empty cartridges...were in a little circle whose diameter was not more than 10 inches." CMA, p. 3024.

"Macklin swore to this." SD-389, p. 92. Also see PGCM-P, p. 1237.

"Those shells were brought down from Fort Niobrara...": CMA, p. 3025

"I think they were taken out there and put there." Ibid., p. 3025.

That rifle, this fourth gun, serial number 45683. CMA, p. 1748. See all of Sergeant Blaney's testimony. Ibid., pp. 1748-1752.

It was still locked in the arms chest. SD-389, pp. 96-97; 98-99.

"...there was, among those papers, the ballistic tests report (Microscopic Investigation Report)." NA. Also see CMA Vol.2, pp. 1309-1326.

Chapter 33. Pardon or *Exoneration*?

"...give him some instances...where commanders have discharged men without honor and without court-martial." Letter from the White House, 12/ 7/ 1906, signed by Roosevelt. NA.

"...no precedents in the regular army had been found." SD 155-Part 1, p. 311.

Huge amounts of information were distilled into a two-page summary sheet: DAML, file symbol: DAPE-MPE (18 JUL 72).

Summary Sheet. Affirmative Action by DA to Re-characterize Discharges as a Result of the Brownsville Incident. Contact Officer Baker.

Chapter 36. Who Actually Did the Shooting?

Judge Welch was found murdered in his bed: Alberto Cabrera was convicted for the murder in 1908. It appears that it was a political murder. "The Handbook of Texas Online, Welch, Stanley. The Texas State Historical Association.

Thought he could shake down the U.S. government for $10,000 in a lawsuit. SR 355, Part 2, p. 42.

"My examination of the death certificate revealed…" See Certified Copy of Inquest Proceeding dated 8/14/06, verbal by Victoriano S. Fernandez. NA.

"It doesn't work." CMA, p. 2515.

"It's probably been like that for a long time." Ibid. Also see, p. 2386. Op.cit.

It started with firing from the porches of their barracks (alleged by the citizens): Katie Leahy said the shooting started from the balconies. PGCM-P, pp. 73-74. Herbert Elkins testified he saw the soldiers shooting from the barracks. Ibid., p. 452.

"Mack Hamilton…overheard [white] civilian conspirators…cooking up a plot to attack the fort." CI, p. 980.

"…examined the sworn testimony of ex-corporal Willie H. Miller." CMA, pp. 855-867, also see CI, pp. 333-343.

"He seemed to be in a terror-stricken frame of mind…" Ibid., p. 980.

"There is no money to bring Hamilton here." CI, p. 981.

"It was their purpose to shoot over the buildings..." Ibid., p. 981.

"...as a case of 'extreme humanity.'" CI, p. 982.

Chapter 37. The Officers' Fates *and Seeds of Doubt*

"When you turned those niggers out of the army at Brownsville," Owen Wister asked Roosevelt, "Why didn't you order a court of enquiry for the commissioned officers?"
"Because I listened to the War Department, and I shouldn't," Roosevelt replied.... "Of course, I can't know all about everything."

"Defensively, he [Roosevelt] launched into a long disquisition on the fickleness of financial advisors. Wister heard him out." Roosevelt continued, "And so, the best you can do is to stop, look, and listen—...and then jump.... Yes. And then jump. And hope I've jumped right." pp. 474-475. *Theodore Rex*, Edmund Morris.

ACKNOWLEDGEMENTS

Books and great works evolve because of the largess of people. I have many to thank.

I would first like to state my deep appreciation and indebtedness to the late Major General Harry W. Brooks, Jr., who gave me the Brownsville project while I was stationed at the Pentagon in 1972 and who set me on the path to writing this book.

I would also like to thank the late Lieutenant General DeWitt C. Smith, Jr., Army Deputy Chief of Staff, Personnel and the longest serving Commandant of the U.S. Army War College, who believed in civil rights and supported my research at the Pentagon in 1972; Dr. Bruce Aiken, historian, author, and member of the Texas Historical Commission; the staff at the National Archives Division and Pentagon Law Library; Louise A. Arnold-Friend, Chief, Library Collections Manager, U.S. Army Military History Institute, U.S. Army War College, Carlisle Barracks, Carlisle, PA.

Additionally, I thank my lifelong friend Lieutenant Colonel Benjamin L. Swinson (Ret), who was a sounding board for my efforts to move the exoneration process through the Pentagon; David C. Lott of Vineyard Haven, Martha's Vineyard, Massachusetts, who surely made the story better; Carl Holt, Director of Martha's Vineyard Television, who filmed my initial efforts in recording the Brownsville story and assisted in archival photo research on the men of the First Battalion 25th Infantry; and my daughter, Janet L. Baker, Esq.

I also want to thank the supporters of my literary efforts: Richard Purdy of Gettysburg, Pennsylvania; Sam Feldman of Martha's Vineyard, Massachusetts; my son William Rhett Baker; and, finally, my wife, Bettye Foster Baker, who inspired me daily.

Lt. Col. (Ret) William Baker

As has been mentioned before, this book is being published after my husband's death. It has been my labor of love to see his manuscript through to completion.

I would like to thank my editor, Elaine C. Henderson, for her insight and dedication and for staying true to my husband's voice. I also want to acknowledge S.A. Boak, who copy edited the final manuscript. I also thank my daughter, Janet L. Baker, Esq., who encouraged my efforts, and David Lott, who believed deeply in Bill Baker's work.

Dr. Bettye Foster Baker

INDEX

10th Cavalry, 415
12th Street, 118, 119
25th Infantry, 1, 3, 6, i, 1, 2, 11, 16, 21, 25, 26, 37, 46, 47, 50, 52, 53, 59, 73, 164, 170, 188, 203, 209, 211, 231, 232, 233, 271, 272, 308, 334, 358, 407, 410, 412, 414, 417, 429, 449
25th United States Infantry Regiment (Colored), 25
26th Infantry, 47, 51, 153, 225
369th Infantry, 338
Aiken, Bruce 398, 449
Alanis, Nicholas 108
Aldrich, Nelson W. 254
Allen, Loma Colonel 373
Allison's Saloon, 72, 73, 75, 80, 90, 200
Ash, Roy 376
Bailey, Wesley 98
Baker, A.Y 80
Baldwin, William J. 248
Belnap, Mr. Richard 261
Blaney, William, Sergeant 330
Blocksom, Augustus P. Major 150
Blythe, Samuel G. 239
Board for Correction of Military Records, 299, 300, 381
Bowers, Verne General 261, 354, 372
Brooks, Harry Colonel, 259
Brown, Donald 388
Browne, Herbert J. 246, 253
Brownsville Affray, 3, 16, 238, 267, 277, 350, 401, 420, 424, 425, 426
Brownsville Daily Herald 1, 28, 149, 425
Brownsville Historical Society, 394
Bryan, William Jennings 216, 221
Buffalo Soldiers, 13, 25, 46, 430
Cabrera, Alberto 395, 446
Callaway, Bo Army, 381
Clarke, C.T. Major 225
Combe, Frederick J. Mayor 23
Combe, Joe 110, 112, 125
Congressional Black Caucus 19, 259

Connolly, John 339
Connor, George 111
Constitution Avenue, 346
Constitutional League, 216, 218, 219, 223
Conyers, Boyd Private 61, 409
Copperhead, 150, 269
Cornelius, Mr. J.C. 352
Coronado, José 121
Cowen, Anna 91, 92, 95, 99, 100, 105, 107, 122, 135, 433
Cowen, Louis 91, 100, 122, 123, 129, 130, 247, 394, 433, 441
Cowen, Ralph 93, 394, 395
Cowen's Alley, 91, 99, 104, 106, 131, 132, 190, 433
Cowen's House, 92, 100, 432
Creager, Renfro B. 132
Crews, Ester 250
Crixell, Teofilo 101
Crixell, V.L. 62
Culberson, Senator 153
Currier, Roger 386
Daggett, Aaron Brigadier General S., 402
Dalling, Blaze 157
Davis, George B. Judge Advocate General, 211
Dellums, Ron Congressman 259
Dews, Robert Lieutenant Colonel, 18

Dominguez, Joe 107, 149, 249, 323, 400
Dreyfus Affair, ii, v, 6, 428
Du Bois, W.E.B. 215
Edger Benjamin J. Jr. Captain 23
Ehrlichman, John 383
El Caney, 2, 35, 36, 210, 233, 430
El Reno, 172, 176, 236
Elizabeth Street, 51, 57, 58, 59, 60, 61, 69, 72, 79, 90, 101, 105, 107, 109, 121, 125, 126, 145, 151, 395, 398
Ellsberg, Daniel 373
Evans, Lon 82, 83
Evans, Mrs. 82, 83, 84, 90, 93, 432
Fernandez, John G. 141
Foraker, Joseph Benson Senator 237, 275
Fort Brown, 14, 20, 21, 22, 23, 34, 42, 47, 50, 51, 53, 54, 63, 64, 74, 83, 96, 97, 106, 107, 116, 121, 139, 149, 153, 156, 158, 159, 163, 164, 170, 171, 184, 194, 234, 269, 309, 316, 330, 353, 359, 394, 395, 402, 403, 438
Fort Leavenworth, 140
Fort Niobrara, 25, 46, 54, 64, 162, 328, 329, 330, 331, 445

Fort Reno, 14, 164, 174, 175, 176, 183, 184, 187, 189, 192, 194, 203, 217, 219, 222, 223, 224, 230, 236, 270, 272, 429, 437
Fort Riley, 62, 67
Fort Sam Houston, 164, 174, 175, 188, 194, 195, 196, 229, 271, 272
Fraser, Donald M. Congressman 352
Frazier, Ernie Colonel 348
Frazier, Jacob First Sergeant, 115
Froehlke, Secretary, 301, 302, 351, 364, 371
Gard, Bobby General 373
Gardner, John Congressman 168
Garlington, Ernest A. General 194, 271
Garrison Road, 20, 42, 50, 57, 99, 112, 118, 152, 202
Garza, Celedonio, 30, 119
Garza, Jose 399
General of the Army, 260, 271
Gomez, Vincent 388
Goodrich, E.H., 136, 141
Goodwin, Doris Kearns 7, 405
Grant, Ulysses S. General 220
Gray, Dorian 232
Gray, Wallace L. 251
Grier Lieutenant, 118, 142, 143, 227, 229, 230
Hamilton, Mack 119, 158, 161, 402, 446
Hanson, Martin 101
Harlan, Supreme Court Justice 243
Harris, Stella 203
Hartke, Vance Senator 380, 381, 383, 384
Hattie, wife of Jacob Frazier 113
Hawkins, Augustus F. Congressman 15, 351
Henry, John 62
Herron, Curtis Reverend, 360
Holmes, Dr. 269
Holoman, John 59, 63, 65, 72, 77, 174, 198, 236, 249, 252, 254, 270, 410
Howard, Joseph H. 96, 413, 432
Howland Captain, 403
Hughes, Charles Evans 215
Hulen, John A. 165
Hume, David 303
Humphrey, Senator 380, 381, 385, 387
Johnson, Donald 371, 372, 376, 387
Jones, William E. Private, 56, 413
Kauffman, White Storekeeper 12
Keaton, Ned ii, 11, 416
Kerwin General, 260, 284,

293, 353
Kibbe, Frank W. 30
Kirk, Robert J. Colonel 360
Kleindienst Attorney General, 266
Krause, Henry 394, 395
Laird, Melvin 16, 344, 346, 371
Lanham, S.W.T. 165
Library of Congress, 3, 277, 307, 321, 422
Lyon, Samuel P. Captain 3, 115, 406
Macklin, Edgar A. Captain 3, 406
Malcolm, Andrew H. 357, 368
Marshal, Napoleon B. 402
Martinez, Amada 92, 100, 123
Martinez, Teofilo 320
McCaskey General, 187, 309
McCurdy, Walker Quartermaster-Sergeant 330
McDonald, Bill Captain 154, 269, 426
McDonnel, James P. 145
Milholland, John 216, 219
Miller, Don 338, 339, 344
Minneapolis Star, 350
Mondale, Walter Senator 380
Monroe, 71, 249, 250, 251, 252, 253
Morgan, Emily West 432

Morgan, J.P. 240
Morris, Edmund 405, 447
Murdoch, Jim Captain 261
National Archives, 3, 4, 307, 328, 331, 332, 333, 338, 339, 344, 346, 356, 357, 358, 397, 398, 420, 421, 422, 424, 449
National Association of Colored Women, 219
Natus, Frank 59, 65, 94, 101, 102, 108, 122, 137, 139, 149, 249, 397, 398, 399, 400
Nixon administration, 262, 283, 286, 293, 371, 376, 377, 380, 381, 383, 384, 385
Orr, Mr. John H. 358
Padron, Genaro 107, 110, 146
Parsimony, Rule of 302
Patton, George General 380
Pennington, J.C. Colonel 351, 378
Penrose, Charles W. 3, 47, 50, 420
Pentagon, ii, 3, 4, 14, 15, 17, 259, 261, 277, 285, 286, 344, 346, 348, 356, 364, 373, 376, 385, 386, 387, 388, 417, 422, 449
Point Isabel, 26
Powers, Jim 31
Preciado, Paulino 108, 139,

434
President Nixon, ii, 14, 263, 335, 339, 376, 386, 387
Prugh, Major General 262
Purdy, Milton D. 237
Ramirez, Macedonio 121
Rendall, George W. 146
Rio Grande, 20, 71, 80, 81, 82, 193, 304, 305, 395
Rogers, Bernie General 353, 375
Rogers, Henry 240
Roosevelt, Theodore 1, 3, 5, 6, 7, ii, 1, 2, 4, 5, 16, 140, 209, 213, 417, 425, 426, 429, 438
Ruby Saloon, 24, 59, 63, 65, 68, 78, 79, 92, 93, 94, 95, 101, 102, 108, 122, 135, 138, 149, 199, 200, 309, 324, 396, 397, 402
Sandburg, Carl 20
Sanders, Mingo 8, 25, 50, 75, 76, 90, 113, 114, 159, 171, 174, 176, 177, 208, 210, 212, 225, 226, 227, 228, 231, 243, 254, 255, 308, 409, 438
Scott, Emmett J. 237
Senate Military Affairs Committee, 3, 309, 420
Shannon, Hal 102
Smith, Dewitt C. Major General 364
Starck, Fred 81, 109, 137, 434
Stewart, Gilchrist 216, 218
Sutton, Willie 373
Tackaberry, Thomas H. Major General 384
Taliaferro, Sergeant 86, 88
Tate, Fred 69
Taylor, Zachary General 20
Terrell, Mary Church 219, 220, 221, 222, 439
Thornton, Luther T. Sergeant 204, 409
Tillman, Ben 195
Tillman, John 24, 59, 78, 108, 199, 200, 396, 398, 402
Togo West, 339, 364, 384
Wall Street Journal, 216
Washington Bee, 216
Washington, Booker T. 5, 195, 215, 237
Washington, D.C., 3, 39, 219, 387, 408, 426, 440
Waterville Maine Sentinel, 216
Welch, Stanley District Judge, 156
Wheeler, Jesse 30, 31, 32, 35
Wheeler, Jessie 260
Wheeler, Samuel 96, 414
White Elephant, 62, 101, 102, 111
Wiegenstein, Henry Lieutenant, 311
William of Ockham, 302

455

Williamson, Wade Colonel 19, 260, 296
Willis, Dorsie W. Private 59, 118, 178, 224, 234, 348, 349, 350, 352, 353, 355, 356, 357, 358, 360, 362, 363, 364, 365, 366, 367, 368, 371, 374, 383, 387, 388, 389, 390, 393, 394, 396, 414, 421
Wister, Owen, 406, 447
Wolff, L. Thomas Doctor 360
Wreford, Sam 25, 29, 30, 31, 32, 34, 36, 37, 38, 44, 136, 138, 430
Yturria, 104, 138, 309, 433
Zola, Émile v, 6, 217